Historians used to know — and it was not too long ago — that the War Between the States had more to do with economics than it did with slavery. The current obsession with slavery as the "cause" of the war rests not on evidence but on ideological considerations of the present day. Gene Kizer has provided us with the conclusive case that the invasion of the Southern States by Lincoln and his party (a minority of the American people) was due to an agenda of economic domination and not to some benevolent concern for slaves. This book is rich in evidence and telling quotations and ought to be on every Southern bookshelf.

Clyde N. Wilson
Emeritus Distinguished Professor of History
University of South Carolina
December 16, 2014

Other books by Gene Kizer, Jr.

The Elements of Academic Success

*How to Graduate Magna Cum Laude from College
(or how to just graduate, PERIOD!)*

Charleston, SC Short Stories, Book One

*Six Tales of Courage, Love, the War Between the
States, Satire, Ghosts & Horror from the Holy City*

Slavery

Was Not the Cause of the War Between the States

Charleston Athenaeum Press

Slavery

Was Not the Cause of the War Between the States

The Irrefutable Argument.

Gene Kizer, Jr.

CHARLESTON ATHENAEUM PRESS
Charleston and James Island, S.C.

Charleston Athenaeum Press

www.CharlestonAthenaeumPress.com
www.BonnieBluePublishing.com

Post Office Box 13012
Charleston, South Carolina 29422-3012

PLEASE ORDER COPIES
from any of our websites

ISBN: 978-0-9853632-7-7 *(softcover)*
Library of Congress Control Number: 2014917730
ISBN: 978-0-9853632-6-0 *(eBook)*

Publisher's Cataloging-in-Publication Data (by QBI)

Kizer, Gene, Jr.
   Slavery was not the cause of the War Between the
States : the irrefutable argument / Gene Kizer, Jr.—
First print edition.
   pages cm
   Includes bibliographical references and index.
   LCCN 2014917730
   ISBN 978-0-9853632-7-7 (softcover)
   ISBN 978-0-9853632-6-0 (eBook)

   1. United States—History—Civil War, 1861-1865—Causes.
2. United States—History—Civil War, 1861-1865—Economic
aspects. 3. Slavery—Political aspects—United States—History—
19th century. 4. Secession—Southern States. 5. Fort Sumter
(Charleston, S.C.)—Siege, 1861. 6. Lincoln, Abraham, 1809-1865.
I. Contains (work): Ramsdell, Charles W. (Charles William),
1877-1942. Lincoln and Fort Sumter. II. Title.

E458.K59 2014   973.7'11
                                             QBI14-600167

First Print Edition
November, 2014

To Dad

Thank you for showing me, by the sterling example of your life and personality, how to be tough, strive, work hard, succeed and accomplish important things, and always how to live a vigorous satisfying life while doing so. Proud to be your son. Love you!

To Mom,
Rest in peace

Thank you for insisting that I take typing at James Island High School the summer when I was in the sixth grade before it was common for boys to do so. You empowered me with a tool for writing and expression that has been a huge influence in my life.

To My Children Trey and Travis,
and to Trey's Heather,
and Travis's Ashley

Proud of my boys and their beautiful ladies!
And, of course, we all embrace the values of
Lt. Richard Sharpe, Commander of the 'Chosen Men,'
the Sharpshooters of the 2nd Battalion in His
Britannic Majesty's 95th Rifle Corps, and of
Sergeant Patrick Harper.

> *Then fall in lads behind the drum*
> *With colours blazing like the sun.*
> *Along the road to come what may*
> *Over the hills and far away.*

To My Stepmother, Elaine Bonner

Glad you made a world traveler out of Dad! From Muni to the Seine!

To Aunt Betty Ann Kizer, and Natalie Durant

Our last Pedicab ride (May, 2014) in downtown Charleston was a hoot! I love you both very much!

To Clay and Kimberly "Pamela" Martin

Good people, Best Friends one can always count on! Same as family since "straight spaghetti" in the ninth grade! Thanks for inviting us into your beautiful home near the start of the Cooper River Bridge Run every year before the race at 6 a.m.!

To Kathie Martin Dudley

So glad you triumphed (I expected no less!) and are back on top of the world and still feisty as hell!

Contents

(with each chapter's epigraph)

Part I

The Irrefutable Argument.

Chapter 1

Abraham Lincoln and His Proclamation

Page 5

The Emancipation Proclamation states that it is a war measure. It deliberately freed no slaves (or few). Lincoln had no control over slaves in Confederate territory that the Emancipation Proclamation purported to free, and the slaves under Union control that Lincoln could have freed easily — nearly a million — were purposely left in slavery. Europeans such as Charles Dickens made fun of Lincoln.

Chapter 2

The North Did Not Go to War to End Slavery

Page 14

If they had, they would have started by passing a constitution amendment abolishing slavery. They did the opposite. They overwhelmingly passed the Corwin Amendment, which left black people in slavery forever, even beyond the reach of Congress. This alone proves,

unequivocally, that the North did not go to war to end
slavery or free the slaves.

Chapter 3

Northern Economic Annihilation:
The True Cause of the War

Page 35

The North cut off from Southern cotton, rice, tobacco,
and other products would lose three fourths of her
commerce, and a very large proportion of her manufactures. And thus those great fountains of finance would
sink very low. . . . Would the North in such a condition
as that declare war against the South?

Henry L. Benning
November 19, 1860

Chapter 4

Panic in the Volatile North

Page 56

In one single blow our foreign commerce must be reduced to less than one-half what it now is. Our coastwise trade would pass into other hands. One-half of
our shipping would lie idle at our wharves. . . . Our
manufactories would be in utter ruins. . . . millions of
our people would be compelled to go out of employment.

Daily-Chicago Times
December 10, 1860

Chapter 5

The Confederate States of America

Page 70

The formation of the Confederate States of America by the people of the South through their secession conventions was the greatest expression of democracy and self-government in the history of the world.

Chapter 6

The Perfect Storm for Economic Disaster in the North

Page 76

Secession cost the North its Southern manufacturing market. The Morrill Tariff threatened to cost the North its shipping industry as U.S. trade was immediately rerouted away from the high-tariff North and into Southern ports where protective tariffs were unconstitutional.

Chapter 7

The Only Thing That Can Save the North Is War

Page 87

Major Robert Anderson, Union commander inside Fort Sumter, emphatically blames Lincoln for starting the war Lincoln had to have to save the North.

Part III

Lincoln and Fort Sumter
by Charles W. Ramsdell

About Charles William Ramsdell

Page 199

In all that pertained to the history of the Southern
Confederacy, his scholarship was decisive.

In Memoriam
Charles William Ramsdell
University of Texas

Lincoln and Fort Sumter

by Charles W. Ramsdell

Page 203

We are to have civil war, if at all, because
Abraham Lincoln loves a party better than he loves his
country. . . . Mr. Lincoln saw an opportunity to inaugurate civil war without appearing in the character of
an aggressor.

"WHY?"
Providence (R.I.) Daily Post
The day after the commencement of
the bombardment of Fort Sumter
April 13, 1861

Contents

Introduction

Slavery was and is a horrible institution. There is nothing in this book, whatsoever, that defends slavery in any way, form or fashion. Slavery was/is a blight on humanity.

The purpose of this book is historical truth. The War Between the States is the central event in American history and, by far, our bloodiest war. It is important to know exactly what sparked it and why. Interpreting the past truthfully and accurately is a debt we owe to the people of the past, and to the future.

In Part I of this book, I argue that slavery was not the cause of the War Between the States. There is absolute, irrefutable proof that the North did not go to war to free the slaves or end slavery. The North went to war to preserve the Union as Abraham Lincoln said over and over.

The reason Lincoln needed to preserve the Union was because, without it, the North faced economic annihilation, the magnitude of which easily made war preferable. Economic problems multiply geometrically. By the time Lincoln was inaugurated on March 4, 1861 there was gloom, despair and panic in the North with thousands of business failures, hundreds of thousands of people out of work, serious trouble with the stock market, threatened runs on banks, and Northern ship captains heading South because of the South's low tariff. There was no talk whatsoever of ending slavery.

Just the opposite. There were guarantees galore of preserving slavery forever.

Just use common sense. If your house is on fire,
you don't care about your neighbor's barking dog or
anything your neighbor is doing. You have to put out
the fire or lose your house. It's just that simple.

The North's economic house caught fire in the winter of 1860 to 61 when the first seven Southern States
seceded. The North quickly discovered that manufacturing and shipping for the South were the sources of
most of its employment, wealth and power. Cotton
alone was 60% of U.S. exports in 1860. Without the
South, the North was headed for bankruptcy. By the
spring of 1861, the North's house was a raging inferno.

The latest death statistics for the War Between
the States have raised it from 620,000, to between
650,000 and 850,000. These are the widely accepted
statistics of historian J. David Hacker of Binghampton
University. He splits the difference and uses 750,000.[1]
I believe it was on the higher end of his range so I use
800,000 in this book.

The wounded usually end up, statistically, as a
multiple of deaths. For example, in WWII we lost
405,399 and had 670,846 wounded, which is 1.65.[2]

---

[1] Rachel Coker, "Historian revises estimate of Civil War dead,"
published September 21, 2011, Binghampton University Research News — Insights and Innovations from Binghampton
University, http://discovere.binghamton.edu/news/
civilwar-3826.html, accessed July 7, 2014.

[2] United States military casualties of war,
http://en.wikipedia.org/wiki/United_States_military_casualties_
of_war, accessed August 1, 2014.

Sometimes the multiplier is higher, sometimes lower, and I realize that a higher percentage died of disease in the War Between the States, but the number of wounded would still be astronomical, well over a million to add to the 800,000 dead.

If the soldiers of World War II were killed at the same rate as the War Between the States, we would have lost 3,870,000 instead of 405,399; and we would have had 6,385,500 wounded instead of 670,846.

That the South, with 1/4th the white population of the North, did not hesitate to fight for its rights and liberty, says everything about the courage of Southerners and their desire for independence. Especially when one considers the other huge advantages of the North: in weapon manufacturing (perhaps 40-to-1, or even more), merchant shipping, a standing army, a substantial navy with fleets of war ships, and a functioning government with access to the *unlimited* immigration of the world's wretched refuse with which to feed Union armies.

The War Between the States was a completely unnecessary war.

Historians know that the Crittenden Compromise (late 1860) would almost certainly have prevented the war. It was based on the old Missouri Compromise line that had worked well for 30 years. Slavery had been prohibited north of the line and allowed south of it.[3]

---

[3] The Missouri Compromise was superseded by the Kansas-Nebraska Act in 1854, which opened up the territory north of the Missouri Compromise line (latitude 36° 30' north) to slavery. This made the Missouri Compromise irrelevant.

The Crittenden Compromise had widespread support, North and South, from good men trying to prevent war, but Abraham Lincoln shot it down. Lincoln
had political allies to pay back so he would not compromise on slavery in the West. He had no problem with
slavery where it existed. He just didn't want it "extended," so he supported the Corwin Amendment,
which left black people in slavery forever, even beyond
the reach of Congress, where slavery already existed.

The defeat of the Crittenden Compromise at the
behest of the partisan Lincoln is a major tragedy of
world history, and more bitterly so because slavery
was not extending into the West. There were few
slaves in the West after being open to slavery for 10
years. Esteemed historian David M. Potter writes that
the Crittenden Compromise had widespread support
from Southerners as prominent as Robert Toombs as
well as strong support in the North and West, and "if
these conclusions are valid, as the preponderance of
evidence indicates, it means that when Lincoln moved
to defeat compromise, he did not move as the cham-
pion of democracy, but as a partisan leader."[4] Potter's
choice of words is far too kind.

Abraham Lincoln was the first sectional president
in American history. The loser in the next five presidential elections got more popular votes than Lincoln.
Of the total 4,682,069 votes cast in 1860, Lincoln received 1,866,452, which is 39.9%. The eighteen states

---

[4] David M. Potter, *Lincoln and His Party in the Secession Crisis* (New Haven: Yale University Press, 1942; reprint, New Haven: Yale University Press, 1979), 200.

voting for him were all above the Mason-Dixon line. He received no electoral votes in fifteen of the thirty-three states. His name was not even on the ballot in ten Southern states. Lincoln's opponents together totaled 2,815,617, which was almost a million votes more than he got.

Potter makes it clear that Lincoln had absolutely no voter mandate to not compromise with the South at this critical juncture in our country's history. With a large majority of voters, excluding slavery from the territories was a non-issue. Potter writes:

> [A] majority, not only of the voters as a whole, but even of the voters in states which remained loyal to the Union, regarded the exclusion of slavery from the territories as non-essential or even undesirable, and voted against the candidate who represented this policy. When Lincoln was inaugurated, the states which accepted him as President were states which had cast a majority of more than a half a million votes against him, and even when the outbreak of war caused four more states to join the Confederacy, the remaining Union still contained a population in which the majority of the electorate had opposed the Republican ticket.[5]

---

[5] Potter, *Lincoln and His Party in the Secession Crisis*, 200.

Potter notes that part of Lincoln's uncompromis-
ing position was political fear that any compromise on
slavery in the territories, after campaigning on it,
meant the dissolution of the Republican Party, which
was made up loosely of so many diverse groups of non-
related voters such as those who wanted a tariff or
bounty or subsidy for their business, or free land, or
were Northern racists who didn't want blacks near
them in the West.

It is a tragedy of unfathomable proportion that
Lincoln killed the Crittenden Compromise. The Crittenden Compromise would have prevented the war
and 800,000 deaths and over a million wounded, and
would have given the country time to work on ending
slavery.

Most other nations on earth, as well as the Northern States, used gradual, compensated emancipation
to end slavery. The Northern capital, Washington, DC,
freed its slaves a year into the war with compensated
emancipation, which proves slavery could have been
abolished quickly and bloodlessly if the will had been
there, North and South.

It is a regretable fact, but slaves were property
and governments that wanted to end slavery in their
countries were glad to compensate slaveowners for the
loss of their property.[6] It is not just racial either. One

---

[6] As stated, ending slavery did not have to be too gradual as
long as compensation to slaveowners was included. The successful Washington, DC 1862 compensation program proved
it could work and be more immediate than gradual, although
that is a small example. There would definitely need to be programs in place to help the new freedmen incorporate into so-

of the largest slaveowners in South Carolina was William Ellison, the famous cotton gin maker in Sumter County, who was black. There were a lot of black slaveowners and I'm sure they would want to be compensated along with whites. Gradual, compensated emancipation was Lincoln's strong belief and desire as well, as he stated in the Preliminary Emancipation Proclamation with respect to the Union slave states.[7] Lincoln talked and wrote about gradual compensated emancipation at many other times and places as well.

---

ciety but that could have been done and is what serious people, as opposed to fanatics, were pushing. It was certainly Lincoln's position most of his life. Historian Richard N. Current believed slavery would not last another generation, and that seems a reasonable assessment.

[7] Paragraph two of Abraham Lincoln's *Preliminary Emancipation Proclamation* issued September 22, 1862 "By the President of the United States of America" reads:

> That it is my purpose, upon the next meeting of Congress to again recommend the adoption of a practical measure **tendering pecuniary aid** to the free acceptance or rejection of all slave States, so called, the people whereof may not then be in rebellion against the United States [Maryland, Delaware, Missouri, Kentucky and later West Virginia] and which States may then have voluntarily adopted, or thereafter may voluntarily adopt, immediate or gradual **abolishment [sic] of slavery** within their respective limits; and that the efforts to colonize persons of African descent, with their consent, upon this continent, or elsewhere, with the previously obtained consent of the Governments existing there, will be continued. (Emphasis added.)

But ending slavery was not the goal of the Republican Party in 1856 and 1860. Taking over the government so they could rule the country for their own benefit and aggrandizement was their goal. George Washington had warned that sectional political parties would destroy the country but Wendell Phillips proudly proclaimed that the Republican Party is the first sectional party in American history and is the party of the North pledged against the South.

For the entire decade of the 1850s, Republicans used the most virulent hatred against the South to rally their votes. Republicans celebrated John Brown's terrorism and murder of Southerners, and Republicans endorsed Hinton Helper's *The Impending Crisis of the South* as a campaign document. Helper's book

> urged class agitation against slavery or, failing that, the violent overthrow of the slave system by poorer whites. Helper concluded that slaves would join with nonslaveholders because 'the negroes . . . in nine cases out of ten, would be delighted with the opportunity to cut their masters' throat.'[8]

---

[8] Ronnie W. Faulkner, 2006, "The Impending Crisis of the South," NCpedia sketch on Hinton Rowan Helper's book, *The Impending Crisis of the South: How to Meet It* (New York: Burdick Brothers, 1857). NCpedia is the Encyclopedia of North Carolina, The University of North Carolina Press: http://ncpedia.org/print/2723, accessed July 31, 2014. The article also states that Hinton Helper was "A racist to the core, he advocated white supremacy."

William H. Seward, soon to be Lincoln's secretary of state, said "I have read the 'Impending Crisis of the South' with great attention. It seems to me a work of great merit, rich yet accurate in statistical information, and logical in analysis."

Lincoln's predecessor, President James Buchanan, in an article he wrote entitled "Republican Fanaticism as a Cause of the Civil War," said *The Impending Crisis* "became at once an authoritative exposition of the principles of the Republican Party. The original, as well as a compendium, were circulated by hundreds of thousands, North, South, East, and West."[9]

Southerners would have been crazy not to secede from a country now ruled by a party that called for their throats to be cut. Republicans were not a great political movement trying to solve the difficult slavery issue with good will. Most people in the North (95 to 98% according to historians Lee Benson and Gavin Wright) were not abolitionists.[10] They did not care about freeing the slaves who would then come North and be job competition.

---

[9] The quotations of William H. Seward and President James Buchanan come from an article by Buchanan, "Republican Fanaticism as a Cause of the Civil War," an essay in Edwin C. Rozwenc, ed., *The Causes of the American Civil War* (Boston: D.C. Heath and Company, 1961), 62.

[10] Lee Benson, "Explanations of American Civil War Causation" in *Toward the Scientific Study of History* (Philadelphia: J. B. Lippincott, 1972), 246, 295-303, in Gavin Wright, *The Political Economy of the Cotton South, Households, Markets, and Wealth in the Nineteenth Century* (New York: W. W. Norton & Company, 1978), 136.

No Republican could be elected in the North on the platform of directly ending slavery but they could agitate on slavery in the West with good results. It was a hot political issue driven as much by rallying votes — vote Republican: 'Vote yourself a farm,' 'Vote yourself a tariff!' — as it was by Northern racism. Lincoln himself stated in the Lincoln-Douglas Debates that the West was to be reserved for white people from all over the earth.

The West was important in the presidential campaigns of 1856 and 1860 because the North needed the West for its surplus population, as both Horace Greeley and Lincoln stated. "Go West, young man!" said Horace Greeley. Lincoln added that he wanted those white Northerners and immigrants to reach the West with Northern institutions in place, which meant no blacks allowed. Period. Neither slaves nor free blacks were welcome in Lincoln's West.

Slavery in the West was a bogus issue anyway, as stated earlier. Slavery was not going beyond the Mississippi River and they all knew it. Republican James G. Blaine said that slavery in the West was "related to an imaginary Negro in an impossible place." Lincoln scholar Richard N. Current writes that "Lincoln and his fellow Republicans, in insisting that Congress must prohibit slavery in the West, were dealing with political phantoms." He points out that Congress "approved the organization of territorial governments for Colorado, Nevada, and Dakota without a prohibition of slavery" because they did not think it was necessary. In 1860, there were only two slaves in Kansas and 15 in Nebraska, and that was after being open to slavery for 10 years. As stated above, Current did not believe slavery would have lasted another generation, even in the deep South.[11]

Charles W. Ramsdell wrote an article entitled "The Natural Limits of Slavery Expansion" and he also concluded "that slavery had about reached its zenith by 1860 and must shortly have begun to decline, for the economic forces which had carried it into the region west of the Mississippi had about reached their maximum effectiveness. It could not go forward in any direction and was losing ground along its northern border."[12]

The New Mexico territory had also been open to slavery for ten years and there were only twenty-nine there in 1860, though that figure was challenged by William H. Seward. He said there were twenty-four.[13]

It is a great irony that Northern anti-slavery was mostly economic or racist. Paraphrasing historian

---

[11] Richard N. Current, *The Lincoln Nobody Knows* (New York: McGraw-Hill Book Company, Inc., 1958), 95-97.

[12] Charles W. Ramsdell, "The Natural Limits of Slavery Expansion" in Edwin C. Rozwenc, ed., *The Causes of the American Civil War* (Boston: D. C. Heath and Company, 1961), 150-162

[13] For an excellent report on an in-depth conversation between U. S. Supreme Court Justice John A. Campbell, William H. Seward, Stephen A. Douglas, John J. Crittenden and others on the extension of slavery, see Honorable John A. Campbell, "Memoranda Relative to the Secession Movement in 1860-61," in the "Papers of Honorable John A. Campbell - 1861-1865.," *Southern Historical Society Papers*, New Series - Number IV, Volume XLII, September, 1917, (Reprint: Broadfoot Publishing Company and Morningside Bookshop, 1991), 3-45.

David Potter, Northern anti-slavery was in no sense a pro-black movement but was anti-black and designed to get rid of blacks. Many Northern and Western States had laws on the books forbidding free black people from even visiting, much less living there, including Lincoln's own Illinois. If a black person stayed too long in Illinois he was subject to arrest and imprisonment by the sheriff. In 1859, Oregon became the 33rd state and this was part of its constitution:

> No free negro, or mulatto, not residing in this state at the time of the adoption of this constitution, shall ever come, reside, or be within this state, or hold any real estate, or make any contract, or maintain any suit therein; and the legislative assembly shall provide by penal laws for the removal by public officers of all such free negroes and mulattoes, and for their effectual exclusion from the state, and for the punishment of persons who shall bring them into the state, or employ or harbour them therein.[14]

In Part II of this book, I argue the right of secession. No American who believes in the Declaration of Independence — in the just powers of the government

---

[14] Taliaferro P. Shaffner, *The War in America: being an Historical and Political Account of the Southern and Northern States: showing the Origin and Cause of the Present Secession War* (London: Hamilton, Adams, 1862), 337-38.

coming from the consent of the governed — can doubt
the right of secession. Horace Greeley certainly didn't.
He believed in it thoroughly until he realized it was
going to affect his money.

The secession conventions of the South and the
creation of the Confederate States of America are the
greatest expression of democracy and self-government
in the history of the world. In state after state, in a
landmass as great as Europe, Southerners rose up
against what they viewed as a dangerous, economically
confiscatory government now run by people who hated
them and whose campaign documents called for their
throats to be cut.

The Southern states called conventions to decide
the one issue: Secession. A convention to decide one
issue is closer to the people than even their legislatures. That's why the Founding Fathers in the Constitutional Convention of 1787 decided that conventions
of the people in each state would be used to ratify the
Constitution. That's where the convention precedent
started, with the Founding Fathers and the ratification of the Constitution. Southerners followed suit
with their conventions to decide secession. They debated the issue fiercely then elected delegates as Unionists and Secessionists who went into their state conventions and debated more.

Seven states voted to secede, then they formed a
democratic republic that was the mirror image of the
republic of the Founding Fathers of 1776 but with
States' Rights strengthened and an economic system
based on free trade. Southerners had always wanted

free trade with the world as opposed to the heavy pro-
tectionist tariffs that had benefited the North to the
detriment of the South the entire antebellum period.

Slavery was not the cause of the War Between the
States. Once you understand the true cause — the imminent economic annihilation of the North which was
coming fast — all other actions taken by Lincoln and
everybody else make infinitely more sense.

Abraham Lincoln needed to start his war as
quickly as he could. He needed the blockade of the
South in place as fast as possible to keep Europeans
and especially the English from forming trade and
military alliances with the South, which the South had
been aggressively pursuing. Lincoln announced his
blockade before the smoke had cleared from the bombardment of Fort Sumter.

In Part III, Charles W. Ramsdell's famous treatise, *Lincoln and Fort Sumter*, shows in magnificent
detail how Lincoln started the war in Charleston Harbor. I hadn't read this brilliant piece in several years
but had to type in every word for this book and I am
deeply pleased that every single word written by Mr.
Ramsdell strongly supports the argument of this book
— that the inevitable economic annihilation of the
North is the reason Abraham Lincoln had to have his
war and get it started as quickly as he could. Mr.
Ramsdell states also that the North's gaping self-in-
flicted wound, the Morrill Tariff, kicked in and greatly
added to the panic and call for war in the North as the
Northern shipping industry was largely rerouted, in
one fell swoop, away from the high-tariff North and

into the low-tariff South where protective tariffs were unconstitutional.

Arguing history is very much like arguing a case in a court of law. All you can do is present your evidence in as persuasive a manner as possible and hope the jury agrees with you.

My argument is thoroughly documented and I believe it is irrefutable.

Gene Kizer, Jr.
Charleston, South Carolina
October 31, 2014

Slavery

Was Not the Cause of the
War Between the States

Part I

The Irrefutable Argument.

Chapter 1

Abraham Lincoln and His Proclamation

> *The Emancipation Proclamation states that it is a war measure. It deliberately freed no slaves (or few). Lincoln had no control over slaves in Confederate territory that the Emancipation Proclamation purported to free, and the slaves under Union control that Lincoln could have freed easily — nearly a million — were purposely left in slavery. Europeans such as Charles Dickens made fun of Lincoln.*

African-American scholar, Lerone Bennett Jr., opens his book *Forced Into Glory, Abraham Lincoln's White Dream*, with an anecdote about Lincoln. The election of 1860 was over and the victorious Lincoln was relaxed and talking to friends in the state capitol in Springfield, Illinois. Somebody commented that it was too bad the first thing he would have to deal with was the slavery issue.

> The president-elect's eyes twinkled and he said he was reminded of a story. Ac-

5

cording to eyewitness Henry Villard,
President-elect Abraham Lincoln "told
the story of the Kentucky Justice of the
Peace whose first case was a criminal
prosecution for the abuse of slaves. Unable to find any precedent, he exclaimed
angrily: 'I will be damned if I don't feel
almost sorry for being elected when the
niggers is the first thing I have to attend
to.'[15]

Bennett, who predictably has drawn the ire of Lincoln worshipers and mythmakers, has built a solid
case against Lincoln using Lincoln's own words and
other highly credible primary sources. *Forced Into
Glory* is a book everyone should read because it cuts
right to the chase and tells it like it is without the lay-
ers of adulation that some historians and most history
professors lovingly place on Lincoln.

---

[15] Lerone Bennett Jr., *Forced Into Glory: Abraham Lincoln's
White Dream* (Chicago: Johnson Publishing Company, 2000),
5. The back cover of *Forced Into Glory* states: "Lerone Bennett
Jr. is the author of the classic study of African-American his-
tory, *Before the Mayflower*. In 1965, he won the Patron Saints
Award of the Society of Midland Authors for his biography of
Martin Luther King Jr., *What Manner of Man*. He received the
Literature Award of the American Academy of Arts and Letters
in 1978." Bennett was also editor of *Ebony* magazine for dec-
ades. Villard's quote comes from Henry Villard, *Lincoln on the
Eve of '61*, edited by Harold G. and Oswald Garrison Villard,
published in New York in 1941.

Some have criticized this book but Bennett is a well-thought-of African-American author and scholar and his take on things is important. You walk away with flashes of indisputable truth because of the extensive use of primary sources and a person's own words. You are guaranteed to develop a more veracious perspective than by reading much of the past 149 years of Lincoln hagiography.

Bennett said racial insensitivity "colored Lincoln's whole presidency."

> General James Samuel Wadsworth, who saw Lincoln almost every day at the height of the crisis and who was with him "frequently for 5 or 6 hours at the War Department," was shocked by the racism in the Lincoln White House, where Lincoln "frequently" spoke of "the nigger question" and debated whether this or that act would "touch the nigger." . . . General Wadsworth said that Lincoln was contemptuous of abolitionists and "spoke often of the slaves as cattle."[16]

Bennett proves (as historians know) that the Emancipation Proclamation was a war measure that

---

[16] Bennett, *Forced Into Glory*, 14. Lerone Bennett's documentation for the quotations herein are in his footnote #4: "The Wadsworth letter cited was listed by the historian James F. Rhodes (4:64)."

freed no slaves (or few). He argues that Lincoln actually *reenslaved* 500,000 who were about to be freed by
the Second Confiscation Act.

The Second Confiscation Act passed the Northern
Congress July 17, 1862. According to Bennett, it would
have freed all the slaves in captured Confederate territory that was under control of the Union Army.[17]

Lincoln "reenslaved" a half-million slaves by signing the Preliminary Emancipation Proclamation on
September 22, 1862, *one day* before the Second Confiscation Act was to go into effect.

This nullified the emancipation part of the Second
Confiscation Act and caused the Emancipation Proclamation to apply.

The Emancipation Proclamation freed no slaves
(or few). Lincoln had no control over slaves in Confederate territory that the Emancipation Proclamation
purported to free, and the slaves Lincoln could have
freed easily were purposely left in slavery. Europeans

---

[17] The Second Confiscation Act was not blanket emancipation
but it unquestionably put hundreds of thousands of slaves on a
path to freedom and that is something Lincoln could not toler-
ate at the time. Lincoln was working on a plan of gradual, compensated emancipation followed by the recolonization of black
people back to Africa or into a place suitable for them. The
emancipation timetable of the Second Confiscation Act was
too soon for Lincoln so he slammed the door shut with the
Preliminary Emancipation Proclamation *the very day before
the Second Confiscation Act was to go into effect.* The slaves
affected — approximately a half-million — stayed in slavery
along with the half-million slaves in the five Union slave states
until well after the end of the war, though they could have been
freed by Lincoln and the Northern Congress at any time.

such as Charles Dickens made fun of Lincoln. William H. Seward, Lincoln's own secretary of state, did too, stating that "We show our sympathy with slavery by emancipating slaves where we cannot reach them and holding them in bondage where we can set them free."[18]

Most scholars agree with Dickens and Seward. Bennett writes:

> The same points have been made with abundant documentation by twentieth-century scholars like Richard Hofstadter, who said the Proclamation "did not in fact free any slaves" (169). Some of the biggest names in the Lincoln establishment have said the same thing. Roy P. Basler, the editor of the monumental *Collected Works of Abraham Lincoln*, said the Proclamation was "itself only a promise of freedom . . . " (1935, 219-20). J. G. Randall, who has been called "the greatest Lincoln scholar of all time," said the Proclamation itself did not free a single slave (1957, 357). Horace White, the *Chicago Tribune* correspondent who covered Lincoln in Illinois and in Washington, said it is doubtful that the Procla-

---

[18] James G. Randall and David H. Donald, *The Civil War and Reconstruction* (Lexington, Mass: D.C. Heath, 1969), 371.

mation "freed anybody anywhere"
(222).[19]

The Emancipation Proclamation states that it is "a fit and necessary war measure for suppressing said rebellion." It lists the states "in rebellion against the United States" because the slaves in those states would now be free. The slaves in the states not in rebellion — the Union slave states of Maryland, Delaware, Kentucky, Missouri, and the counties of Virginia that became the fifth Union slave state, West Virginia, as well as captured Confederate territory specifically listed (which was most of it at the time) — "are, for the present, left precisely as if this proclamation were not issued" — in other words, left in slavery.

So, not only did Lincoln free no slaves (or few) with the Emancipation Proclamation, an argument can be made that he prevented the freedom of 500,000 — Bennett says "reenslaved" — who would have been free or on a path to freedom within 24 hours of his signing the Preliminary Emancipation Proclamation.[20]

---

[19] Bennett, *Forced Into Glory*, 6-7.

[20] As stated in footnote #17, the Second Confiscation Act was not blanket emancipation but it definitely gave hundreds of thousands of slaves some kind of chance at freedom. If one loves Lincoln, as James M. McPherson does, then one tends to believe that the chance at freedom granted by the Second Confiscation Act was too torturous and improbable to ever work, therefore Lincoln really wasn't "reenslaving" anybody with the Preliminary Emancipation Proclamation. That may have some truth, but as a war president who had already suspended habeas corpus, shut down newspapers, arrested and

Historian James M. McPherson seems to admit that the Emancipation Proclamation freed no slaves. He calls that argument an "old canard" but he does not tell us which slaves *were* freed (because none, or few, were). Instead, he tells us that the Emancipation Proclamation made the Union Army an army of liberation as it invaded deeper into the South.[21] The only problem with that argument is that the performance of Lincoln and the Union Army up to that point in the war was mixed so there was no guarantee that the Union Army would take any more Confederate territory — but there was an *absolute guarantee* that the Emancipation Proclamation would keep hundreds of thousands — nearly a million — black people in slavery in the five Union slave states and the already-captured Confederate territory exempted in the EP. And it is an absolute fact that Lincoln and the North could have freed those slaves easily if they had wanted to.

---

imprisoned critics, rigged elections and done many other dictatorial things, Lincoln considered himself to have vast powers to interpret a law any way he wanted to. Think about President Barack Obama, who is not even a wartime president, and his 41 changes to the Affordable Care Act. There is little doubt that if Lincoln had wanted to free some slaves with the Second Confiscation Act, he would have. He didn't, and as a result, a half-million black people stayed in slavery, along with another half-million in the five Union slave states, for a total approaching one million, until after the end of the war.

[21] James M. McPherson, "Lincoln the Devil," book review of Lerone Bennett Jr.'s *Forced into Glory, Abraham Lincoln's White Dream*, New York Times on the Web, August 27, 2000, http://www.nytimes.com/books/00/08/27/reviews/000827.27mcphert.html, accessed 7/4/2014.

Here is how Lerone Bennett calculated the
500,000 slaves that he maintains Lincoln reenslaved.
This is his footnote #3 on page 627 of *Forced into
Glory*:

> Appletons' *Annual Cyclopaedia* 1863 re-
> ported that the Emancipation Proclama-
> tion only applied to slaves in Confeder-
> ate-held areas — where Lincoln did not
> have the power to free them. The Proc-
> lamation did not apply to the 429,396
> slaves in the "loyal" [Union] slave states
> of Kentucky, Maryland, Missouri, and
> Delaware, and left in slavery the
> 402,863 slaves in Union-controlled areas
> Lincoln could have freed: 275,719 in
> Tennessee, 87,812 in Louisiana, and
> 39,332 in Virginia. The AC estimate was
> based on the 1860 Census and did not
> take into consideration population
> growth and the large number of slaves
> who flocked to Union-controlled areas in
> Tennessee, Louisiana, and Virginia. I
> have therefore used a conservative esti-
> mate of 500,000 for the number of slaves
> Lincoln could have freed and deliber-
> ately did not free.

Slavery was not the cause of the War Between the
States. In the weeks leading up to the war, Lincoln
and the North were not discussing emancipation. Their

actions were driven by the disastrous collapse of the Northern economy that was fast approaching, and the threatened dissolution of the Republican Party because of extreme dissatisfaction with the state of affairs in the North

.

Chapter 2

The North Did Not Go to War
to End Slavery

*If they had, they would have started by
passing a constitution amendment
abolishing slavery. They did the opposite. They overwhelmingly passed the
Corwin Amendment, which left black
people in slavery forever, even beyond
the reach of Congress. This alone
proves, unequivocally, that the North
did not go to war to end slavery or free
the slaves.*

The North does not get to redefine, in the middle of the
war, its reason for going to war. What the North proclaimed in the *beginning,* stands, as its reason for going to war — and it is unchangeable. War measures
halfway through the war, such as the Emancipation
Proclamation that freed no slaves (and prevented close
to a million slaves from achieving their freedom), have
nothing to do with why the North went to war in the
first place.

A near-unanimous resolution entitled the *War
Aims Resolution* established early-on what the North

was fighting for. It was passed by the Northern Congress in July, 1861, three months after the bombardment of Fort Sumter:

> ... That this war is not waged upon our
> part in any spirit of oppression, nor for
> any purpose of conquest or subjugation,
> nor for the purpose of overthrowing or
> interfering with the rights or institu-
> tions [slavery] of the States, but to de-
> fend and maintain the supremacy of the
> Constitution [which allowed and pro-
> tected slavery], and to preserve the
> Union. . . .[22]

Throughout the antebellum years as the country achieved its Manifest Destiny marching westward, winning the Mexican War, growing in wealth and power, no credible Northern leader said they should march armies into the South to end slavery.[23]

---

[22] The War Aims Resolution is also known by the names of its sponsors, Representative John J. Crittenden of Kentucky and Senator Andrew Johnson of Tennessee: the Crittenden-Johnson Resolution, or just the Crittenden Resolution. It passed the U.S. House of Representatives July 22, 1861, and the Senate July 25, 1861. There were only two dissenting votes in the House and five in the Senate.
http://en.wikipedia.org/wiki/Crittenden-Johnson_Resolution, accessed March 29, 2014.

[23] Indeed, there is much evidence that illegal slave trading was still being conducted by many Northern ship captains right up to the beginning of the war, though slave trading had officially been outlawed since 1808.

Throughout the first two years of the war, almost
nobody in the North said they were fighting to end
slavery. To do so would risk racist Union soldiers de-
serting because they signed up to fight for the Union,
not to free slaves whom they feared would move north
and inundate their towns and cities and be job competition. Julia Dent Grant, wife of Ulysses S. Grant,
might have freed her four slaves if she had thought it
was an abolition war and not a war for the Union.[24]

---

[24] There is a well-known story about Ulysses S. Grant wherein
Grant states that he is fighting to preserve the Union and if
anybody accuses him of fighting to free the slaves, he will
promptly go join the Confederacy and fight on their side. There
may be some truth to it, and maybe not. Grant did own one
slave whom he freed in 1859, but his wife, Julia, owned four
throughout much of the war, therefore Grant's household was
a slaveholding household. Grant's supposed quotation was
published in 1868 in the *Democratic Speaker's Hand-Book*,
which was a Democratic Party campaign document in the
1868 campaign when Grant was running for president as a
Republican. However, in 1861, Grant was a Democrat, and, as
stated, living in a slaveholding household. *The Democratic
Speaker's Hand-Book* on page 33 states that Grant was the
Colonel of the Twenty-first Illinois, stationed near Mexico in
1861, and that Grant's quotation was provided by the editor of
the *Randolph Citizen*, a Missouri newspaper. It starts: "In a
public conversation in Ringo's banking-house, a sterling Union
man put this question to him [Grant]: 'What do you honestly
think was the real object of this war on the part of the Federal
Government?'"

> 'Sir, said Grant, 'I have no doubt in the world
> that the sole object is the restoration of the
> Union. I will say further, though, that I am a
> Democrat—every man in my regiment is a
> Democrat—and whenever I shall be con-

Most Northerners, excluding a few truly good-hearted abolitionists, accepted slavery. As stated earlier, historians Lee Benson and Gavin Wright maintain that the percentage of abolitionists in the North was "probably no more than 2 per cent, almost certainly no more than 5 per cent, of the Northern electorate,"[25] and, ironically, many of them didn't like slavery because they didn't like blacks and did not want to associate with them. Prominent abolitionist Elijah Lovejoy had been murdered by an outraged Northern mob in Lincoln's own Illinois in 1837. The mob was trying to destroy Lovejoy's abolitionist materials and his press.

---

vinced that this war has for its object anything else than what I have mentioned, or that the Government designed using its soldiers to execute the purposes of the abolitionists, I pledge you my honor as a man and a soldier that I will carry my sword to the other side, and cast my lot with that people.'

Source: *Democratic Speaker's Hand-Book: Containing every thing necessary for the defense of the national democracy in the coming presidential campaign, and for the assault of the radical enemies of the country and its constitution*, compiled by Matthew Carey, Jr. Cincinnati: Miami Printing and Publishing Company, 1868.

[25] Benson, "Explanations of American Civil War Causation" in Wright, *The Political Economy of the Cotton South,* 136. David M. Potter also points out that Northern antislavery had a strong anti-black bias and was not designed to help black people but to get rid of them. See David M. Potter, *The Impending Crisis, 1848-1861*, completed and edited by Don E. Fehrenbacher (New York: Harper & Row, Publishers, 1976), 35-36.

By 1861, Northerners had been supporting slavery for 241 years and would continue supporting it throughout the War Between the States since five slave states, as noted earlier, fought for the North. Again, those states are Maryland, Delaware, Kentucky, Missouri and West Virginia, which came into the Union during the war as a slave state.[26]

If the North was fighting to end slavery, it would *never* permit slave states to fight for the Union — or, it would have ended slavery in the Union slave states immediately.

It did the opposite and made sure by constitutional amendment and proclamation that slavery in the Union was protected, just as it was, and had always been, by the Constitution.

That's how the North really felt about slavery and freeing the slaves.

Lincoln himself took it a step further. He supported the first Thirteenth Amendment to the U.S. Constitution — the Corwin Amendment — which would have left black people in slavery forever, even beyond the reach of Congress. It passed March 2, 1861, two days before Lincoln's first inaugural. It reads:

> No amendment shall be made to the
> Constitution which will authorize or give

---

[26] The District of Columbia, which included the Northern capital, Washington, permitted slavery for the first year of the war. Slavery was abolished in DC with compensation to slaveowners in 1862, but it continued in the five Union slave states throughout the war and a while afterward.

to Congress the power to abolish or interfere, within any State, with the domestic institutions thereof [slavery], including that of persons held to labor
[slaves] or service by the laws of said
State.[27]

About the Corwin Amendment, Lincoln said, in his
first inaugural on March 4, 1861:

I understand a proposed amendment to
the Constitution — which amendment,
however, I have not seen — has passed
Congress, to the effect that the Federal
Government shall never interfere with
the domestic institutions of the States,
including that of persons held to service.
To avoid misconstruction of what I have
said, I depart from my purpose not to
speak of particular amendments so far
as to say that, holding such a provision
to now be implied constitutional law, I
**have no objection to its being made ex-
press and irrevocable.**
(Emphasis added.)

Before Lincoln took office, President James Buchanan actually signed the Corwin Amendment after it

---

[27] Corwin Amendment,
http://en.wikipedia.org/wiki/Corwin_Amendment. Accessed
March 26, 2014.

had been approved by Congress and was ready to be
sent to the states for ratification. Buchanan's act was
symbolic only.

It is important to note that the Corwin Amendment had required a two-thirds vote in the House and
Senate and it had passed with mostly Northern votes
because seven Southern states were out of the Union
by then and did not vote. Indeed, the bill's sponsor,
Representative Thomas Corwin, was from Ohio.

Three Northern states ratified the Corwin Amendment — Ohio, Maryland and Illinois — before the war
made it moot.

After the Corwin Amendment's passage, Lincoln
sent a letter with a copy of the Corwin Amendment to
each state's governor pointing out that Buchanan had
signed it. Lincoln was making sure everyone knew of
his strong support of slavery forever, even beyond the
reach of Congress.

Before even mentioning the Corwin Amendment in
his first inaugural, Lincoln made it clear that he
strongly supported slavery and had "no inclination" to
end it:

> Apprehension seems to exist among the
> people of the Southern States that by
> the accession of a Republican admini-
> stration their property and their peace
> and personal security are to be endan-
> gered. There has never been any reason-
> able cause for such apprehension. In-
> deed, the most ample evidence to the

contrary has all the while existed and
been open to their inspection. It is found
in nearly all the published speeches of
him who now addresses you. I do but
quote from one of those speeches when I
declare that "I have no purpose, directly
or indirectly, to interfere with the institution of slavery in the States where it
exists. I believe I have no lawful right
to do so, and I have no inclination to do
so." Those who nominated and elected
me did so with full knowledge that I had
made this and many similar declara-
tions, and had never recanted them.
And, more than this, they placed in the
platform for my acceptance, and as a law
to themselves and to me, the clear and
emphatic resolution which I now read:

> Resolved, That the main-
> tenance inviolate of the
> rights of the States, and
> especially the right of each
> State to order and control
> its own domestic institu-
> tions according to its own
> judgment exclusively, is
> essential to that balance of
> power on which the perfec-
> tion and endurance of our
> political fabric depend,

and we denounce the law-
less invasion by armed
force of the soil of any
State or Territory, no matter under what pretext, as
among the gravest of
crimes.

I now reiterate these sentiments; and, in
doing so, I only press upon the public
attention the most conclusive evidence of
which the case is susceptible, that the
property, peace, and security of no section are to be in any wise endangered by
the now incoming administration.
(Emphasis added.)

On August 22, 1862, sixteen months into the war,
Lincoln wrote to Horace Greeley, editor of the *New
York Tribune*, in response to a letter Greeley had sent
him, and reiterated:

. . . My paramount object in this struggle
is to save the Union, and is *not* either to
save or to destroy slavery. If I could save
the Union without freeing *any* slave I
would do it, and if I could save it by freeing *all* the slaves I would do it; and if I
could save it by freeing some and leaving
others alone I would also do that—What
I do about slavery, and the colored race,

I do because I believe it helps to save the
Union; and what I forbear, I forbear be-
cause I do *not* believe it would help the
Union. [28] (Lincoln's italics.)

Exactly one month — September 22, 1862 — after
writing his letter to Horace Greeley, Lincoln issued the
Preliminary Emancipation Proclamation and the very
first paragraph states clearly that the war is being
fought to restore the Union and not to free the slaves:

I, Abraham Lincoln, President of the
United States of America, and Commander-in-Chief of the Army and Navy
thereof, do hereby proclaim and declare
that **hereafter, as heretofore, the war
will be prosecuted for the object of practically restoring the constitutional relation between the United States, and
each of the States,** and the people
thereof, in which States that relation is,
or may be, suspended or disturbed.
(Emphasis added.)

Clearly, the North did not instigate a war to end
slavery.

The focus on slavery as the primary cause of the
War Between the States — even indirectly — is a

---

[28]Letter, A. Lincoln to Horace Greeley, August 22, 1862, in Roy
P. Basler, ed., *The Collected Works of Abraham Lincoln* (New
Brunswick, NJ: Rutgers University Press, 1953) V:388.

fraud of biblical proportions and it prevents real understanding of American history.

Pulitzer Prize winning historian and Lincoln scholar, David H. Donald, back in the 1960s, was concerned about the overemphasis of slavery as the cause of the war. He said the Civil Rights Movement seems to have been the reason for stressing slavery as the cause of the war.

I have already proven that the North did not go to war to end slavery. There is much more evidence but the following is a good summary of the things in the beginning that show, beyond the shadow of a doubt, that the North did not go to war to free the slaves or because of slavery:

> 1) The North's War Aims Resolution,
> which states clearly that they are fight-
> ing to preserve the Union and not "for
> the purpose of overthrowing or interfer-
> ing with the rights or institutions [slav-
> ery] of the States."

> 2) Lincoln's constant promises in high
> profile forums such as his first inaugural
> address, to protect slavery where it ex-
> isted.

> 3) The United States Congress's over-
> whelming passage of the Corwin Amend-
> ment, which would have left black peo-
> ple in slavery forever, even beyond the

reach of Congress. **If the North was fighting to end slavery, it would have passed a constitutional amendment ending slavery, and not one that guaranteed that black people would be in slavery forever, even beyond the reach of Congress.** Three Northern states ratified the Corwin Amendment including Lincoln's own Illinois before the war made it moot. This alone proves, unequivocally, that the North did not go to war to free the slaves or to end slavery. (Emphasis added.)

4) Lincoln's strong support for the Corwin Amendment as stated in his first inaugural and in personal letters to the governors.

5) The North's historical support for slavery and slave-trading.

6) The fact that, when Lincoln sent his hostile military mission to Charleston to start the war, just prior to the bombardment of Fort Sumter, there were more slave states in the Union than in the Confederacy.[29]

---

[29] The eight slave states in the Union on April 12, 1861 when Fort Sumter was bombarded are Virginia, Tennessee, Arkansas, North Carolina, Maryland, Delaware, Kentucky and Mis-

7) Northern leaders — no credible
Northern leader throughout the antebel-
lum period said they ought to march ar-
mies into the South to free the slaves.
Indeed, abolitionists were hated in the
North. Elijah Lovejoy was murdered in
Lincoln's Illinois.

8) Northerner leaders — almost none of
whom for the first two years of the war
said that they were fighting to free the
slaves. Ulysses S. Grant's wife, Julia,
owned four slaves. It would be hard for
Grant to say he had gone to war to end
slavery when his own house was a slaveholding household.

9) The five slave states that fought for
the North throughout the war: Maryland, Delaware, Missouri, Kentucky, and
West Virginia.

10) The Preliminary Emancipation Proclamation issued September 22, 1862,
that states clearly in the very first paragraph that "**hereafter, as theretofore,**
the war will be prosecuted for the object

---

souri. West Virginia was admitted to the Union as a slave state
during the war. The seven states first to secede and form the
Confederate States of America are South Carolina, Georgia,
Florida, Alabama, Louisiana, Mississippi and Texas.

of practically restoring the constitutional relation" between the U.S. and seceded states i.e., the Union. There is no mention of slavery. (Emphasis added.)

11) The Emancipation Proclamation that freed no slaves (or few) and deliberately left at least 832,259, who were under Northern control, in slavery. Most of those black people officially stayed slaves until well after the end of the war. They could have been freed easily if the North had wanted to free them.[30]

---

[30] The argument that Lincoln *had* to word the Emancipation Proclamation to protect slavery in the Union slaves states because he did not have the constitutional authority to end slavery in the those states has some merit and makes my point — that **Northerners did not go to war to end slavery. If they had, they would have started by passing a constitutional amendment abolishing slavery. As stated above, they did the opposite and overwhelmingly passed the Corwin Amendment, which would have left black people in slavery forever, even beyond the reach of Congress. It was ratified by three Northern states before the war made it moot.** ALSO, if one buys the argument that Lincoln didn't have the constitutional authority to end slavery in the Union slaves states, then how did he get the authority to end slavery in the Southern slave states, which, according to Lincoln, were still part of the Union? As Lincoln stated, the Emancipation Proclamation was a *war measure* and its authority came from Lincoln's power as commander-in-chief. It was not designed to help black people but designed to help Union armies win the war by encouraging slaves in the South to rise up and kill women and children in the South, which would cause men in the Confederate Army to want to go home to protect their fami-

The Emancipation Proclamation states,
literally, that it is a war measure, and it
was not issued early on.

It was not issued before Lincoln took office, or after the bombardment of Fort
Sumter, or during Lincoln's first inaugural. It was issued two years into the war
— and it freed no slaves (or few).

The conditions around the issuance of
the Emancipation Proclamation and its
timetable establish the fact that the
North most certainly did not go to war
on April 12, 1861 to end slavery or free
the slaves.

---

lies. Of course, this didn't happen because the slaves were
loyal to the South for the most part throughout the war. The EP
would, however, cause slaves, in the excitement of impending
battle, to run off as the Union Army invaded further into the
South. This would be advantageous to the North. **Two other
HUGE reasons the EP was issued: To get the North favorable press in Europe, and to help stymie official recognition of the Confederacy, which would almost certainly
bring military assistance.** But, getting back to the constitutional argument, the North allowed slave states to be part of
the Union, and the South allowed free states to be part of the
Confederacy. The South anticipated that several free states
with economic ties to the South would join the CSA and this
bothered Lincoln greatly. In keeping with its States' Rights philosophy, slavery in the CSA was up to an individual state.
(Emphasis added.)

The North's support for slavery goes back to the beginning of the country when Northern (and British) slave traders brought most of the slaves here and made huge fortunes in the process. Dr. Edgar J. McManus in his excellent book, *Black Bondage in the North*, writes that "Boston merchants entered the African trade as early as 1644, and by 1676 they were bringing back cargoes from as far away as East Africa and Madagascar."[31] McManus writes:

> [The slave trade] quickly became one of the cornerstones of New England's commercial prosperity . . . which yielded enormous commercial profits.[32]

Virtually the entire infrastructure of the Old North was built on profits from the slave trade and slave traders such as Boston's Peter Faneuil of Faneuil Hall, the ironically named "Cradle of Liberty," which might have been a cradle for him but sure wasn't for the tens of thousands of black Africans he was responsible for snatching from their families and forcing into the horrors of the Middle Passage.

McManus explains the importance of the slave trade to the New England economy:

> [The slave trade] stimulated the growth of other industries. Shipbuilding, the

---

[31] Edgar J. McManus, *Black Bondage in the North* (Syracuse: Syracuse University Press, 1973), 9-10.
[32] Ibid.

distilleries, the molasses trade, agricultural exports to the West Indies, and the
large numbers of artisans, sailors, and
farmers were all dependent upon the
traffic in Negroes. It became the hub of
New England's economy.[33]

See also the excellent 2005 book *Complicity, How
the North Promoted, Prolonged, and Profited from
Slavery*, by Anne Farrow, Joel Lang, and Jenifer
Frank of *The Hartford Courant.*[34]

Let's go beyond the North's guilt for enthusiastic,
widespread slave trading and look at the whole picture.

The North could not have gotten cargoes of slaves
without tremendous help from blacks themselves.
Black African tribal chieftains had captives from tribal
warfare rounded up and waiting in places like Bunce
Island off modern Sierra Leone to be picked up by
slave traders from all over the world. The constant un-
rest in Africa today with genocides, kidnappings,
never-ending warfare, people hacked to death, makes
it easy to understand. Black tribal chieftains were
worse then because there was no media attention on
them. They made slavery easy. White people did not
even have to get off the ship and usually didn't. Slavery could never have happened without those blacks in

---

[33] Ibid.
[34] Anne Farrow, Joel Lang, and Jenifer Frank, *Complicity, How
the North Promoted, Prolonged, and Profited from Slavery*
(New York: Ballantine Books, 2005).

Africa who were all too willing to sell other blacks into slavery for profit.[35]

Slavery has always existed including today. Indians enslaved other Indians. The Romans would conquer a place and kill all the men and take all the women and children into slavery. Most cultures, worldwide, had slavery at one time or another. American slavery is not the first. Only 5% of slaves in the exodus from Africa, called the African Diaspora, ended up in the United States. Many ended up in Brazil and other places in South America and the Caribbean.

Slavery is a blight on humanity but a fact of human history and we should understand the truth of it and not the politically correct lie that blames only the South. All Americans, but especially African-Americans, deserve to know the entire truth about slavery and not some white-washed version. "Truth" is why Lerone Bennett wrote *Forced into Glory*, to reveal that racist Abraham Lincoln deliberately did not free any slaves (or freed very few) with the Emancipation Proclamation, and, most of Lincoln's life (Lerone Bennett says *all* of his life) supported sending African-Americans back to Africa or into a climate suitable to them. The Preliminary Emancipation Proclamation confirms this long-held belief of Lincoln's that "the effort to colonize persons of African descent, with their consent, upon this continent, or elsewhere, with the previously

---

[35] See James Walvin, *Slavery and the Slave Trade, A Short Illustrated History* (Jackson: University Press of Mississippi, 1983) and numerous other books on the slave trade.

obtained consent of the Governments existing there, will be continued."

There would have been no American slavery without black tribal chieftains in Africa, and British and Yankee slave traders.

The reason the South gets all the blame is because of a half-century of political correctness[36] in which only one side of the story has been told[37] because, if you tell the Southern side, even in a scholarly manner, you open yourself up to charges of being a racist and member of the KKK who wishes we still had slavery. Esteemed historian, Eugene D. Genovese, writes:

> To speak positively about any part of

---

[36] Political correctness — to be correct "politically" — is the opposite of being correct in a scholarly manner. Scholarship seeks truth. Politics does not. Politics seeks to persuade or intimidate so power can be won. Sometimes truth is used. Oftentimes lies are used such as President Obama's "If you like you healthcare plan, you can keep your healthcare plan. Period." which was labeled by Politifact the *Lie of the Year* for 2013.

[37] Joe Gray Taylor, in attempting to examine the causes of the war 25 years ago, notes that **David H. Donald "seems to have been correct when he said in 1960 that the causation of the Civil War was dead as a serious subject of historical analysis"** and that **"A 'Southern' point of view on the secession crisis no longer exists among professional historians."** These quotations come from Joe Gray Taylor, "The White South from Secession to Redemption," in John B. Boles and Evelyn Thomas Nolen, *Interpreting Southern History, Historiographical Essays in Honor of Sanford W. Higginbotham* (Baton Rouge: Louisiana State University Press, 1987), 162-164. (Emphasis added.)

this Southern tradition is to invite charges of being a racist and an apologist for slavery and segregation. **We are witnessing a cultural and political atrocity** — an increasingly successful campaign by the media and an academic elite to strip young white Southerners, and arguably black Southerners as well, of their heritage, and therefore, their identity. They are being taught to forget their forebears or to remember them with shame.[38] (Emphasis added.)

NAACP resolutions passed in 1987 and 1991 spewing hatred on the Confederate battle flag also intimidate scholars who would rather not weigh in or who will take the anti-South side without a fair examination of the issues. Professors know that they stand almost no chance of getting tenure if they say anything good about the South in the War Between the States. They know that we live in a shallow and superficial time and just an accusatory whiff in the air that someone is a racist, whether they are or not, will end a college history career or prevent one from getting started.[39]

---

[38] Eugene D. Genovese, *The Southern Tradition, The Achievement and Limitations of an American Conservatism* (Cambridge, MA and London: Harvard University Press, 1994), xi-xii. Dr. Genovese passed away September 26, 2012.

[39] The 1987 NAACP anti-Confederate-battle-flag resolution was passed at their Southeast Region Convention in March of that year and can be found in Don Hinkle, *Embattled Banner,*

But, remember the old proverb: "The one who states his case first seems right, until the other comes and examines him"[40]

The War Between the States is the central event in American history. It should be examined thoroughly just as Lerone Bennett has examined Abraham Lincoln and given us a fresh perspective on old Honest Abe the racist who used the "n" word more than the Grand Wizard of the Ku Klux Klan, the same Abe Lincoln who wanted to ship black people back to Africa and who deliberately freed no slaves with the Emancipation Proclamation when he could have freed close to a million under Union control. There is a lot to know and think about in order to understand what really happened.

A Reasonable Defense of the Confederate Battle Flag (Paducah, KY: Turner Publishing Company, 1997), 23-25. The 1991 resolution can be found in NAACP convention minutes from that year, as cited in Hinkle, *Embattled Banner*, 157-186.

[40] English Standard Version of the Bible, Proverbs 18:17.

Chapter 3

Northern Economic Annihilation: The True Cause of the War

The North cut off from Southern cotton, rice, tobacco, and other products would lose three fourths of her commerce, and a very large proportion of her manufactures. And thus those great fountains of finance would sink very low. . . . Would the North in such a condition as that declare war against the South?[41]

Henry L. Benning
November 19, 1860

The cause of the war itself is not complicated — the South seceded and the North immediately began a dramatic economic collapse.

Northerners quickly discovered that their great wealth and employment depended on the South — on

---

[41] Benning was a justice on the Georgia Supreme Court at the beginning of the war. He became one of Gen. Robert E. Lee's most able brigadier generals in the Army of Northern Virginia. See footnote #51 for the source of this quotation.

manufacturing for the South, on financing Southern
agriculture, on shipping Southern commodities around
the world. Cotton alone made up 60% of U.S. exports
in 1860.

This was the era of the Pax Britannica and Great
Britain ruled world trade, not the North. The North's
biggest customer, by far, was the South.

Economic historian Philip S. Foner wrote extensively on business in the North. In his excellent book,
*Business & Slavery, The New York Merchants & the
Irrepressible Conflict,* he explains with crystal clarity
why the North quickly decided that war was preferable
to economic ruin:

> It was also exceedingly logical that when
> all the efforts to save the Union peace-
> fully had failed, the merchants, regard-
> less of political views, should have en-
> dorsed the recourse to an armed policy.
> They had conducted their long struggle
> to prevent the dissolution of the Union
> because they knew that their very exis-
> tence as businessmen depended upon
> the outcome. When they finally became
> aware of the economic chaos secession
> was causing, when they saw the entire
> business system crumbling before their
> very eyes, they knew that there was no
> choice left. **The Union must be**

preserved. Any other outcome meant
economic suicide.[42] (Emphasis added.)

That was the choice the North was facing. Preserve the Union or face economic disaster which meant
the collapse of the entire North into anarchy. Northerners were not concerned about slavery when their
economic house was a raging inferno.

The most prominent economist of the antebellum
era, Thomas Prentice Kettell, wrote a famous book entitled *Southern Wealth and Northern Profits as Exhibited in Statistical Facts and Official Figures: Showing
the Necessity of Union to the Future Prosperity and
Welfare of the Republic.* He argued that Southerners
were producing the wealth of the United States with
cotton and other commodities but Northerners were
taking all the profits. Kettell understood the extensive
interaction between the two regions and the North's
dependence on the South:

> These transactions influence the earn-
> ings, more or less direct, of every North-
> ern man. A portion of every artisan's
> work is paid for by Southern means.
> Every carman draws pay, more or less,
> from the trade of that section [the
> South]. The agents who sell manufac-

---

[42] Philip S. Foner, *Business & Slavery, The New York Merchants & the Irrepressible Conflict* (Chapel Hill: The University
of North Carolina Press, 1941), 322.

tures, the merchants who sell imported
goods, the ships that carry them, the
builders of the ships, the lumbermen
who furnish the material, and all those
who supply means of support to them
and their families. The brokers, the dealers in Southern produce, the exchange
dealers, the bankers, the insurance companies, and all those who are actively
employed in receiving then distributing
Southern produce, with the long train of
persons who furnish them with houses,
clothing, supplies, education, religion,
amusement, transportation, etc., are dependent upon this active interchange, by
which at least one thousand millions of
dollars come and go between the North
and South in a year.[43]

There were two components of the North's enormous economic success. The first was simply the luck
of having an agricultural region as successful as the
South to do for. The South was vast, warm, fertile and
productive. Southerners were as ambitious as Northerners and wanted to make money too. They did so

---

[43] Thomas Prentice Kettell, *Southern Wealth and Northern
Profits as Exhibited in Statistical Facts and Official Figures:
Showing the Necessity of Union to the Future Prosperity and
Welfare of the Republic* (New York: Geo. W. & John A. Wood,
1860; reprint: University: University of Alabama Press, 1965),
75.

with agriculture. It had been this way since Jamestown when colonists found they could make fortunes with tobacco, then later when the cotton gin made short-staple cotton profitable. Per capita income in the South, in the years before the war, was roughly the same as in the North. So, supplying the successful South with goods and services, and shipping for the South, gave Northerners jobs.

The second was the utterly unfair taxation of the South for the direct benefit of the North: 3/4ths of the federal treasury was supplied by the South, yet 3/4ths of federal tax revenue was spent in the North. It was mostly Southerners who had to pay the high tariffs that protected Northern businesses and industry. It was a direct transfer out of the South and into the pockets of Northerners.

In a frank editorial, "What Shall Be Done for a Revenue?" March 12, 1861, one month before the bombardment of Fort Sumter, the *New York Evening Post* writes:

> That either the revenue from duties
> must be collected in the ports of the re-
> bel states, or the ports must be closed to
> importations from abroad, is generally
> admitted. If neither of these things be
> done, our revenue laws are substantially
> repealed; **the sources which supply our
> treasury will be dried up;** we shall have
> no money to carry on the government;
> the nation will become bankrupt before

the next crop of corn is ripe. There will
be nothing to furnish means of subsis-
tence to the army; nothing to keep our
navy afloat; nothing to pay the salaries
of the public officers; the present order
of things must come to a dead stop.[44]
(Emphasis added.)

Think about the American Revolution and the
taxation without representation issue. Those taxes
were minuscule compared to 1860 when millions of
dollars per year were flowing straight out of the South
and into the pockets of Northerners.

Those Northerners had not earned a penny of it. It
was through government manipulation that they had
managed to get monopoly status for most Northern
industries and shipping, which killed competition and
allowed Northerners to charge high rates. There was a
protective tariff, and bounties and subsidies to Northern businesses that were like tax credits and payments
from the federal treasury, even though most of the
money *in* the federal treasury — 3/4ths of it — had
come from the South.

The *Report on the Causes of the Secession of Georgia* stated it clearly:

The material prosperity of the North

---

[44] *New York Evening Post*, March 12, 1861, "What Shall Be
Done for a Revenue?", in Howard Cecil Perkins, ed., *Northern
Editorials on Secession*, Vol II (Gloucester: Peter Smith,
1964), 598.

was greatly dependent on the Federal
Government; that of the South not at
all.[45]

The great Southern writer, William Gilmore
Simms, knew the North well and concluded the same:

> No doubt that, in one sense, they cherish
> the Union, but only as the agency by
> which they prosper in uncounted pros-
> perity. It is to them, the very breath of
> life; it has made them rich and powerful,
> & keeps them so. No doubt they love the
> South, but it is as the wolf loves the
> lamb, coveting and devouring it.[46]

---

[45] *Report on the Causes of the Secession of Georgia,* adopted
by the Georgia Secession Convention, Tuesday, January 29,
1861, in the *Journal of the Georgia Convention,* in *The War of
the Rebellion: A Compilation of the Official Records of the Union and Confederate Armies* (Washington: Government Printing Office, 1900; reprint, Historical Times, Inc., 1985), Series
IV, Volume 1, 81-85.

[46] William Gilmore Simms, "Antagonisms of the Social Moral.
North and South.", unpublished 1857 lecture housed in the
Charles Carroll Simms Collection of the South Caroliniana Library, University of South Carolina, Columbia, 38-42; herein-
after cited as "Antagonisms." Simms (1806-1870) had a brilliant literary career. There is a bust of him in White Point Gardens at the Battery in Charleston. Edgar Allan Poe said Simms
was the greatest American writer of the 19th century. Simms
wrote 82 book-length works in his career, 20 of which are very
important in American history and literature. Simms understood the mind of the North. His books had been published in
the North. He knew the national publishing industry inside and

Southerners woke up one day and realized that they were being robbed blind and from then on, they would have no way to protect themselves. Henceforth in American history, the South would be outvoted by the North and any manner of confiscatory economic manipulation could and would continue. The North had four times the white voting population and the Republican Party had rallied them.

The governance of the entire country would now be by the North, for the North. George Washington had warned against sectional parties but Wendell Phillips proudly stated that the Republican Party was the party of the North pledged against the South.

Alexis de Tocqueville had predicted that if any one state gained enough power to control the government, it would make the rest of the country tributary to its power and would rule for its benefit. That's exactly what happened except it wasn't one state, it was the Northern States with their similar commercial interests.

This section from *The Address of the People of South Carolina, Assembled in Convention, to the People of the Slaveholding States of the United States* in December, 1860 explains precisely why the Southern States were now in the exact same position toward the North that the Colonies had been toward Great Britain:

The Revolution of 1776 turned upon one

---

out and had many friends and associates in the North.

great principle, self-government — and
self-taxation, the criterion of self-government. Where the interests of two peoples
united together under one Government,
are different, each must have the power
to protect its interests by the organization of the Government, or they cannot
be free. The interests of Great Britain
and of the Colonies were different and
antagonistic. Great Britain was desirous
of carrying out the policy of all nations
towards their Colonies, of making them
tributary to her wealth and power.

The Southern States now stand exactly
in the same position towards the Northern States that the Colonies did towards
Great Britain. The Northern States,
having the majority in Congress, claim
the same power of omnipotence in legislation as the British Parliament. "The
General Welfare," is the only limit to the
legislation of either; and the majority in
Congress, as in the British Parliament,
are the sole judges of the expediency of
the legislation this "General Welfare"
requires. Thus, the Government of the
United States has become a consolidated
Government; and the people of the
Southern States are compelled to meet

the very despotism their fathers threw
off in the Revolution of 1776. . . .

For the last forty years, the taxes laid by
the Congress of the United States, have
been laid with a view of subserving the
interests of the North. The people of the
South have been taxed by duties on imports, not for revenue, but for an object
inconsistent with revenue — to promote,
by prohibitions, Northern interests in
the productions of their mines and
manufacturers. [47]

---

[47] "Duties on imports for revenue" and "a tariff for revenue"
mean the same thing. They both refer to a small import tariff
whose sole purpose is to generate the small amount of revenue needed to run the government. The paragraph above, to
which this footnote belongs, points out the difference between
a small tariff for revenue, which the South always wanted because they craved free trade, verses a high protective tariff
designed to protect Northern industry from competition. A tariff
is a penalty, it's punitive, thus a high protective tariff worked by
making certain imported goods so expensive Southerners
could not afford them and would have to buy from the North.
To make matters more unfair, a tariff allowed Northerners to
ignore market competition and simply charge what they
wanted, up to the level of the tariff. A product which cost $100
on the free market might cost Southerners $400 by the time
they paid the protective tariff or the jacked-up Northern price.
This is exactly what is meant by "to promote, by prohibitions,
Northern interests." Protective tariffs promoted Northern goods
by putting cost prohibitions on any other goods. An additional
outrage occurred if a Southerner decided to go ahead and buy
an imported item and pay the tariff because 3/4ths of the
money the Southerner had to pay would go straight into the

The people of the Southern States are
not only taxed for the benefit of the
Northern States, but after the taxes are
collected, three-fourths of them are ex-
pended at the North. This cause, with
others, connected with the operation of
the General Government, has made the
cities of the South provincial. Their
growth is paralyzed; they are mere sub-
urbs of Northern cities. The agricultural
productions of the South are the basis of
the foreign commerce of the United
States; yet Southern cities do not carry
it on. . . . No man can, for a moment, believe that our ancestors intended to establish over their posterity, exactly the
same sort of Government they had over-
thrown.[48]

All of this had started right after the Revolution
when Northerners begged for federal protection for
their industries to get them going so they could com-

---

pockets of Northerners. It is not hard to see the unfairness of
this system nor why Southerners wanted free trade with the
rest of the world. Southerners were in a **far** worse position
verses the North than the Colonists had been with Great Britain in 1776. (Emphasis added.)

[48] *The Address of the People of South Carolina, Assembled in
Convention, to the People of the Slaveholding States of the
United States*, in John Amasa May and Joan Reynolds Faunt,
South Carolina Secedes (Columbia: University of South Caro-
lina Press, 1960), 82-92.

pete with Great Britain. Southerners had gone along
with it out of the good feelings from winning the Revolution, and patriotism.

But, like Ronald Reagan said, the closest thing to
eternal life is a government program and none of the
measures protecting Northern industry ever ended.
The North became dependent on them, like a drug ad-
dict, and clamored for more and more.

It was nothing but Northern greed for other people's money and it — not slavery — was the seed that
grew into war. Texas Representative John H. Reagan
told Northern representatives in early 1861:

> You are not content with the vast mil-
> lions of tribute we pay you annually un-
> der the operation of our revenue law, our
> navigation laws, your fishing bounties,
> and by making your people our manufac-
> turers, our merchants, our shippers. You
> are not satisfied with the vast tribute we
> pay you to build up your great cities,
> your railroads, your canals. You are not
> satisfied with the millions of tribute we
> have been paying you on account of the
> balance of exchange which you hold
> against us. You are not satisfied that we
> of the South are almost reduced to the

condition of overseers for northern capi-
talists.[49]

The most quoted phrase from the secession debate
in the South in the months leading up to secession
comes from the Declaration of Independence:

> Governments are instituted among Men,
> deriving their just powers from the con-
> sent of the governed, That whenever any
> Form of Government becomes destruc-
> tive of these ends, it is the Right of the
> People to alter or to abolish it, and to
> institute new Government, laying its
> foundation on such principles and orga-
> nizing its powers in such form, as to
> them shall seem most likely to effect
> their Safety and Happiness.

Any government that forces a region to pay 3/4ths
of the country's taxes then turns around and spends
3/4ths of the tax money in a different region for the
benefit of those who demanded the taxes but pay little

---

[49] John H. Reagan, "Speech of Representative John H.
Reagan of Texas, January 15, 1861," in *Congressional Globe*,
36 Congress, 2 Session, I, 391, as cited in abridged version of
Kenneth M. Stampp, ed., *The Causes of the Civil War*, 3rd
revised edition (New York: Simon & Schuster, Inc., 1991), 89.
Reagan served as Confederate Postmaster General and in
Jefferson Davis's cabinet as one of Davis's most trusted ad-
visors.

themselves — is a thief and a far worse tyranny than Great Britain in 1776.

The federal government in 1860 did not have the consent of the governed in the South or any "just powers." It had become the enemy of nine million Southerners, just as Great Britain had become the enemy of three million colonists in 1776. There is not one iota of difference in 1776 and 1861.

That's why Northern-biased and politically correct "historians" are so determined to keep the focus on slavery as the cause of the war with the implication that Northerners are the good guys and Southerners the bad, even though slavery as the cause of the American War Between the States is one of the biggest frauds in world history, as noted by Charles Dickens, who was a contemporary.

Northerners don't want to be the British in the second American Revolution but they were. They were far worse.

Georgia Senator Robert Toombs created an apt metaphor — a suction pump — to describe the Northern confiscation of Southern money which was made up of

> bounties and protection to every interest
> and every pursuit in the North, to the
> extent of at least fifty millions per an-
> num, besides the expenditure of at least
> sixty millions out of every seventy of the
> public expenditure among them, thus
> making the treasury a perpetual fertil-

izing stream to them and their industry,
and a suction-pump to drain away our
substance and parch up our lands.[50]

Henry L. Benning, nicknamed "Rock" and for
whom the sprawling U.S. Army base, Fort Benning,
near Columbus, Georgia is named, calculated the exact
amount flowing through Toombs's suction pump:

Eighty-five millions is the amount of the
drains from the South to the North in
one year, — drains in return for which
the South receives nothing.[51]

Benning argues that this $85,000,000 — a gargan-
tuan sum in 1861 — was not legitimately-earned profit
but the extra *above* normal profit that Southerners
had to pay because prices were higher than they
should have been. Monopolies protecting Northern
businesses and shipping exempted them from market
competition therefore they had no incentive to keep
costs down. They could charge what they wanted, and,
of course, it was going to be as much as they could get.

---

[50] Robert Toombs, "Secessionist Speech, Tuesday Evening,
November 13" delivered to the Georgia legislature in Milledgeville, November 13, 1860, in William W. Freehling, and
Craig M. Simpson, *Secession Debated, Georgia's Showdown
in 1860* (New York: Oxford University Press, 1992), 38.
[51] Henry L. Benning, "Henry L. Benning's Secessionist
Speech, Monday Evening, November 19," delivered in Milledgeville, Georgia, November 19, 1860, in Freehling and Simpson, *Secession Debated, Georgia's Showdown in 1860*, 132.

When a customer needs a product but the govern‐
ment says you can only buy from one supplier — you
have to pay that supplier's price, even though a hun‐
dred suppliers might make the exact same product and
charge half the price.

Say it's 1860 and you need a widget on your farm
that costs $50 from any of several different European
companies.

You would have your choice — but then the fed‐
eral government steps in and says you can ONLY buy
from Monopoly Company of the North and their price
is $175.

The $125 difference is what Benning is talking
about. It is unearned money sucked out of the South
and deposited into the pockets of Northerners simply
because the Northern owners of Monopoly Company of
the North lobbied the federal government to grant
them monopoly status.

The same thing happened with monopoly shipping
rates.

The tariff worked similarly too. It allowed North‐
ern businesses to ignore market competition and
charge right up to the level of the tariff. The higher a
tariff they could get, through political manipulation,
the more money that went into their pockets.

Preserving the Union, the North's money machine
— its suction pump, its cash cow — was critical, not
just desirable. As the Northern businessmen con‐
cluded: "The Union must be preserved. Any other out‐

come meant economic suicide,"[52] which meant bankruptcy, anarchy, and societal collapse. Lincoln and the
Northern Congress understood this completely and
agreed wholeheartedly, which is why they said over
and over and over: The War Between the States is
about preserving the Union, not ending slavery.

Slavery, obviously, is not why the North went to
war. In the weeks before the bombardment of Fort
Sumter, Northerners either bent over backwards to
protect slavery or were virtually silent on the slavery
issue — but they were screaming at the threshold of
pain about the impending economic catastrophe.

The prescient Benning asked a question which
predicted the violent future with 100% accuracy:

> The North cut off from Southern cotton,
> rice, tobacco, and other Southern prod-
> ucts would lose three fourths of her com-
> merce, and a very large proportion of her
> manufactures. And thus those great
> fountains of finance would sink very low.
> . . . Would the North in such a condition
> as that declare war against the South?[53]

These are the issues that caused the War Between
the States. It had nothing whatsoever to do with

---

[52] Foner, *Business & Slavery,* 322.
[53] Benning, "Henry L. Benning's Secessionist Speech, Monday
Evening, November 19" in Freehling and Simpson, *Secession
Debated, Georgia's Showdown in 1860,* 132.

slavery, especially not with any kindness on the part of the North toward black people, or desire by the North to end slavery. It was all about money, power and the ascendence of one region's economic interests over another's.

Charles Dickens, author of *A Christmas Carol, David Copperfield*, and so many other wonderful books, who is thought of as a literary colossus and the greatest novelist of the Victorian period, also published a periodical, *All the Year Round.* He was up on current events and horrified by the American war. He correctly identified it as a tariff war over economic issues and "Slavery has in reality nothing on earth to do with it."[54]

Dickens said the federal government compelled the South "to pay a heavy fine into the pockets of Northern manufacturers" so that "every feeling and interest on the one side [South] calls for political partition, and every pocket interest on the other side [North] for union."[55]

Dickens said the North "having gradually got to itself the making of the laws and the settlement of the

---

[54] The short quotations from Charles Dickens come from articles that are all quoted in Charles Adams, *When in the Course of Human Events, Arguing the Case for Southern Secession* (Lanham, MD: Rowman & Littlefield Publishers, Inc., 2000), 90-91: Charles Dickens, "The Morrill Tariff," *All the Year Round*, 28 December 1861, 328-330; "The American Tariff Bill," *Saturday Review*, 9 March 1861, 234-235; Dickens, "American Disunion," 411.

[55] See Note 54.

Tariffs . . . taxed the South most abominably for its own advantage . . . ."[56]

He noted the hypocrisy of the North and its bad treatment of black people, and the South's right to secede:

> Every reasonable creature may know, if
> willing, that the North hates the Negro,
> and that until it was convenient to make
> a pretence that sympathy with him was
> the cause of the War, it hated the abo-
> litionists and derided them up hill and
> down dale. For the rest, there is not a
> pin to choose between the two parties.
> They will both rant and lie and fight un-
> til they come to a compromise; and the
> slave may be thrown into that compro-
> mise or thrown out of it, just as it hap-
> pens. As to Secession being Rebellion, it
> is distinctly provable by State Papers
> that Washington considered it no such
> thing — that Massachusetts, now loud-
> est against it, has itself asserted its
> right to secede, again and again — and
> that years ago when the two Carolinas
> began to train their militia expressly for
> Secession, commissioners were sent to
> treat with them and to represent the dis-
> astrous policy of such secession, who

---

[56] See Note 54.

never dreamed of hinting that it would
be rebellion.[57]

Dickens was adamant that "the quarrel between
North and South is, as it stands, solely a fiscal quarrel" because "Union means so many millions a year
lost to the South; secession means the loss of the same
millions to the North. The love of money is the root of
this as of many many other evils."[58]

Of course, it is the Northern love of other people's
money that is the root of all evil Dickens is talking
about. Southerners were simply trying to keep their
money from being confiscated by the government and
given to Northerners — just as the Colonists were trying to keep their money from being confiscated by King
George III and distributed throughout the British Empire. Every man and woman can understand that. Nobody wants their hard-earned money confiscated by
the government and given to somebody else.

Dickens's famous biographer, Peter Ackroyd, used
Scrooge's favorite word to describe the Northern lie
later in the war that slavery was suddenly their reason
for fighting even though the Emancipation Proclamation freed no slaves (or few), deliberately left close to a
half-million in slavery in the five Union slave states,
and left hundreds of thousands in slavery in captured

---

[57] Charles Dickens, letter to W. W. De Cerjat, 16 March 1862,
in Graham Storey, ed., *The Letters of Charles Dickens* (Oxford: Clarendon Press, 1998), Vol. Ten, 1862-1864, 53-54.
[58] See Note 54.

Confederate territory. Ackroyd writes:

> The Northern onslaught upon slavery
> was no more than a piece of specious
> humbug designed to conceal its desire
> for economic control of the Southern
> states.[59]

---

[59] Peter Ackroyd, *Dickens* (London, 1990), 271, as quoted in
Adams, *When in the Course of Human Events*, 89.

Chapter 4

Panic in the Volatile North

*In one single blow our foreign com-
merce must be reduced to less than
one-half what it now is. Our coastwise
trade would pass into other hands.
One-half of our shipping would lie idle
at our wharves. . . . Our manufactories
would be in utter ruins. . . . millions of
our people would be compelled to go
out of employment.*

Daily-Chicago Times
December 10, 1860

When Northerners began realizing how truly dependent they were on the South, they flew into a panic.
Horace Greeley is the embodiment of the North and he
proved himself a hypocrite of the first order.

On December 17, 1860, the day South Carolina's
Secession Convention began, Greeley published a long
emotional editorial in the *New York Daily Tribune* af-
firming and supporting the right of secession as not
only legal but moral. He is known for saying that our
"erring sisters should be allowed to depart in peace."

In "The Right of Secession," Greeley writes:

— We have repeatedly asked those who
dissent from our view of this matter to
tell us frankly whether they do or do not
assent to Mr. Jefferson's statement in
the Declaration of Independence that
governments "derive their just powers
from the consent of the governed; and
that, whenever any form of government
becomes destructive of these ends, it is
the right of the people to alter or abolish
it, and to institute a new government,"
&c., &c. We do heartily accept this doctrine, believing it intrinsically sound,
beneficent, and one that, universally accepted, is calculated to prevent the shedding of seas of human blood. And, if it
justified the secession from the British
Empire of Three Millions of colonists in
1776, we do not see why it would not justify the secession of Five Millions of
Southrons from the Federal Union in
1861. If we are mistaken on this point,
why does not some one attempt to show
wherein and why? . . . — we could not
stand up for coercion, for subjugation,
for we do not think it would be just. We
hold the right of Self-Government sacred, even when invoked in behalf of
those who deny it to others . . . if ever

'seven or eight States' send agents to
Washington to say 'We want to get out of
the Union,' we shall feel constrained by
our devotion to Human Liberty to say,
Let Them Go! And we do not see how we
could take the other side without coming
in direct conflict with those Rights of
Man which we hold paramount to all political arrangements, however convenient and advantageous.[60]

But three months later, as the Northern economy collapsed around him and genuine panic ensued with plummeting property values, business failures, factory closures, an imminent stock market crash, people in the streets, goods rotting on New York docks, and ut-ter disaster on the horizon, he wanted war. The entire North wanted war. They all agreed with the *New York Times*: "At once shut down every Southern Port, de-stroy its commerce and bring utter ruin on the Confed-erate states."[61]

The hypocrisy of Greeley, as the embodiment of the North, is breathtaking.

He writes in his newspaper that "We hold the right of Self-government sacred," and we believe in the

---

[60] "The Right of Secession," *The New-York Daily Tribune*, De-cember 17, 1860, in Howard Cecil Perkins, ed., *Northern Edi-torials on Secession* (Gloucester, MA: Peter Smith, 1964), 199-201.
[61] *The New-York Times*, 22-23 March, 1861, as quoted in Ad-ams, *When in the Course of Human Events*, 65.

American Revolution and the Declaration of Independence, and we believe in the "just powers" of the government coming from the "consent of the governed," and we believe in the "Right of the People to alter or to abolish" a tyrannical government — and we believe in a "devotion to Human Liberty" and the "Rights of Man" no matter how "convenient and advantageous" our current situation — and his most hypocritical of hypocritical statements, that "we could not stand up for coercion, for subjugation, for we do not think it would be just."

He then casts all his sacred principles to the ground and spits all over them. He spits on the Revolutionary War and the Founding Fathers too, and he grinds the Declaration of Independence into the dirt with his heel because they all were secondary to his money — and the North was with him in lockstep.[62]

---

[62] If the North had granted the right of secession as Greeley had so strongly supported at first, there would have been no War Between the States. Greeley and the North could have formed a new relationship with the South and traded, done business, and been friends. However, Northerners saw their economic collapse and loss of wealth and power with no hope of regaining it. They knew 60% of U.S. exports had been cotton, alone, which they got wealthy shipping. They knew those cargoes would be irreplaceable. They knew Great Britain would supply manufactured goods to the South cheaper than the North, and that Southerners would soon manufacture for themselves. So, **Northerners weighed their enormous advantages at that point in history and decided a bloody war of invasion and conquest to maintain their economic supremacy over a peace-seeking, independent South was better for them than fair economic competition in the world market. It would solve all Lincoln's political prob-**

Backtrack to December, 1860, as South Carolina's Secession Convention gets underway. South Carolina Governor Francis Wilkinson Pickens reflected the utter thrill and ecstasy of the South over its forthcoming independence. He said in his inaugural message that South Carolina would "open her ports free to the tonnage and trade of all nations, ... She has fine harbors, accessible to foreign commerce, and she is in the centre of those extensive agricultural productions, that enter so largely into the foreign trade and commerce of the world."[63] He said South Carolina would immediately seek free trade relationships with all countries, especially England, and

> it is for the benefit of all who may be interested in commerce, in manufactories, and in the comforts of artizans and mechanic labor everywhere, to make such speedy and peaceful arrangements with us as may advance the interests and happiness of all concerned.[64]

Contrast that with Northern panic in the same week from *The Chicago Times:*

---

lems by causing Northerners to rally to the flag. It would also put people to work. (Emphasis added.)
[63] Francis Wilkinson Pickens, "Inaugural Message of South Carolina Governor Francis Wilkinson Pickens," published 18 December 1860 in *The (Charleston, S.C.) Courier.*
[64] Ibid.

In one single blow our foreign commerce
must be reduced to less than one-half
what it now is. Our coastwise trade
would pass into other hands. One-half of
our shipping would lie idle at our
wharves. We should lose our trade with
the South, with all its **immense profits**.
Our manufactories would be in utter ruins. Let the South adopt the free-trade
system, or that of a tariff for revenue,[65]
and these results would likely follow. If
protection be wholly withdrawn from our
labor, it could not compete, with all the
prejudices against it, with the labor of
Europe. We should be driven from the

---

[65] See also Footnote #47 for the difference between tariff for
revenue and protective tariff. What is meant by "a tariff for
revenue" is a small tariff to raise a small amount of revenue to
pay for the operation of a small federal government such as
the government of the Confederate States of America. Southerners had always wanted free trade with the world. They believed in as small a tariff as possible. Contrast a small tariff for
revenue with the huge protective tariffs the North loved that
were punitive and meant to deter free trade so that one would
be forced to buy from the North at jacked-up rates that were
not determined by market competition but were jacked-up to
the level of the tariff. The tariff is the perfect thing to contrast
the differences in North and South. The moment the South
was out of the Union, they made protective tariffs unconstitutional while the North passed the astronomical Morrill Tariff.
The Morrill Tariff prevented the recovery of the Northern economy and made war Abraham Lincoln's only choice to save the
North from economic annihilation. Of course, Lincoln's choice
resulted in 800,000 deaths and over a million wounded out of
a population of approximately 31 million.

market, and millions of our people would
be compelled to go out of employment.[66]
(Emphasis added.)

New York City was petrified and ready to secede
from New York State over the certain loss of its commercial trade with the South. The situation was too
"gloomy and painful to contemplate" according to
Mayor Fernando Wood. He issued his "Recommenda-
tion for the Secession of New York City" on January 6,
1861 to make it clear that New York supported the
South and valued its trade with the South and wanted
to keep it:

> When Disunion has become a fixed and
> certain fact, why may not New York dis-
> rupt the bands which bind her to a venal
> and corrupt master — to a people and a
> party [Lincoln's Republicans] that have
> plundered her revenues, attempted to
> ruin her commerce, taken away the
> power of self-government, and destroyed
> the Confederacy [meaning the pre-seces-
> sion Union with the Southern States in-
> tact] of which she was the proud Empire
> City? Amid the gloom which the present

---

[66] *Daily Chicago Times*, "The Value of the Union," December
10, 1860, in Perkins, ed., *Northern Editorials on Secession*,
Vol. II, 573-574.

and prospective condition of things must
cast over the country, New York, as a
Free City, may shed the only light and
hope of a future reconstruction of our
once blessed Confederacy. . . .[67]

Northern society was volatile, anyway, wild and
unstable, subject to economic panics (severe reces-
sions/depression, bank failures, etc.). The entire decade before the war, the North was chaotic, dangerous,
often a wretched place to live. The scenes in Martin
Scorsese's *Gangs of New York* are true to life but don't
even begin to tell the real story.

Widespread poverty kept the working classes hungry and in turmoil. Constant immigration from Europe
increased the pressure steadily and made the North a
boiler on the verge of exploding. Most immigrants arrived with little or no money yet had to survive. They
headed straight to factories and "industrial misery"
where a man could work for only a few brutal years
before his body was ruined by black lung and other dis-
eases due to unhealthy conditions in crude factories.

Industrial turmoil in the North mirrored Europe.
European agitation was transferred to the North with
"strikes and demonstrations, far-reaching, prolonged

---

[67] Mayor Fernando Wood, "Mayor Fernando Wood's Recom-
mendation for the Secession of New York City," January 6,
1861, in Henry Steele Commager, ed., *Documents of American History*, Sixth Edition (New York: Appleton-Century-Crofts,
Inc.), 374-376.

and repeated, never more volcanic in character than in the decade that preceded the Civil War."[68]

There was genuine concern that if the enfran-chised but miserable poor ever got organized, they would vote themselves into power then confiscate the property of wealthy people and redistribute it. It had happened in other places.

Some historians believe it did happen in the North but the property taken was not that of a ruling class. It was the western lands. That is why the West was such a huge campaign issue in 1860. When Horace Greeley said, "Go West, young man, and grow up with the country," it was not just a good idea. It was the pres-sure valve of the Northern boiler that was about to ex-plode — and it released the North's surplus population to the West like steam into the wind.

William Gilmore Simms had toured the North on a lecture tour in 1856 and noted that Republican prom-ises are "Addressed to a class, counting millions of des-perate men, whom a grinding daily necessity makes reckless of every consideration of law, justice and the constitution."[69] He also said the North "is all wild, dis-ordered, anarchical, ready for chaos and disruption. And, the Northern mind, where not fanatical, is marked by a frivolity, a levity, which makes it reluc-tant to grapple seriously with serious things."[70] In the

---

[68] Charles A. Beard and Mary R. Beard, *The Rise of American Civilization* (New York: The MacMillan Company, 1936), Vol. 1, 633-634.

[69] Simms, "Antagonisms," 72-74.

[70] Simms, "Antagonisms," 36-39.

Panic of 1857, tens of thousands of hungry workers had roamed the streets of Northern cities in mobs shouting "bread or blood!"

Republicans had rallied those voters with slogans like "Vote yourself a tariff" and "Vote yourself a farm." Historian Mary Beard wrote that "when the Republicans in their platform of 1860 offered free land to the workingmen of the world in exchange for a protective tariff" they got a "tumultuous response."[71]

Northern anti-slavery was in no sense a pro-black movement but was anti-black. It was a way to rally votes. Might as well substitute the term "anti-South" for "anti-slavery" because it was anti-South — against the South — not pro-black.

Historian James L. Huston states well the Northern attitude toward slavery:

> If opposition to slavery had involved
> only antagonism toward racial oppres-
> sion, then the northern attack would
> have barely existed. The North was not
> a racially egalitarian section seeking to
> establish equitable race relations in the
> slaveholding South.[72]

Many of the genuine abolitionists in the North — the 2 to 5% mentioned by Lee Benson and Gavin

---

[71] Beard and Beard, *The Rise of American Civilization,* 649.
[72] James L. Huston, "Property Rights in Slavery and the Coming of the Civil War," *Journal of Southern History,* Volume LXV, Number 2, May, 1999, 263-264.

Wright — were racists. This is a great irony but many
hated slavery because they hated blacks and did not
want to associate with them, especially in the West.

David M. Potter states that Northern anti-slavery
was "not in any clear-cut sense a pro-Negro movement
but actually had an anti-Negro aspect and was designed to get rid of the Negro."[73]

Abraham Lincoln also wanted to "get rid of the Negro." He had always supported recolonization. As
stated earlier, Lincoln's Preliminary Emancipation
Proclamation is clear that "the effort to colonize persons of African descent, with their consent, upon this
continent, or elsewhere, with the previously obtained
consent of the Governments existing there, will be continued."

Some abolitionists such as William Lloyd Garrison
had real concern for black people. Robert Toombs said
Garrison was a man of conviction who would not take
an oath to the U.S. Constitution because it protected
slavery. Toombs said the good abolitionists like Garrison did not trust the "political abolitionists" and
wanted nothing to do with them.

These political abolitionists — the other 95 to 98%
of the Northern electorate — wanted something from
the government such as free land in the West, a protective tariff, bounty, subsidy or monopoly for their
businesses. Some were working men afraid of competition with slave labor, especially in the West. All had
been led to believe that if they voted Republican, the

---

[73] Potter, *The Impending Crisis, 1848-1861*, 35-36.

Republican Party would bring them riches beyond their wildest imaginations, farms, tariffs, land, whatever they wanted. This was not a pro-black movement in any way. It was a carnival of greed and special interests.

Charles P. Roland in *An American Iliad, The Story of the Civil War* acknowledges the economic and racist character of Northern anti-slavery:

> There was a significant economic dimension in the Northern antislavery sentiment, the fear of competition from slave labor and the awareness that work itself was degraded by slavery. Finally and paradoxically, a racial factor contributed to the Northern attitude. Antipathy against slavery often went hand in hand with racism that was similar in essence, if not in pervasiveness of intensity, to the Southern racial feeling. Many Northerners objected to the presence of slavery in their midst, in part, because they objected to the presence of blacks there.[74]

Alexis de Tocqueville observed the Northern racist attitude as well and said "Race prejudice seems stronger in those states that have abolished slavery than in those where it still exists, and nowhere is it

---

[74] Charles P. Roland, *An American Iliad, The Story of the Civil War* (Lexington: University Press of Kentucky, 1991), 3.

more intolerant than in those states where slavery was never known."[75]

Many Northern and Western states had laws prohibiting free blacks from settling there including Lincoln's own Illinois. In Illinois, it was called "An act to prevent the immigration of free Negroes into this State" and it said that any free black person staying longer than 10 days "was subject to arrest and imprisonment."[76]

Wars are not fought over issues like slavery.

Mothers and fathers do not send their precious sons off to die because they don't like the domestic institutions in other countries.

No country in history had a war to end slavery, and neither did we. Most nations ended slavery with gradual, compensated emancipation, or some variation thereof. That's what Lincoln always favored.

The domestic institutions in other countries affect no one, but a threat to one's economy affects everyone and is extremely dangerous. It must be dealt with immediately before it gets out of hand.

An economic collapse progresses with lightning speed into panic, runs on banks, mob violence, anarchy, and the collapse of the government itself. People

---

[75] Alexis de Tocqueville, *Democracy in America*, trans. by George Lawrence (New York: Harper & Row, 1969), v. 1, 342, in Jeffrey Rogers Hummel *Emancipating Slaves, Enslaving Free Men, A History of the American Civil War* (Chicago: Open Court, 1996), 26.

[76] H. Newcomb Morse, "The Foundations and Meaning of Secession," *Stetson Law Review* of Stetson University College of Law, Vol. XV, No. 2, 1986, footnote #28, 423.

are desperate, have no food, no money. Men have no way to protect their wives and daughters from rape, murder, violence. Civil law breaks down and is replaced by the law of the jungle.

No government is going to let that happen. That's why we fought two Gulf Wars. Any threat to the free-flow of oil from the Middle East is a threat to our economy.

Chapter 5

The Confederate States of America

*The formation of the Confederate
States of America by the people of the
South through their secession conventions was the greatest expression of
democracy and self-government in the
history of the world.*

Southerners revered the Founding Fathers and quoted
the Declaration of Independence extensively in the secession debate in the South in the months before seceding from the Union. As stated earlier, George
Washington is front and center on the Great Seal of
the Confederacy. The most widely quoted phrase of the
secession debate comes from the Declaration of Independence:

> Governments are instituted among
> Men, deriving their just powers from
> the consent of the governed, That when-
> ever any Form of Government becomes
> destructive of these ends, it is the Right
> of the People to alter or to abolish it, and
> to institute new Government, laying its

foundation on such principles and organizing its powers in such form, as to
them shall seem most likely to effect
their Safety and Happiness.
(Emphasis added.)

The formation of the Confederate States of America by the people of the South through their secession
conventions was the greatest expression of democracy
and self-government in the history of the world.

How could it not be? Millions of people in a land
mass as great as Europe rose up in state after state
and invoked Thomas Jefferson, Patrick Henry, George
Washington and others of their Revolutionary sires.
There were only 85 years between 1776 and 1861. The
Revolution and Declaration of Independence were still
fresh in the minds and hearts of Southerners.

They withdrew from an economically confiscatory
government run by people who hated them, and
formed a new one more to their liking "laying its foundation on such principles and organizing its powers in
such form, as to them shall seem most likely to effect
their Safety and Happiness."[77] And they stood ready,

---

[77] The Confederate States of America was the mirror image of
the original American republic of 1776 but with improvements.
The Confederate Constitution strengthened States' Rights and
eliminated the "general welfare" language that gave the federal government too much power.

Protective tariffs were outlawed. Never again would one
section of the country benefit at the expense of another as the
North had so greatly benefited at the expense of the rest of the
country and especially the South. Taxation would be uniform
as the Founding Fathers intended.

with great enthusiasm, to fight for their sacred right of self-government.

Sovereignty resides with the people. The people are the sovereign.

Conventions of the people in their respective states to decide *one* issue, such as secession, are the infallible way to express the will of the people — the consent of the governed. Conventions of the people are closer to the sovereign than even their legislatures, and the precedent of using a convention to decide an extremely important issue comes straight from the Founding Fathers who instructed that states use conventions to ratify the Constitution rather than their legislatures.

Southerners were committed to free trade with the world and hoped that would include the North as Jefferson Davis said in his inaugural.

Spending for infrastructure improvements from the general treasury was also outlawed because it had been so unfair in the Union for the South to pay 3/4ths of the taxes while 3/4ths of the tax money was spent in the North.

Southerners were not against internal improvements whatsoever. They strongly encouraged them but wanted each state to decide for itself what it wanted to spend money on. They felt it was unjust to take money from the people of one state and give it to the people in another.

The Confederate Constitution, while similar to the U.S. Constitution, had a lot of practical things in it such as a single six-year term for the president so he wasn't constantly campaigning. Also, every bill had to be truthfully labeled.

Of course, slavery was not required. It was up to each individual state. Southerners expected many free states would join the Confederacy for economic reasons and this was a great concern to Abraham Lincoln.

The just powers of the government of the Confederate States of America were granted by the people of the South in their secession conventions. The United States Government in 1861 no longer had the consent of the governed in the South or any just powers. The government of the United States had become the government of the North pledged against the South, as Wendell Phillips had proclaimed about the Republicans now in power.

Southerners were fed up with massive unfair taxation that greatly benefited the North, and years of hatred used by Republicans to rally their votes. Southerners did not trust the North and for good reason. They felt that the North was already at war with them via terrorists like John Brown who was financed in the North, then celebrated in the North for murdering Southerners. William Gilmore Simms said:

> Do you not see that, when Hate grows
> into open insolence, that the enemy is
> prepared to gratify all his passions? —
> that, having so far presumed upon our
> imbecility as to spit his scorn and venom
> into our very faces, he feels sure of his
> power to destroy![78]

---

[78] William Gilmore Simms, "South Carolina in the Revolution. The Social Moral. Lecture 1", unpublished 1857 lecture housed in the Charles Carroll Simms Collection of the South Caroliniana Library, University of South Carolina, Columbia, 4-5.

In each Southern state, Southerners debated se-cession vigorously, even ferociously, before calling con-ventions. They elected delegates as Unionists or Seces-sionists who went into the conventions and debated the issue further, then they voted. In only two states was the vote unanimous for secession: South Carolina, the first state to secede; and North Carolina, after the bombardment of Fort Sumter, when Lincoln called for 75,000 volunteers to invade the South.

It is extremely important to note that only seven states seceded and formed the Confederate States of America at first. Virginia had called a convention but voted not to secede. Tennessee, Arkansas and North Carolina had not seceded either. That meant that when the guns of Fort Sumter sounded, there were more slave states in the Union than in the Confeder-acy.[79]

Beyond the shadow of a doubt, the secession of Virginia, Tennessee, Arkansas and North Carolina had NOTHING to do with slavery. They seceded after the bombardment of Fort Sumter when Lincoln called for 75,000 volunteers to invade the South, and they did so because they were against federal coercion of a sover-eign state, which they found illegal, unconstitutional

---

[79] As previously stated in Note #29, the eight slave states in the Union on April 12, 1861 when Fort Sumter was bombarded are Virginia, Tennessee, Arkansas, North Carolina, Maryland, Delaware, Kentucky and Missouri. West Virginia was admitted to the Union as a slave state during the war. The seven states to first secede and form the Confederate States of America are South Carolina, Georgia, Florida, Alabama, Louisiana, Mississippi and Texas.

and immoral. The federal government was supposed to be the agent of the people in their respective states, and not their master. No one group of states had any right or authority to make war on another group.

Chapter 6

The Perfect Storm for Economic Disaster in the North

Secession cost the North its Southern manufacturing market. The Morrill Tariff threatened to cost the North its shipping industry as U.S. trade was immediately rerouted away from the high-tariff North and into Southern ports where protective tariffs were unconstitutional.

Contrast the North and South.

Virginia Governor John Letcher was thrilled about the future of Virginia out of the Union. He had told the House of Delegates three months earlier that "We have the best port in the country; . . . if direct trade were established between Norfolk and Europe, it would give increased prosperity to every interest in the commonwealth. It would secure for us a commercial independence" and it would give us a "great interior and exterior trade" the latter from "ships sailing directly to

Europe, at regular intervals from the port of
Norfolk."[80]

The feeling in the North was the polar opposite.
There was panic. Shortly after Letcher's speech, *The
Manchester* (N.H.) *Union Democrat* warned:

> The Southern Confederacy will not em-
> ploy our ships or buy our goods. What is
> our shipping without it? Literally noth-
> ing. The transportation of cotton and its
> fabrics employs more ships than all
> other trade. The first result will be that
> Northern ships and ship owners will go
> to the South. They are doing it even
> now.[81]

Governor Letcher continued with great enthusiasm:

> I am entirely satisfied, that if direct
> trade were established between Norfolk
> and Europe, it would result in the
> enlargement of our cities, the increase of

---

[80] Governor John Letcher, "Governor John Letcher's Message
on Federal Relations to the legislature of Virginia in extraordinary session on January 7, 1861," in *Journal of the House of
Delegates of the State of Virginia, for the Extra Session, 1861*
(Richmond: William F. Ritchie, Public Printer, 1861), Document I, iii-xxvii.

[81] *The Manchester* (N.H.) *Union Democrat*, "Let Them Go!",
editorial of February 19, 1861, in Perkins, ed., *Northern Editorials on Secession*, Vol. II, 592.

our agricultural products, the development of our resources, the creation of
manufactures, the enhancement of the
value of lands, the opening of the coal
and mineral beds, make the stock which
the state owns in her rail roads productive — and the end would be a diminu-
tion of the state debt, as well as lower
taxes.[82]

The *Union Democrat* continued with despair:

In the manufacturing departments, we
now have the almost exclusive supply of
10,000,000 of people. Can this market be
cut off, and we not feel it? Our mills run
now—why? Because they have cotton.
. . . **But they will not run long. We hear
from good authority that some of them
will stop in sixty days.** We don't need
any authority—everybody knows they
must stop if our national troubles are
not adjusted. An inflexible law cannot be
violated. The shoe business is completely
prostrate. . . .[83] (Emphasis added.)

---

[82] Letcher, "Governor John Letcher's Message on Federal Relations to the legislature of Virginia in extraordinary session on
January 7, 1861," Document I, iii-xxvii.

[83] *The Manchester* (N.H.) *Union Democrat*, "Let Them Go!",
editorial of February 19, 1861 in Perkins, ed., *Northern Editorials on Secession*, Vol. II, 592.

The *Union Democrat* gave the North 60 days before their mills would stop because they would have no
cotton. It is no coincidence that in 55 days, Abraham
Lincoln called for 75,000 volunteers to invade the
South.

On February 18, 1861, Jefferson Davis had said in
his inaugural address as Provisional President of the
Confederate States of America that the South would
immediately establish the "freest trade" possible with
the rest of the world:

> . . . [As] an agricultural people, whose
> chief interest is the export of a commod-
> ity required in every manufacturing
> country, our true policy is peace, and the
> freest trade which our necessities will
> permit. It is alike our interest, and that
> of all those to whom we would sell and
> from whom we would buy, that there
> should be the fewest practicable restric-
> tions upon the interchange of commodi-
> ties. There can be little rivalry between
> ours and any manufacturing or navigat-
> ing community, such as the Northeast-
> ern States of the American Union. It
> must follow, therefore, that a mutual
> interest would invite good will and kind
> offices.[84]

---

[84] Jefferson Davis, "Inaugural Address," as Provisional President of the Confederate States of America, 18 February 1861,
at Montgomery, Alabama in Lynda Lasswell Crist, ed., *The*

But Davis's good will could not touch the impending disaster in the North. There was no mention of
slavery by the *Union Democrat* or anywhere else in the
North because slavery was not the cause of the war.
The North could care less about slavery or helping
black people. The *Union Democrat* writes the day after
Davis's inaugural:

> [W]hen people realize the fact that the
> Union is permanently dissolved, real es-
> tate will depreciate one half in a single
> year.—Our population will decrease
> with the decline of business, and matters
> will go in geometrical progression from
> bad to worse—until all of us will be
> swamped in utter ruin. Let men con-
> sider—apply the laws of business, and
> see if they can reach any different con-
> clusion.[85]

Northern businessmen had already concluded that
the Union had to be preserved or there would be "economic suicide" in the North as Philip S. Foner pointed
out.

The North's Morrill Tariff, adopted March 2, 1861,
two days before Lincoln's first inaugural and six weeks

Papers of Jefferson Davis (Baton Rouge: Louisiana State University Press, 1992), Volume 7, 46-50.
[85] *The Manchester* (N.H.) *Union Democrat*, "Let Them Go!",
editorial of February 19, 1861 in Perkins, ed., *Northern Editorials on Secession*, Vol. II, 592.

before the bombardment of Fort Sumter, was like pumping gasoline into a fire. It was astronomical and made entry of goods into the North 37 to 50% higher than entry into the South.

Southerners were brilliant. They had always wanted free trade so they made protective tariffs un-constitutional. Northerners were not only greedy but utterly ignorant of basic economics.

The Morrill Tariff immediately re-routed most of the trade of the United States away from the North and into the South in one fell swoop.

The North was unquestionably going to lose most of its trade and a huge amount of its wealth and power all at once. Nobody in the world wanted to do business with the North and pay 37 to 50% more for the pleas-ure when the beautiful sultry ports of the South — Charleston, Savannah, New Orleans, Galveston, Mo-bile, et al. — beckoned. The world, and Northern ship captains, were beating a path to the South where free trade reigned and the most demanded commodities on earth were abundant, and where protective tariffs were unconstitutional.

Harper's Weekly lampooned the Morrill Tariff :

(next page):

Harper's Weekly
April 13, 1861

The New Tariff on Dry Goods.

Unhappy condition of the Optic Nerve
of a Custom House Appraiser who has
been counting the Threads in a Square
Yard of Fabric to ascertain the duty
thereon under the New MORRILL Tariff. The Spots and Webs are well-known
Opthalmic Symptoms. It is confidently
expected that the unfortunate man will
go blind.

The Morrill Tariff is the epitome of Northern
greed and abuse of the economic system, which are

major, primary causes of the War Between the States. Its imminent passage had caused "a fierce onslaught by all sorts of interests." Ida Tarbell, historian and Lincoln biographer, said that protection of 20% was even given to wood-screws though there was "but one small factory for wood-screws in the country." The Rhode Island senator who had gotten this protection, Sen. James F. Simmons, was from then on known as "Wood-Screw Simmons."[86]

Wood-Screw Simmons is a cute story but there is nothing cute about the 800,000 lives lost in the War Between the States or the million who were wounded.

The Morrill Tariff slammed the door shut on any possibility that the North would be able to deal with the loss of its captive Southern market and now its shipping industry. Northerners had said over and over that their labor needed protection, that they could not compete on an even basis with Europe. Out of a sense of entitlement from long years of protectionism that benefited the North at the expense of the rest of the country, they were not even willing to try.

They were also petrified of the industrialization of the South, which was a certainty. Southerners were extremely excited about developing their own manufacturing.

The secession of the South and the Morrill Tariff were the perfect storm of economic disaster for the

---

[86] Adams, *When in the Course of Human Events,* 65; and Ida M. Tarbell, *The Tariff in Our Times* (New York: The Macmillan Company, 1911), 8-11.

North. The Morrill Tariff guaranteed that the Northern economy would not recover but that wasn't the
worst of it.

With the goods of the world flowing into Southern
ports, they would then be floated up the Mississippi
and distributed throughout the rest of the country.
Southerners had always wanted more trade with the
West and now they would have it.

The *New York Evening Post* ten days after the
passage of the Morrill Tariff stated the hopelessness of
the Northern position:

> [A]lllow railroad iron to be entered at Sa-
> vannah with the low duty of ten per
> cent., which is all that the Southern
> Confederacy think of laying on imported
> goods, and not an ounce more would be
> imported at New York: the railways
> would be supplied from the southern
> ports. Let cotton goods, let woolen fab-
> rics, let the various manufactures of iron
> and steel be entered freely at Galveston,
> at the great port at the mouth of the
> Mississippi, at Mobile, at Savannah and
> at Charleston, and they would be imme-
> diately sent up the rivers and carried on
> the railways to the remotest parts of the
> Union.[87]

---

[87] *New York Evening Post*, March 12, 1861, "What Shall Be
Done for a Revenue?" in Perkins, ed., *Northern Editorials on
Secession*, Vol II, 598.

Philip S. Foner confirms the position of the *New York Evening Post*:

> A Southern Confederacy made economi-
> cally independent of the North meant, of
> course, the total loss [to the North] of
> Southern trade [and] would very likely
> attract to it the agrarian sections of the
> Southwest and Northwest. The [North-
> ern] merchants knew that the South had
> sought for years to cement economic ties
> with the West. Prior to the secession
> movement it had failed. But direct trade
> with England on the basis of a low tariff
> or free trade, together with the aid of
> English capital for railroad connections
> with the West, would be too attractive to
> be rejected by the Western states.[88]

English capital would build factories and rail-
roads, and the South, with its free trade philosophy
and control of King Cotton, would not only dominate
United States trade thanks to the Morrill Tariff, but
would manufacture, ship, and compete in every respect
in world commerce. There was nothing preventing this
and every reason for the South to rush forward. Free
trade is what it had always wanted.

Cotton and other bountiful Southern commodities
would be a hop and a skip to Southern manufacturing

---

[88] Foner, *Business & Slavery*, 284.

facilities, which would be a hop and a skip to Southern ports. People would immigrate into the South and increase its wealth and power as had happened in the North for the past half century. Southerners did not need high tariffs and protectionism. They would compete on a level playing field with the rest of the world. They were enthusiastic, confident, and anxious to get going.

Chapter 7

The Only Thing That Can Save the North Is War

*Major Robert Anderson, Union com-
mander inside Fort Sumter, emphatically blames Lincoln for starting the
war Lincoln had to have to save the
North.*

Lincoln needed to start the war as fast as he could before Southerners completed trade and military alliances with England and other European countries,
which they had been pursuing with great enthusiasm
for months. With every second that went by, the South
got stronger and the North got weaker. Lincoln knew
there was no advantage, whatsoever, to waiting.

He also worried greatly about free states joining
the South. The Confederate Constitution allowed it.
Slavery was not required. Slavery was up to an individual state, and Southerners anticipated that many
free states with economic ties to the South, especially
along the Mississippi and in the West, would join the
Confederacy.

The Boston Transcript saw what was happening
and realized that the protection to slavery that the

North was quite willing to give was not what the
South wanted:

> [T]he mask has been thrown off and it is
> apparent that the people of the principal
> seceding states are now for commercial
> independence. They dream that the cen-
> tres of traffic can be changed from
> Northern to Southern ports. The mer-
> chants of New Orleans, Charleston, and
> Savannah are possessed of the idea that
> New York, Boston, and Philadelphia
> may be shorn, in the future, of their
> mercantile greatness, by a revenue sys-
> tem verging on free trade.[89]

The South wanted to be INDEPENDENT just as
the Colonists had wanted to be independent in 1776.
The South wanted freedom and self-government. It
was tired of the confiscation of its hard-earned money
by the North and the federal government. It was tired
of 10 years of Northern hatred and terrorism.

Northern panic and Southern jubilation grew
steadily until they reached a crescendo on April 12,
1861, and the orchestra wore gray in the forts and batteries encircling Charleston Harbor, and it wore blue
inside Fort Sumter, led by Union Major Robert Anderson.

---

[89] *The Boston Transcript*, 18 March 1861, in Adams, *When in
the Course of Human Events*, 65.

Anderson saw the events of the day clearly and put the blame squarely on Abraham Lincoln for starting the war that Lincoln had to have to save the Union and the North. Lincoln and Secretary of War Simon Cameron wrote to Anderson and informed him that warships and a military mission to reinforce him were en route.

Anderson and the Southerners in Charleston were standing face to face, each with a cocked gun on a hair-trigger aimed at the other's head. It had been this way for weeks, but Lincoln couldn't wait any longer. He was anxious to get a blockade set up around the ports of the South that would slow the European rush to military and trade treaties with the South. This was a critical thing for Lincoln or suddenly it would have been like the French in the American Revolution who came to the aid of the Colonists and helped mightily to secure American independence.

Once Lincoln got the war started, he could throw up his blockade and force Europeans to take a wait-and-see attitude.

Lincoln knew that sending his warships and soldiers to Charleston during the most critical hour in American history would start the war. That's why it was well publicized nationally, so everybody could get ready. He hoped the Confederates would fire first. Everything he did was designed to get that result. See Charles W. Ramsdell's famous treatise, "Lincoln and

Fort Sumter,"[90] Part III of this book, for proof that Lincoln started the war.

Anderson was at ground zero on April 12, 1861
and could judge both sides and pass judgment on who
started the war, and he clearly blames Lincoln. This is
what he writes in his response to Lincoln and Cameron:

> . . . a movement made now when the
> South has been erroneously informed
> that none such will be attempted, would
> produce most disastrous results through-
> out our country. . . . We shall strive to do
> our duty, though I frankly say that my
> heart is not in the war **which I see is to**
> **be thus commenced.** . . .
> (Emphasis added.)

Anderson sees that the war "is to be thus commenced" by Abraham Lincoln, who had to hurry up
and get it started or soon the South with European
trade and military alliances would be unbeatable.

Northern greed, hatred and terrorism drove the
South out of the Union and cost the North its huge
captive manufacturing market in the South. It also
cost the North unfettered access to bountiful Southern
commodities needed in manufacturing.

---

[90] Charles W. Ramsdell, "Lincoln and Fort Sumter", *The Journal of Southern History*, Volume 3, Issue 3 (August, 1937),
Pages 259 - 288.

More Northern greed in the form of the Morrill Tariff threatened to destroy the Northern shipping industry and send Northern ship captains South where protective tariffs were unconstitutional. The Morrill Tariff guaranteed that the Northern economy would not recover.

Northern leaders knew that they were headed for an unimaginable disaster and at the same time would have to face the South as a major competitor owning most of the trade of the United States, strongly backed militarily and financially by Europe, and with control of the most demanded commodity on the planet: cotton.

Abraham Lincoln, the first sectional president in American history, was president of the North and the North was clamoring for war. There was gloom, despair and extreme agitation in the North. Hundreds of thousands were unemployed, angry, in the street. The "clangor of arms" had been heard. Every day that went by the South got stronger and the North got weaker. There was no advantage whatsoever to waiting a second longer, so, after agonizing for weeks, Lincoln saw a way to get the war started without appearing to be the aggressor, and he took it. This was the view of several Northern newspapers as Charles W. Ramsdell points out in Part III in "Lincoln and Fort Sumter."

The threatened annihilation of the Northern economy and the rise of the South are what drove all actions in that fateful spring of 1861. Certainly not any mythical desire on the part of the North to end slavery.

The North's choices had been clear: descend into economic hell and mob rule, or fight.

If they fought, because of their overwhelming advantages at that point in history (4 to 1 in manpower, perhaps 40 to 1 in weapon manufacturing, army, navy, unlimited immigration, etc.), they knew they had an excellent chance of winning everything and gaining total control of the country.

If they didn't fight, the South would surely ascend to predominance.

Of course they were going to fight and use their advantages before they lost them.

Lincoln figured the North would win easily but First Manassas proved him wrong, thus we had the bloodiest war in American history with 800,000 deaths and over a million wounded. The South was invaded and destroyed but fought until it was utterly exhausted before it was all over. It had nothing left to give or the war would certainly have continued on.

It was World War II, seventy-five years later, before the South began to recover from the destruction, but it is a certainty that if 1861 rolled around again and Southerners had the opportunity to fight for independence, they would. To the South, 1861 was 1776 all over. They believed the Founding Fathers had bequeathed to them by the Declaration of Independence, the right of self-government, and they would pay any price to achieve it.

Basil Gildersleeve, still known today as the greatest American classical scholar of all time, was a Confederate soldier from Charleston, South Carolina. He sums it up nicely in *The Creed of the Old South,* published 27 years after the war:

> All that I vouch for is the feeling; . . .
> there was no lurking suspicion of any
> moral weakness in our cause. Nothing
> could be holier than the cause, nothing
> more imperative than the duty of up-
> holding it. There were those in the South
> who, when they saw the issue of the war,
> gave up their faith in God, but not their
> faith in the cause.[91]

---

[91] Basil L. Gildersleeve, *The Creed of the Old South*, Baltimore: The Johns Hopkins Press, 1915; reprint: BiblioLife, Penrose Library, University of Denver (no date given), 26-27.

Chapter 8

Slavery Was Not the Cause of the War Between the States

Two things caused the war.

The first was Northern greed that abused the economic system and made it unfair and confiscatory toward the South. Unearned money was flowing directly through Robert Toombs's suction pump out of the South and into the pockets of Northerners. Southerners were forced to pay 3/4ths of the taxes, yet 3/4ths of the tax money was being spent in the North to enrich Northerners and build up their cities. This was blatantly unfair just as British taxes had been in 1776. The monopoly status that Northerners were able to get for their industries destroyed market competition and allowed them to raise rates and prices and put extra money in their pockets simply because of economic manipulation, and that would unquestionably continue.

Southerners have to accept some of the blame for this because they were part of the government too and allowed it to go on, though they did try to control it with the Nullification movement of 1832 brought on by the Tariff of Abominations. The country was supposed to be heading toward free trade but it never came close to getting there, and, by the elections of 1856 and 1860, it was too late. The events of the day were too volatile and could not be controlled.

What Southerners did have control over was their own government once they seceded and formed the Confederate States of America. They immediately made protective tariffs unconstitutional at the same moment that Northerners passed the astronomical Morrill Tariff, which rerouted most of the trade of the United States away from the North and into the South in one fell swoop.

The North and South simply had different economic needs and desires just as any industrial society would with any agrarian society. But there was a huge difference in America: The South could easily industrialize and was moving fast to do so, but the North would never be able to produce the most demanded commodity on the planet, cotton, or any of the other Southern commodities that were in such high demand worldwide and had made the North so rich.

The South without the North was in great shape, but the North without the South was dead.

Philip S. Foner analyzed the situation perfectly as panic in the North took over in the spring of 1861:

> On April 1, the Morrill tariff would go
> into effect, and after that date the duties
> on the principal articles of import would
> be nearly twice as heavy at New York as
> they would be at New Orleans, Charles-
> ton, and Savannah. The consequences of

this difference in duties were not difficult to see. Anything that had happened
thus far in the secession crisis was mild
compared with what the immediate future would bring.[92]

It is clear to Foner that the South's free trade philosophy and low tariff verses the North's astronomical
Morrill Tariff was a huge factor in bringing on the war.
Slavery had nothing to do with any of these critical
economic issues. Foner writes:

The war of the tariffs has been ignored
in most studies devoted to the antebellum period, yet it is doubtful whether
any event during those significant
months prior to the outbreak of the Civil
War was as influential in molding public
opinion in the North. Certainly in New
York City, it caused a political revolution. It brought to an end any hope that
Union could be preserved peacefully.[93]

The second thing that caused the War Between
the States was the sectional takeover of the United
States Government by the Republican Party, which
was the party of the North — now the *government* of
the North — pledged against the South. George Wash-

---

[92] Foner, *Business & Slavery,* 277-278.
[93] Foner, *Business & Slavery,* 282.

ington had warned that the establishment of sectional political parties would destroy the country. Washington stressed that the country should be ruled by national parties that had the best interest of the entire country at heart.

But abolitionist Wendell Phillips with great enthusiasm acknowledged that the Republican Party "is the first sectional party ever organized in this country. It does not know its own face, and calls itself national; but it is not national—it is sectional. The Republican Party is a party of the North pledged against the South." Indeed, Lincoln was not even on the ballot south of the Mason-Dixon line in the election of 1860.

Thomas Prentice Kettell, the most credible economist alive in 1860, with tremendous knowledge of the interconnection of North and South, writes:

> It [the North] had before it a most brilliant future, but it has wantonly disturbed that future by encouraging the growth of a political party [Republican] based wholly upon sectional aggression,—a party which proposes no issues of statesmanship for the benefit of the whole country; it advances nothing of a domestic or foreign policy tending to national profit or protection, or to promote the general welfare in any way.[94]

---

[94] Kettell, *Southern Wealth and Northern Profits*, 147.

That same Northern greed of the Republican Party told Northerners to "Vote yourself a farm" and "Vote yourself a tariff" and hate your fellow countrymen of the South. Republicans used hate and greed to rally their voters because everything was at stake: The takeover of the entire country which they could rule for their own enrichment and aggrandizement. They were drooling like a pack of snarling wolves surrounding a lamb before tearing it to shreds.

This was the party of the North pledged against the South, not the party of the United States trying to solve the difficult slavery problem with good will and concern for all, as most other slaveholding countries on earth had done.

No country had to have a war to end slavery and neither did we. Virtually every country ended slavery with gradual compensated emancipation or some variation thereof, which is what Abraham Lincoln himself favored. That's how the North, itself, had ended slavery — with gradual, compensated emancipation — though ever-thrifty Yankees never freed their slaves. It is well-known that they sold them back into slavery in the South just before they were to be freed, such as before the slave's 21st birthday. Alexis de Tocqueville said that Northerners didn't free their slaves, they simply changed the slave's master from a Northern to a Southern one.

Kettell had acknowledged the Republican hate which had been used to rally Northern voters:

[T]he North has for more than ten years
constantly allowed itself to be irritated
by incendiary speakers and writers,
whose sole stock in trade is the unrea-
soning hate against the South that may
be engendered by long-continued irritat-
ing misrepresentation.[95]

Southerners came to the realization that people
who hated them and had committed acts of terrorism
and murder against them were about to rule over
them. From then on in American history, Southerners
would be outvoted by those same people. Any manner
of hate and economic confiscation could and would continue, and would likely be worse than ever.

Of course, Northerners had every right to form a
party and try to take over the government, which they
finally did.

But Southerners, believing in the Declaration of
Independence and the consent of the governed, had
every right to secede from the Union that had become
a worse tyranny than the Colonists faced with the
British — 1861 was an even more compelling and jus-
tifiable secession from tyranny than 1776.

Southerners were well aware of their revolutionary heritage and the beliefs of the Founding Fathers
and the sacred words of the Declaration of Independence. They believed with every ounce of their beings

---

[95] Ibid.

that

> Governments are instituted among Men,
> deriving their just powers from the con‐
> sent of the governed, That whenever any
> Form of Government becomes destruc‐
> tive of these ends, it is the Right of the
> People to alter or to abolish it, and to
> institute new Government, laying its
> foundation on such principles and orga‐
> nizing its powers in such form, as to
> them shall seem most likely to effect
> their Safety and Happiness.

Northerners, as Horace Greeley proved, had be‐
lieved in it too until it threatened their money.

South Carolina stated it accurately in "The Ad‐
dress of the People of South Carolina, Assembled in
Convention, to the People of the Slaveholding States of
the United States":

> [W]hen vast sectional interests are to be
> subserved, involving the appropriation
> of countless millions of money, it has not
> been the usual experience of mankind,
> that words on parchments can arrest
> power. [96]

---

[96] "The Address of the People of South Carolina, Assembled in Convention, to the People of the Slaveholding States of the United States".

The idea that the good North killed 800,000 people and wounded even more to end slavery, because, otherwise, those evil Southerners would have had slavery to this very day, is an absurdity of biblical proportions.

Southerners were the heirs of the Founding Fathers from a region steeped in Christianity and the Ten Commandments, the Golden Rule. Alexis de Tocqueville acknowledged that race relations were better in the South than anywhere in America. Southerners would have ended slavery with some kind of compensated emancipation, the same method that Lincoln believed in and most other nations on earth had used. Slavery was not extending beyond the Mississippi River and it is unfathomable that slavery would exist in the age of the telephone and automobile. Southerners wanted the same options as Northerners, to hire and fire people as business demanded without a birth-to-death commitment. The industrialization of the South would have sped up emancipation greatly, and it would have been in the best interest of the South to help newly freed slaves incorporate themselves into Southern society with friendship and good will for all.

It is ludicrous to think otherwise, but the slavery lie must be maintained or the true horror of what happened with the destruction of the republic of the Founding Fathers and the deaths of 800,000 men and wounding of over a million more comes into too shocking a focus.

Slavery was not the cause of the War Between the States. Clearly, the North did not go to war to free the slaves.

The North went to war because it faced economic annihilation due to Southern secession, which Republican hate and greed had caused, and the Morrill Tariff.

Tennessee Representative Thomas A. R. Nelson, who had submitted the Minority Report of the House Committee of Thirty-three, also delivered the "Speech of Hon. Thomas A. R. Nelson, of Tennessee, On the Disturbed condition of the Country." While Southerners were ecstatic over their independence, here's what Nelson observed about the North:

> Three short months ago this great nation was, indeed, prosperous and happy. What a startling, wondrous change has come over it within that brief period! Commercial disaster and distress pervade the land. Hundreds and thousands of honest laboring men have been thrown out of employment; gloom and darkness hang over the people; the tocsin of war has been sounded; the clangor of arms has been heard.[97]

That is why Abraham Lincoln, president of the North, had to have his war, and it had nothing to do with slavery. It had everything to do with Northern

---

[97] Thomas A. R. Nelson, "Speech of Hon. Thomas A. R. Nelson, of Tennessee, On the Disturbed condition of the Country" (Washington: H. Polkinhorn, 1861), 1-12.

"Commercial disaster and distress" and "Hundreds and thousands of honest laboring men" in the North "thrown out of employment."

That's why "the tocsin of war" was sounded by the North because down South there were no such bells of dread or warning. Only beautiful church bells of patri-otism, triumph, thrill and enthusiasm over independ-ence, just as there were on that first 4th of July in 1776.

Georgia Governor Joseph E. Brown sums up the feeling in the South:

> [W]e have within ourselves, all the ele-
> ments of wealth, power, and national
> greatness, to an extent possessed proba-
> bly by no other people on the face of the
> earth. With a vast and fertile territory,
> possessed of every natural advantage,
> bestowed by a kind Providence upon the
> most favored land, and with almost mo-
> nopoly of the cotton culture of the world,
> if we were true to ourselves, our power
> would be invincible, and our prosperity
> unbounded.[98]

---

[98] Joseph E. Brown, "Special Message of Governor Joseph E. Brown on Federal Relations, delivered to the Georgia Senate and House of Representatives in Milledgeville, Georgia, on November 7, 1860," in Allen D. Chandler, *The Confederate Records of the State of Georgia* (Atlanta: Charles P. Byrd, State Printer, 1909), Volume 1, 19-57.

Southerners seceded because they wanted to be independent. They were not going to be ruled over by a sectional political party that came to power using the most vicious kind of hatred, terrorism and murder to rally its votes, a party that demanded that Southerners pay 3/4ths of the country's taxes so that Northerners could spend 3/4ths of the tax money on themselves.

Southerners wanted a country like the republic of the Founding Fathers where states were supreme and the federal government was weak. They believed with all their hearts in the Declaration of Independence and the just powers of the government coming from the consent of the governed. The secession conventions of the South and their debates and votes to secede were the greatest expression of democracy and self-government in the history of the world.

Northerners, as Horace Greeley proved, had believed in the Declaration of Independence and the right of secession too, until they realized it was going to affect their money.

So the war came.

Part II

The Right of Secession

The Right of Secession

The Southern States, in all likelihood,
were exercising a perfectly legitimate
right in seceding from the Union.[99]

H. Newcomb Morse
Stetson University College of Law
Stetson Law Review, 1986

Senator Judah P. Benjamin of Louisiana was a brilliant legal mind who was later attorney general, secretary of war and secretary of state of the Confederacy.
In his farewell speech to the United States Senate on
February 5, 1861 he went into great detail about the
right of secession. He asserted that the denial of that
right is a "pretension so monstrous" that it "perverts a
restricted agency [the Federal Government], constituted by sovereign states for common purposes, into
the unlimited despotism of the majority, and denies all
legitimate escape from such despotism . . . and degrades sovereign states into provincial dependencies."
He said that "for two-thirds of a century this right [of

---

[99] H. Newcomb Morse, "The Foundations and Meaning of Secession," Stetson University College of Law, *Stetson Law Review*, Vol. XV, No. 2, 1986), 436.

secession] has been known by many of the states to be, at all times, within their power."[100]

No American who believes in the Declaration of Independence can ever doubt the right of secession. Our country was born of secession from the British Empire. Secession is defined by Merriam-Webster as "the act of separating from a nation or state and becoming independent."[101] The Declaration of Independence starts with:

> When in the Course of human events, it becomes necessary for one people to dissolve the political bands which have connected them with another, and to assume among the powers of the earth, the separate and equal station to which the Laws of Nature and of Nature's God entitle them, . . .

The Southern States unquestionably had the right to secede from the Union. There is a preponderance of direct evidence supporting the right of secession.

Historian Kenneth M. Stampp in his book *The Imperiled Union* points out that "the case for state sover-

---

[100] Judah P. Benjamin, "Farewell Address to the U.S. Senate" delivered February 5, 1861, in Edwin Anderson Alderman, and Joel Chandler Harris, eds., *Library of Southern Literature* (Atlanta: The Martin and Hoyt Company, 1907), Volume 1, 318-319.
[101] Merriam-Webster online definition of "secession," http://www.merriam-webster.com/dictionary/secession, accessed August 11, 2014.

eignty and the constitutional right of secession had flourished for forty years before a comparable case for a perpetual Union had been devised," and even then its logic was "far from perfect because the Constitution and the debates over ratification were fraught with ambiguity."[102]

Historians such as Professor Stampp are like lawyers who have clients they know are guilty but they still have to defend them.[103]

If, as Professor Stampp (along with Judah Benjamin, Horace Greeley, Alexis de Tocqueville, Charles Dickens, George Washington, Thomas Jefferson, Massachusetts, and most leaders North and South including Abraham Lincoln in 1847[104]) said — "the case for state sovereignty and the constitutional right of seces-

---

[102] Kenneth M. Stampp, *The Imperiled Union, Essays on the Background of the Civil War* (New York: Oxford University Press, 1980), 35-36.

[103] The right of secession is like the bright sun in front of Professor Stampp's face but he can't (or won't) see it. He writes on page four of *The Imperiled Union* that "the Unionist case was sufficiently flawed to make it uncertain whether in 1865 reason and logic were on the side of the victors —" but he adds his obligatory disclaimer to cloud the issue by stating that we really can't tell "in the tangled web of claims and counterclaims" if reason and logic "were indisputably on either side." He says on page 11 that "In truth, the wording of the Constitution gives neither the believers in the right of secession nor the advocates of a perpetual Union a case so decisive that all reasonable persons are bound to accept it." At least Professor Stampp knew better than to deny the right of secession as he defends his guilty client.

[104] In 1847, on the floor of the United States House of Representatives, Abraham Lincoln said:

sion had flourished for forty years" — then that means
it was born from the country's founding and created by
its Founding Fathers and it existed. Period. It is indisputable. How could it not be?

The Founding Fathers did not say that states had
the right to secede for 40 years then they lose that
right. The Founding Fathers did not put a time limit
or expiration date on it despite the economic/political
needs of the North to promote a perpetual union to justify its war on the South. Southerners had the right to
secede and there is nothing that could take it away
from them.

It would be so much more truthful if some historians would call an obvious truth a truth, but they
have that guilty client to defend so they cloud the issue
and give their client the benefit of the doubt, lest they
be accused of being unpatriotic or, God forbid, a racist.

It makes no sense for a group of colonies, desig-
nated as individual sovereign states by King George
III at war's end, who had just fought a bloody war to

Any people, anywhere, being inclined and
having the power, have the right to rise up and
shake off the existing government, and form a
new one that suits them better. This is a most
valuable, a most sacred right, a right which we
hope and believe is to liberate the world.

SOURCE: Abraham Lincoln, 1847 Congressional debate in
the United States House of Representatives in John Shipley
Tilley, *Lincoln Takes Command* (Nashville: Bill Coats, Ltd.,
1991), xv. Tilley's source, as stated in footnote #4 on page xv,
was Goldwyn Smith, *The United States: An Outline of Political
History*, 1492-1871 (New York and London, 1893), 248.

escape from a political union with the British Empire, to, so casually, lock themselves into another political union that they could not escape from. They wouldn't and didn't.

The right of secession was assumed but three states specifically reserved it before acceding to the Constitution. It was a condition they demanded, and that demand had to be met before they would ratify the Constitution and join the Union. Those states are Virginia, New York and Rhode Island. They specifically put in writing that they had the right to secede from the Union if it should ever become detrimental to their best interests, and *they* get to decide when that has happened. All the other states approved of this right of secession of Virginia, New York and Rhode Island's, therefore, since all the states are equal, they had it too.

That is the kind of guarantee of freedom and self-government the Founding Father's bequeathed to us and it is in direct conflict with Lincoln and the North's idea. Lincoln and the North are often represented in the secession debate in the South by the concept of the "tyranny of the majority" which Judah Benjamin mentioned at the beginning of this essay. The tyranny of the majority is why the Founding Fathers created a republic and not a pure democracy where 50% plus one vote can hang the other 49%.

The ideas developed by Lincoln and the North were a result of their economic situation. They wanted centralization so they could use their majority to rule the entire country for their own wealth, aggrandizement and commercial gain. Alexis de Tocqueville wrote that the urge for centralization in the 19th century was a powerful urge worldwide. That's why the idea that the good North went to war to free the slaves rather than to increase its money and power is a fraud of biblical proportions and easily disproven.

H. Newcomb Morse writes persuasively about the right of secession in the *Stetson Law Review*, a publication of the Stetson University College of Law. In an excellent article entitled "The Foundations and Meaning of Secession," Morse writes that the War Between the States did not prove that secession was illegal because

> many incidents both preceding and following the War support the proposition that the Southern States did have the right to secede from the Union. Instances of nullification prior to the War Between the States, contingencies under which certain states acceded to the Union, and the fact that the Southern States were made to surrender the right to secession all affirm the existence of a right to secede . . .[105]

He adds that the Constitution's "failure to forbid secession" and amendments dealing with secession

---

[105] Morse, "The Foundations and Meaning of Secession," 420.

that were proposed in Congress as Southern states were seceding strengthened his argument that

> the Southern States had an absolute
> right to secede from the Union prior to
> the War Between the States.[106]

Morse argues that because the Constitution did not forbid secession, then every state acceding to the Constitution had the implied right to secede from it. He says that if men of the caliber of Madison, Hamilton, Wilson and the others meant to forbid secession, they definitely would have said so, and the omission of a prohibition on secession in the Constitution is strong proof that the right of secession existed and was assumed.[107]

---

[106] Ibid.

[107] There had to be a specific constitutional prohibition on secession for it to be illegal. Conversely, there did not have to be a specific constitutional affirmation of the right of secession for it to be legal because the 10th Amendment to the United States Constitution states:

> The powers not delegated to the United States
> by the Constitution, nor prohibited by it to the
> States, are reserved to the States respectively,
> or to the people.

There was no constitutional prohibition on secession, nor was there a constitutional sanctioning of any kind of federal coercion to force a state to obey a federal law. To do so would be to perpetrate an act of war on the offending state by the other states, for whom the federal government was their agent.

He quotes James Madison in *The Madison Papers*
who wrote "a breach of any one article by any one
party, leaves all other parties at liberty to consider the
whole convention as dissolved."[108] Vermont and Massachusetts, he points out, nullified with statutes the
Fugitive Slave Law of 1793 and those two breaches of
the compact alone were enough for the South to consider the compact dissolved.

There were many other violations of the Constitution discussed throughout the secession debate in the
South including Northern Personal Liberty Laws that,
in effect, nullified the Fugitive Slave Law of the Compromise of 1850 as well as Article IV, Section 3 of the
Constitution, which dealt with fugitive slaves. At least
ten Northern states had statutes that nullified the two
aforementioned laws.

Other breaches of the Constitution included the
harboring of fugitives from justice in the North, specifically two of John Brown's sons who were with
Brown at Harpers Ferry and were wanted in Virginia
for murder. They were being harbored in Ohio and
Iowa. Brown himself had been backed by Northerners
and financed with Northern money. Fanatical abolitionists with the acquiescence of states like Massachusetts tried desperately to destroy "domestic tranquil-
ity" in the South by sending incendiary abolitionist
material in the mail encouraging slaves to revolt and

---

[108] James Madison, *The Madison Papers* (Philadelphia: 1840),
895, in Morse, "The Foundations and Meaning of Secession,"
420.

murder. There is also, as mentioned earlier, the Republican endorsement of Hinton Helper's *The Impending Crisis of the South,* which called for the throats of Southerners to be cut.

The Republican Party was not a great movement trying to end the difficult slavery problem with good will. Their ranks included murderers and promoters of state-sponsored murder and terrorism. They knew how to end slavery if that had been their desire. They had ended it in the North with gradual, compensated emancipation, which was Lincoln's strong belief and approach, and the method used by most countries on earth. Ending slavery was not the Republican desire. No Republican could be elected suggesting that Northerners spend their hard-earned sweatshop money to free the slaves in the South who would then come North and be job competition. Control of the government for their own wealth and commercial empowerment was the Republican desire. Hate was simply a tool to help them get there.

To prove the right of a state to determine for itself when the Constitution had been violated, Morse quotes Jefferson's *Kentucky Resolutions,* which point out that <u>if the government had the right to determine when the</u> <u>Constitution was violated, then the government would</u> <u>be the arbiter of its own power and not the Constitu-</u> <u>tion.</u> The *Kentucky Resolutions* also reaffirm state sovereignty and independence.[109]

---

[109] Morse, "The Foundations and Meaning of Secession," 422-427.

Morse demonstrates that congressional discus-
sions and proposed legislation during the secession of
Southern states indicated that Congress believed the
right of secession to exist. One piece of legislation was
introduced to deal with the disposition of federal property within a seceding state as well as a seceding
state's assumption of its share of the national debt.
Another scrambled to forbid secession unless approved
by two-thirds of the members of both houses of Congress, the president, as well as all the states.

Morse then points out that thirty-six years earlier,
Chief Justice John Marshall, in *Gibbons v. Ogden*,
wrote that "limitations of a power furnish a strong argument in favor of the existence of that power. . . ."[110]
Morse concludes:

> What would have been the point of the
> foregoing proposed amendments to the
> Constitution of the United States pro-
> hibiting or limiting the right of secession
> if under the Constitution the unfettered
> right of secession did not already exist?
> Why would Congress have even consid-
> ered proposed amendments to the Con-
> stitution forbidding or restricting the
> right of secession if any such right was

---

[110] Chief Justice John Marshall, *Gibbons v. Ogden*, 22 U.S. (9
Wheat.) 1 (1824), 200, in Morse, "The Foundations and Meaning of Secession," 428.

already prohibited, limited or non-exis-
tent under the Constitution?[111]

Morse goes on to discuss the aforementioned conditional ratification of the Constitution by three of the
original thirteen states, which specifically reserved for
those states the right of secession. The states were Virginia, New York and Rhode Island. Virginia referred to
the wording of her conditional ratification of the U.S.
Constitution in her Ordinance of Secession.[112] Morse

---

[111] Morse, "The Foundations and Meaning of Secession," 428.
[112] VIRGINIA: AN ORDINANCE to repeal the ratification of the
Constitution of the United States of America by the State of
Virginia, and to resume all the rights and powers granted under said Constitution.

The people of Virginia **in their ratification of the Constitution of the United States of America, adopted by them in
convention on the twenty-fifth day of June, in the year of
our Lord one thousand seven hundred and eighty-eight,
having declared that the powers granted under said Constitution were derived from the people of the United States
and might be resumed whensoever the same should be
perverted to their injury and oppression,** and the Federal
Government having perverted said powers not only to the injury of the people of Virginia, but to the oppression of the
Southern slave-holding States . . .

Adopted by the convention of Virginia April 17, 1861.

[It should again be noted that Virginia's secession had
NOTHING whatsoever to do with slavery. Virginia, North Carolina, Arkansas and Tennessee seceded because of Lincoln's
call for 75,000 volunteers to invade the South, which they
viewed as illegal, unconstitutional and immoral. Virginia's action was immediate. A brief chronology is illustrative. The bom-

points out that since the other states, which had un-
conditionally ratified the Constitution, consented to
Virginia's conditional ratification, then they "ostensibly assented to the principle that Virginia permissibly
retained the right to secede." He adds that with the
additional acceptance of "New York's and Rhode Island's right to secede, the existing states of the Union
must have tacitly accepted the doctrine of secession."
Further, Morse states that according to the Constitution, all the new states that joined the Union after the
first thirteen also had the right of secession since new
states entered on an equal footing with the exact same
rights as the existing states.[113]

Southerners during the secession debate knew
that Virginia, New York and Rhode Island had reserved the right of secession, thus all the states had
the right of secession. Senator Judah P. Benjamin, in
his farewell speech to the United States Senate on
February 5, 1861, said:

> The rights of Louisiana as a sovereign
> state are those of Virginia; no more, no

---

bardment of Fort Sumter began April 12, 1861. Fort Sumter
surrendered April 13th. Major Anderson, with full military hon-
ors, saluted his flag and marched out of the fort April 14th. On
April 15th, Lincoln called for 75,000 volunteers to invade the
South, and on April 17th, Virginia seceded. She was followed
by Tennessee and Arkansas on May 6th and North Carolina
on May 20th, thus the completion of the Southern republic.]
(Emphasis added.)

[113] Morse, "The Foundations and Meaning of Secession," 428-
32.

less. Let those who deny her right to resume delegated powers, successfully re-
fute the claim of Virginia to the same
right, in spite of her expressed reserva-
tion made and notified to her sister
states when she consented to enter the
Union.[114]

Morse skips forward to Reconstruction and points
out that "the Northern occupational armies were removed from Arkansas, North Carolina, Florida, South
Carolina, Mississippi, and Virginia only after those
former Confederate States had incorporated in their
constitutions a clause surrendering the right to
secede." Morse then argues brilliantly that

by insisting that the former Confederate
States surrender their right to secede,
the United States government had im-
plicitly admitted that those states originally had the right. How could they surrender a right, unless they had it in the
first place?[115]

To summarize, Morse points out that before the
war, under Virginia's conditional ratification of the
Constitution, when the people decided that govern-

---

[114] Judah P. Benjamin, "Farewell Address to the U.S. Senate" delivered February 5, 1861, *Library of Southern Literature,* Vol. 1, 318.
[115] Morse, "The Foundations and Meaning of Secession," 433.

ment power had been "perverted to their injury or oppression," they had the right to secede. When Northern
states passed Personal Liberty Bills and other statutes
nullifying the fugitive slave laws of the Constitution
(Article IV, Section 3), a "perversion" occurred which
gave the Southern states the right to secede. Reinforcing that perversion even further was the federal government's not forcing those Northern states to abide
by the Constitution, therefore

> the Northern States conceivably "per-
> verted" national law to the "injury or op-
> pression" of the people of the Southern
> States. Thus, the reassumption of the
> powers of government by the people of
> the Southern States was a natural con-
> sequence of the Northern States' conduct
> and the federal government's failure to
> prohibit that conduct.[116]

The only other issue, according to Morse, was
whether the Southern states conducted their act of secession legally. Morse points out that the people are
the sovereign having supreme, absolute and perpetual
power, therefore secession would have to be accomplished by the people of each state rather than their
legislatures. He says "convention delegates elected by
the people of the state to decide one question consti-

---

[116] Morse, "The Foundations and Meaning of Secession," 433-
434.

tute authority closer to the seat of the sovereign — the people themselves," therefore a convention in each Southern state would be necessary as a "special agent of the people of the state." Did the Southern States conduct themselves legally and therefore perfect their acts of secession and independence? Morse says:

> When the Southern States seceded from the Union in 1860 and 1861, not one state was remiss in discharging this legal obligation. Every seceding state properly utilized the convention process, rather than a legislative means, to secede. Therefore, not only did the Southern States possess the right to secede from the Union, they exercised that right in the correct manner.[117]

Morse's conclusion is that

> conceivably, it was the Northern States that acted illegally in precipitating the War Between the States. The Southern States, in all likelihood, were exercising a perfectly legitimate right in seceding from the Union.[118]

---

[117] Morse, "The Foundations and Meaning of Secession," 434-436.

[118] Morse, "The Foundations and Meaning of Secession," 436.

Other direct evidence of the right of secession abounds. Albert Taylor Bledsoe wrote in 1866 what is thought to be the best book ever written on the right of secession: *Is Davis a Traitor; or Was Secession a Constitutional Right Previous to the War of 1861?* Richard M. Weaver, who was during his lifetime a professor and author of several noted books on the South, called *Is Davis a Traitor* "the masterpiece of the Southern apologias."[119] Weaver described it as a "brilliant specimen of the polemic" out of the entire "extensive body of Southern political writing."[120]

Clyde N. Wilson, Emeritus Distinguished Professor of History at the University of South Carolina, editor of *The Papers of John C. Calhoun,* and author of many outstanding books, essays and articles, goes even further. In the Introduction to a 1995 reprint of *Is Davis a Traitor*, Dr. Wilson lists the top seven books defending the South and the right of secession and says "Bledsoe did it first and best," his argument for

---

[119] By "apologia," Weaver means a *formal* explanation and defense of a position, not an apology.

[120] George M. Curtis, III, and James J. Thompson, Jr., eds., *The Southern Essays of Richard M. Weaver* (Indianapolis: LibertyPress, 1987), 152. Richard M. Weaver graduated from the University of Kentucky in 1932, earned an M.A. degree at Vanderbilt University, and a doctorate in English from Louisiana State University in 1943. He taught at the University of Chicago until his death in 1963. He wrote scores of essays and published several books. He is best known for his books *Ideas Have Consequences,* and *The Ethics of Rhetoric.*

the right of secession being "absolutely irrefutable to any honest mind."[121]

Bledsoe was born in Frankfort, Kentucky in 1809. He graduated from West Point in 1830 and had been there part of the time with Robert E. Lee, Jefferson Davis, Leonidas Polk and Albert Sydney Johnston. He loved mathematics and theology, but practiced law for nine years in Springfield, Illinois as part of a bar that included Abraham Lincoln and Stephen A. Douglas. Bledsoe faced Lincoln in court several times and "it was said that Bledsoe won six out of eleven cases tried against Lincoln." Also, Bledsoe had given Lincoln lessons, at one point, on using a broadsword because Lincoln had been challenged to a duel.[122]

After his legal career, Bledsoe taught astronomy and mathematics at the University of Mississippi, acquiring a "legendary" genius for mathematics. In 1854,

---

[121] Albert Taylor Bledsoe, *Is Davis a Traitor; or Was Secession a Constitutional Right Previous to the War of 1861?* (Baltimore: Innes & Company, 1866; reprint, North Charleston: Fletcher and Fletcher Publishing, 1995), Introduction to the 1995 reprint by Clyde N. Wilson, i-ii. The other six works that best defend the South and right of secession according to Dr. Wilson are the two-volume work *A Constitutional View of the Late War Between the States* by Alexander H. Stephens; *The Rise and Fall of the Confederate Government* by Jefferson Davis; *A Defence of Virginia and Through Her of the South* by Robert L. Dabney; *The Creed of the Old South* by Basil L. Gildersleeve; *The Southern States of the American Union Considered in their Relations to the Constitution of the United States and the Resulting Union* by Jabez L. M. Curry; and *The Lost Cause* by Edward A. Pollard.

[122] Bledsoe, *Is Davis a Traitor;*, Introduction to the 1995 reprint by Clyde N. Wilson, i-viii.

he began teaching mathematics at the University of Virginia.

During the war, Bledsoe served briefly as the colonel of a regiment of infantry from Virginia, then later in the Confederate War Department, and finally he was sent to Europe by President Davis on what is thought to have been a secret diplomatic mission to influence public opinion in Britain. After the war, until his death in 1877, Bledsoe published *The Southern Review* in which he continued to argue the justice and truth of the Southern cause.[123]

Bledsoe began working on *Is Davis a Traitor* while in England and published it just after the war "as a part of the campaign of Davis's defense." The Confederate President was in prison at Fort Monroe, a U.S. Army installation in Hampton, Virginia where he spent a miserable two years waiting to be tried for treason. He was in irons with a bright light shining in his cell twenty-four hours a day with guards marching back and forth. The bright light was an additional measure of vindictiveness since it was known that Davis had never been able to sleep except in total darkness.

Davis *wanted* to be tried for treason because he was confident he could prove the right of secession. In talking about the effectiveness of *Is Davis a Traitor*, Richard Weaver writes that

---

[123] Ibid.

> Bledsoe witnessed some practical result
> of his labor when Robert Oulds and
> Charles O'Conor, attorneys for Jefferson
> Davis, made use of the book in preparing
> their defense; but the Federal govern-
> ment, apparently feeling the weakness
> of its legal position, allowed the case to
> be dismissed.[124]

Here was the North's big chance to prove the South wrong once and for all in a solemn, dignified court of law in the eyes of the world and for all of posterity, but they refused to take it. Why? They certainly had not suddenly had a change of heart toward the South. It was Reconstruction, the body of the assassinated Lincoln was barely cold in the ground. South-hating radical Republicans held great sway in Congress. Northern troops were in charge of most Southern states while large numbers of former Confederates were disenfranchised. This was exactly the time the Federal Government would have wanted to convict the Southern president if it had a case. It was willing to kill hundreds of thousands of Southerners on the battle field so there can be no doubt it would have relished humiliating Jefferson Davis in a courtroom.

But the Federal Government knew it would lose so it dropped its case. The Federal Government, like that embodiment of the North, Horace Greeley, knew there was an absolute right of secession. The Declaration of

---

[124] Curtis and Thompson, eds., *The Southern Essays of Richard M. Weaver* (Indianapolis: LibertyPress, 1987), 153-154.

Independence is very clear. There were no treason trials against any former Confederates because any one
trial would prove the right of secession, and immi-
nently practical Northerners were not about to lose in
a court of law what they had won on the battlefield.

Bledsoe's "irrefutable" argument in *Is Davis a
Traitor* begins with the Constitution as a compact or
legal agreement among the members to the compact.
The reason Bledsoe starts here is because any member
that has acceded to (agreed to) the terms of a compact,
can secede from that compact if the terms are broken
by one of the other members. This is exactly what
Morse said as well.

Bledsoe produces the writings and statements of
the strongest opponents of the Constitution as compact
— Daniel Webster and others — who have admitted
that if the Constitution is a compact, then states can
secede from it.[125] Webster was the great spokesman for
the North with the credibility and reputation to go
along with it. Bledsoe writes:

> Thus, the great controversy is narrowed
> down to the single question — Is the
> Constitution a compact between the
> States? If so, then the right of secession
> is conceded, even by its most powerful
> and determined opponents; by the great

---

[125] Taking on Webster also takes on most of the others who
did not believe the Constitution was a compact because most
of them quoted Webster and used his argument.

jurist, as well as by 'the great expounder' [Webster] of the North.[126]

If the Constitution was a compact, the North had clearly broken specific terms of the compact. As Morse stated earlier, Northern states had statutes on their books nullifying constitutional and congressional laws with regard to fugitive slaves. Many in the North believed, as William H. Seward stated, that they were operating according to a "higher law" than the Constitution therefore the Constitution meant nothing and did not have to be obeyed. The more radical had long called the Constitution a "covenant with death and agreement with hell."[127]

How could the North be trusted if they were going to violate the Constitution at will? The reason for breaking the law does not justify breaking the law. If one doesn't like a law, one has to change the law, not break it. Breaking laws according to a "higher law" is what ISIS and Bin Laden and their ilk do. Men and

---

[126] Bledsoe, *Is Davis a Traitor;*, 6.

[127] Statement by the famous abolitionist, William Lloyd Garrison, publisher of *The Liberator*, who burned a copy of the Constitution and Fugitive Slave Act on the 4th of July, 1854, to cheers and hisses. Robert Toombs might have disagreed with Garrison but he respected Garrison. Toombs said Garrison believed what he said unlike the "political abolitionists" of the North who were in anti-slavery to vote themselves a farm or a tariff. Quotations from Garrison, Seward and others come from Bledsoe, *Is Davis a Traitor;*, 151-153.

women who believe in the rule of law do not break the law. They change the law when it needs changing.[128]

If somebody breaks the law, they are no longer trustworthy and other parties are not obligated to remain in any arrangement with them. The North's having clearly broken the compact guaranteed that secession was legal if the Constitution was a compact that was "acceded to" by the original makers. Did the original states "accede" to a compact?

Webster railed against the Constitution as a compact. He said that saying "the States acceded to the Constitution" was "unconstitutional language."[129] Discrediting the single word, "accede," was very important to Webster.

So Bledsoe researched in great detail the words of the Founders and finds that in the Constitutional Convention of 1787, "Mr. James Wilson . . . preferred 'a partial union' of the States, 'with a door open for the **accession** of the rest.'"[130]

However, "Mr. Gerry, a delegate from Massachusetts, was opposed to 'a partial confederacy, leaving other States to **accede** or not to **accede**, as had been intimated.'"[131]

Father of the Constitution, James Madison, "used the expression 'to **accede**' in the Convention of 1787, in

---

[128] And certainly the Fugitive Slave Law and similar laws were unfair with huge areas of unfair potential abuse, and they needed changing.
[129] Bledsoe, *Is Davis a Traitor;*, 16, 12.
[130] Bledsoe, *Is Davis a Traitor;*, 12-17.
[131] Ibid.

order to denote the act of adopting 'the new form of government by the States.'"[132]

Virginia Governor Randolph, also at the Convention of 1787, said "That the **accession** of eight States reduced our deliberations to the single question of Union or no Union."[133]

Patrick Henry had said that if the Constitution "be amended, every State will **accede** to it."[134]

Mr. Grayson asks if Virginia will gain anything from her prominent position "by **acceding** to that paper."[135]

Benjamin Franklin, whom Bledsoe says was next in importance at the Constitutional Convention to Washington, later said "Our new Constitution is now established with eleven States, and the **accession** of a twelfth is soon expected."[136]

George Washington, as he watched states join the Constitution, said "If these, with the States eastward and northward of us, should **accede** to the Federal government . . ."[137]

Chief Justice John Marshall used the word "**accede**" in reference to joining the Constitution, and even Mr. Justice Story, a staunch opponent of the belief in Constitution as compact, said "The Constitution has been ratified by all the States; . . . Rhode Island did

---

[132] Ibid.
[133] Ibid.
[134] Ibid.
[135] Ibid.
[136] Ibid.
[137] Ibid.

not **accede** to it, until more than a year after it had
been in operation;".[138]

Webster had attacked the word "accede" as something invented by proponents of the Constitution as
compact. Bledsoe points out that Webster's attack on
"accede" by calling it a "new word" was totally incorrect because "accede" had been exactly "the word of the
fathers of the Constitution" led by Washington. They
had all used the word "accede" in reference to states
joining the Constitution, and, of course, the converse of
"accede" is "secede."[139]

Over and over Bledsoe demolishes each and every
argument that maintains secession was not legal or a
right. He produces the words of the Founding Fathers
specifically calling the Constitution a compact starting
with the Father of the Constitution, James Madison.
In the *Virginia Resolutions* of 1798, Madison states:

> That this assembly doth explicitly and
> peremptorily declare, that it views the
> powers of the Federal Government as
> resulting from the compact, to which the
> States are parties.[140]

Bledsoe further mentions a letter from Madison to
a Mr. Everett in 1830 in which Madison says that the

---

[138] Ibid.
[139] Bledsoe, *Is Davis a Traitor;*, 17.
[140] Bledsoe, *Is Davis a Traitor;*, 25.

Constitution is "'a compact among the States in their highest sovereign capacity.'"[141]

Bledsoe then convicts Webster using Webster's own words. Webster had admitted that the Constitution was a compact in a debate three years earlier on "Foote's resolutions." Bledsoe says "that Mr. Webster himself, had, like everyone else, spoken of the Constitution as a compact, as a bargain which was obligatory on the parties to it." Webster had said:

> [I]t is the original bargain, . . . the com-
> pact — let it stand; let the advantage of
> it be fully enjoyed. The Union itself is
> too full of benefits to be hazarded in
> propositions for changing its original ba-
> sis. I go for the Constitution as it is, and
> for the Union as it is.[142]

Perhaps the strongest argument against the right of secession is based on the words "We the people" in the Constitution's Preamble. Those who argue that the Constitution is not a compact but is a national document, believe that "We the People" means all of the American people in one body and not in their sovereign states. This, says Bledsoe, "is the great stronghold, if it has one, of the Northern theory of the Constitution. The argument from these words appears in every speech, book, pamphlet, and discussion by every advo-

---

[141] Ibid.

[142] Daniel Webster, on Foote's resolutions in Bledsoe, *Is Davis a Traitor;*, 25.

cate of the North. It was wielded by Mr. Webster in his
great debate with Mr. Calhoun, in 1833, . . .".[143] If the
Constitution was written as a document for all of the
American people in one body, then individual states
had no right to withdraw from it.

The Committee on Style of the Constitutional Convention of 1787 was headed by Gouverneur Morris of
Pennsylvania. Here's what Gouverneur Morris said is
meant by "We the people," which he authored:

> The Constitution . . . was a compact not
> between individuals, but between politi-
> cal societies [states], the people, not of
> America, but of the United States, each
> [state] enjoying sovereign power and of
> course equal rights.[144]

Morris himself believed in the right of secession
and supported New England's move to secede during
the War of 1812, which culminated in the Hartford
Convention.[145]

---

[143] Bledsoe, *Is Davis a Traitor;*, 61.

[144] Gouverneur Morris, *Life and Writings*, Vol. iii, p. 193, as
quoted in Bledsoe, *Is Davis a Traitor;*, 64-65. Morris would
have been even more clear if he had not capitalized "United."
It is not capitalized in the Declaration of Independence which
reads "The unanimous Declaration of the thirteen united
States of America." Clearly that is what Morris is saying, that
the individual sovereign states are "united" with equal rights
and sovereign power.

[145] Bledsoe, *Is Davis a Traitor;*, 64-65.

Bledsoe quotes *The Madison Papers* and refers to some 900 pages of the proceedings of the Constitutional Convention of 1787 in which are recorded the debate over *method* of ratification. He points out that nowhere in that vast record is there a discussion of the "people" as meaning the entire American people outside of their states. The big debate was over whether the legislatures of each state would ratify the Constitution, or the "people" of each state in special convention.

It was decided that since a later legislature might rescind the ratification of an earlier legislature, it would be a more sound foundation to have the people of each state ratify the Constitution in special conventions called for the single purpose of ratification.[146]

That is exactly why the Southern States used conventions to secede. The Constitutional Convention of 1787 had set the precedent when it decided that states should use the convention method to ratify the Constitution, and, as Mr. H. Newcomb Morse said in the *Stetson Law Review*, "not one [Southern] state was remiss in discharging this legal obligation" to use a convention of the people when it seceded from the Union.

The reason there is no listing in the Preamble of specific states ratifying the Constitution as had been done in the body of the Articles of Confederation is because nobody knew how many states, or which ones, would ratify the Constitution.

---

[146] Bledsoe, *Is Davis a Traitor;*, 66-73.

If all the states had been listed and one refused to ratify, then the document would be invalid. The number "nine" was decided on, as the number of states necessary to put the Constitution into effect, but, in debating the issue, it was brought up that the Constitution could only apply to those states ratifying it, therefore no references *could* be made to "all" of the American people.

Bledsoe writes that Rufus King suggested adding "between the said states, so as to confine the operation of the government to the States ratifying the same."[147] The words were cleaned up and found their way into the Constitution in Article VII which starts out:

> The Ratification of the Conventions of nine States, shall be sufficient for the Establishment of this Constitution between the States so ratifying the Same.

Bledsoe further clarifies:

> [W]hen it was determined that the Constitution should be ratified by 'the Conventions of the States,' and not by the legislatures, this was exactly equivalent, in the uniform language of the Convention of 1787, to saying that it shall be ratified by 'the people of the States.' Hence, the most ardent friend of State

---

[147] Bledsoe, *Is Davis a Traitor;*, 72.

> rights, or State sovereignty, saw no rea-
> son why he should object to the words,
> 'We, the people of the United States,'
> because he knew they were only in-
> tended to express the mode of ratifica-
> tion by the States . . . in their sovereign
> capacity, as so many political societies or
> peoples, as distinguished from their leg-
> islatures.[148]

Bledsoe goes on by pointing out that the Federal Government had no legal right whatsoever to coerce a state into following its laws, therefore it had no right to force a seceding state back into the Union. President Buchanan had stated in his lame duck period between Lincoln's election of November 6, 1860, and March 4, 1861, when Lincoln would be inaugurated, while state after state was seceding, that as president of the United States, he had no power to coerce a state, even though he denied that secession was legal.

Bledsoe notes the contradiction in Buchanan's position and writes "if we say, that coercion is a consti-tutional wrong, or usurpation, is not this saying that the Constitution permits secession, or, in other words, that it is a Constitutional right?"

He says "Coercion is unconstitutional . . . wrong . . . strikes down and demolishes the great fundamen-tal principle of the Declaration of Independence: The sacred right of self-government itself." About seces-

---

[148] Bledsoe, *Is Davis a Traitor;*, 73.

sion, he says "Secession, on the other hand, asserts the
right of self-government for every free, sovereign, and
independent State in existence."[149]

Bledsoe discussed the views of credible foreign ob-
servers and writes that Alexis de Tocqueville, in *Democracy in America*, said:

> The Union was formed by the voluntary
> agreement of the States; and in uniting
> together they have not forfeited their
> nationality, nor have they been reduced
> to the condition of one and the same peo-
> ple. If one of the States choose to with-
> draw from the compact, it would be dif-
> ficult to disprove its right of doing so,
> and the Federal Government would have
> no means of maintaining its claims di-
> rectly either by force or right.[150]

To Tocqueville, Bledsoe adds "Mackay, and
Spence, and Brougham, and Cantu, and Heeren," then
he goes on "as well as other philosophers, jurists and
historians among the most enlightened portions of
Europe, [who] so readily adopt the Southern view of
the Constitution, and pronounce the American Union
as a confederation of States."[151]

---

[149] Bledsoe, *Is Davis a Traitor;*, 154.

[150] Alexis de Tocqueville, *Democracy in America*, as quoted in
Bledsoe, *Is Davis a Traitor;*, 155. The reference to *Democracy
in America* footnoted by Bledsoe is Vol. i, Chap. xviii., p 413.

[151] Bledsoe, *Is Davis a Traitor;*, 157.

Bledsoe continues with more persuasive argument, the words of Thomas Jefferson and Alexander
Hamilton, who assert, beyond doubt, that the Constitution is a compact and the states, sovereign.

He discusses William Rawl of Philadelphia and his
book, *A View of the Constitution of the United States,*
which stresses the right of secession and was used as a
textbook at West Point during most of the antebellum
era.

He also mentions the States' Rights Hartford Convention of New England states, which strongly supported the right of secession, though it went way beyond its legal right to secede and actually aided the
British in the War of 1812 thus becoming the most
treasonous assembly in American history.[152]

---

[152] The New England states had threatened to secede many
times such as with the Louisiana Purchase, the Mexican War,
anything that added territory to the South that would dilute
New England's political power. During the War of 1812, New
England was deeply aggrieved over trade issues affecting
commerce and shipping. They called the Hartford Convention
and made plans to secede. The Hartford Convention (December 15, 1814 to January 5, 1815, in Hartford, Connecticut)
quickly became the most dishonorable affair in American history. New England governors had deliberately sabotaged the
American war effort by withholding troops and refusing to support the United States against Great Britain. Massachusetts'
Gov. Caleb Strong refused to retake part of Maine captured by
the British, then later sent a secret Massachusetts delegation
to make a separate peace with the British. President James
Madison was truly concerned that all of New England would
make a separate peace with Great Britain. Shortly after the
Hartford Convention, Massachusetts sent three commissioners to Washington, D.C. who arrived in February, 1815 to air
their grievances but Andy Jackson and the Southern boys in

As stated earlier, Horace Greeley, as the embodiment of the North, had thoroughly believed in the
right of secession. He had written in his *New-York
Daily Tribune* on December 17, 1860, just as South
Carolina's secession convention was starting, a brilliant editorial entitled "The Right of Secession." Here
again, is most of it:

> We have repeatedly asked those who dis-
> sent from our view of this matter to tell
> us frankly whether they do or do not as-
> sent to Mr. Jefferson's statement in the
> Declaration of Independence that gov-
> ernments "derive their just powers from
> the consent of the governed; and that,
> whenever any form of government be-
> comes destructive of these ends, it is the
> right of the people to alter or abolish it,
> and to institute a new government," &c.,
> &c. We do heartily accept this doctrine,
> believing it intrinsically sound, benefi-
> cent, and one that, universally accepted,
> is calculated to prevent the shedding of

New Orleans had already whipped the British and the war was
over. The commissioners quickly returned to Massachusetts in
disgrace. The Hartford Convention, thereafter became synony-
mous with treason since they had aided and abetted an enemy
during war. The Federalist Party, which had supported the
Hartford Convention, was all but destroyed, though it continued strong in Massachusetts for some years. See Hartford
Convention, http://en.wikipedia.org/wiki/Hartford_Convention,
accessed August 26, 2014.

seas of human blood. And, if it justified the secession from the British Empire of Three Millions of colonists in 1776, we do not see why it would not justify the secession of Five Millions of Southrons from the Federal Union in 1861. If we are mistaken on this point, why does not some one attempt to show wherein and why? . . . — we could not stand up for coercion, for subjugation, for we do not think it would be just. We hold the right of Self-government sacred, even when invoked in behalf of those who deny it to others . . . if ever 'seven or eight States' send agents to Washington to say 'We want to get out of the Union,' we shall feel constrained by our devotion to Human Liberty to say, Let Them Go! And we do not see how we could take the other side without coming in direct conflict with those Rights of Man which we hold paramount to all political arrangements, however convenient and advantageous.[153]

Horace Greeley and the North had it right until they realized their "devotion to Human Liberty" and belief in "those Rights of Man which we hold para-

---

[153] "The Right of Secession," *The New-York Daily Tribune*, December 17, 1860, in Perkins, ed., *Northern Editorials on Secession*, 199-201.

mount to all political arrangements" meant nothing to them when compared to their money and power. The "shedding of seas of human blood" was OK with them, and that is exactly what they got.

The Southern States unquestionably had the right to secede from the Union, as Horace Greeley just reiterated. That Southerners lost a catastrophic war, which, if it occurred today, would count 8.7 million dead and 10 million wounded, only glorifies and enshrines in the annals of human history, the courage of Southerners and their commitment to democracy, self-government, the Founding Fathers, and especially the Declaration of Independence with its assertion that governments derive their just powers from the consent of the governed.

An Annotated Chronology of the Secession Debate in the South[154]

Here are the debates, conventions, speeches, votes, thrill and triumph of Southerners as they proclaim the Declaration of Independence of 1776 their guiding principle and they establish a democratic republic that is the mirror image of the republic of the Founding Fathers.

---

[154] Please see the Bibliography for complete information on every source used in this chronology, especially primary sources. Most of the quotations herein are used in the previous text and cited, but if not, are cited here. The following sources were used repeatedly: Ralph A. Wooster, *The Secession Conventions of the South* (Princeton, NJ: Princeton University Press, 1962); Charles W. Ramsdell, "Lincoln and Fort Sumter," *Journal of Southern History*, Volume 3, Issue 3 (Aug., 1937); E. B. Long with Barbara Long, *The Civil War Day by Day, An Almanac, 1861 - 1865* (New York: Da Capo Press, 1971; reprint, New York, Da Capo Press, 1985); John Amasa May and Joan Reynolds Faunt, *South Carolina Secedes* (Columbia, SC: University of South Carolina Press, 1962); *The War of the Rebellion: A Compilation of the Official Records of the Union and Confederate Armies* (Washington: Government Printing Office, 1900; reprint, Historical Times, Inc., 1985); W. Buck Yearns, ed., *The Confederate Governors* (Athens, GA: The University of Georgia Press, 1985); John Shipley Tilley, *Lincoln Takes Command* (second printing, Nashville: Bill Coats, Ltd., 1991).

February 24, 1860

Joint Resolutions of the General Assembly of Ala-bama approved. It would trigger, upon the election of a Republican to the presidency, the calling of a convention "to consider, determine and do whatever in the opinion of said Convention, the rights, interests, and honor of the State of Alabama requires to be done for their protection."

Notice that Alabama is talking about taking action "for their protection." They were legitimately concerned as was the rest of the South after 10 years of Republican hatred, terrorism and murder of Southerners. Republicans had printed Hinton Helper's book, *The Impending Crisis of the South*, by the tens of thousands and distributed it to all corners of the country as a campaign document calling for the throats of Southerners to be cut. Southerners believed that John Brown at Harpers Ferry was following the Republican guidebook. Southerners were convinced that there was more murder and terrorism coming, to go along with economic confiscation if they stayed in the Union under Republican rule.

September 21, 1860

Washington, D.C. speech of William Lowndes Yancy, "Equal Rights in a Common Government." The fiery Yancy said

> Revenues have been raised at the rate of
> two or three dollars in the South to one

from any other section for the support of
this great Government, but the South
makes no complaint of mere dollars and
cents. Touch not the honor of my section
of the country, and she will not complain
of almost anything else you may do; but
touch her honor and equality and she
will stand up in their defence, if necessary in arms. . . . No matter who may be
elected, no matter what may be done,
still they [the North] will stand to the
Union as the great cause of their prosperity. . . .[155]

October 19, 1860

Rep. John H. Reagan publishes an excellent letter
pointing out, among other things, the Northern desire
to "strike down the sovereignty and equality of the
States," taking of private property in slaves with no
compensation, promotion of Helper's book which rec-
ommends "treason, blood, and carnage as a proper
campaign document" for the Republicans, etc.

November 5, 1860

South Carolina Governor William H. Gist asks the

---

[155] William Lowndes Yancy, "Equal Rights in a Common Government, Speech in Washington, D.C., September 21, 1860,"
in Alderman and Harris, eds., *Library of Southern Literature.*

legislature for a state convention if the Republicans
win the election.

November 6, 1860

Republican Abraham Lincoln is elected sixteenth
president of the United States with Hannibal Hamlin
of Maine his vice-president. Historian David M. Potter
in *Lincoln and His Party in the Secession Crisis* writes
that Lincoln was elected by a Northern sectional minority representing the smallest plurality of popular
votes in American history. The loser in the next five
presidential elections got more popular votes than Lincoln. Of the total 4,682,069 votes cast, Lincoln received
1,866,452 which is 39.9%. The eighteen states voting
for him were all above the Mason/Dixon line. He received no electoral votes in fifteen of the thirty-three
states. His name was not even on the ballot in ten
Southern states. Lincoln's opponents together totaled
2,815,617, which was almost a million votes more than
he got.

November 7, 1860

Georgia Governor Joseph E. Brown delivers his
long *Special Message on Federal Relations* encouraging separate state action on secession rather than
waiting for a convention of Southern states to jointly
decide the issue. He points out, among many positive
issues, Southern economic strength, and it ends with
"To every demand for further concessions, or compro-

mise of our rights, we should reply, 'The argument is exhausted,' and we now 'stand by our arms.'"

(Some time between November 7-20, 1860, the *Resolutions on Secession from Floyd County, Georgia*, was issued.)

November 10, 1860

South Carolina legislature approves bill calling for secession convention to begin December 17, 1860.

November 12, 1860

Commencement of an entire week of speeches debating secession before the Georgia legislature in Milledgeville. This was a critical debate since Georgia, the Empire State of the South, had the largest population and strongest economy in the lower South.

Georgian Thomas Read Roots Cobb's secessionist speech to the Georgia legislature and guests in Milledgeville. This rousing speech pointed out, among other things, flagrant Northern violations of the Constitution, Northern hatred being promoted at all levels toward the South, Northern fanatical abolitionism, possibility of a wall of free states around the Cotton States, and warns of the "gory head" of civil war.

Prices on the New York financial market drop sharply due to heavy selling.

November 14, 1860

Mississippi Gov. Pettus "issued a call for a special session of the legislature on November 26 to consider necessary future safeguards for Mississippi."

Alabama Governor Andrew B. Moore makes it clear that December 24, 1860, will be the day for election of delegates to a secession convention, and the convention is to convene January 7, 1861.

November 19, 1860

Secessionist Speech of Georgian Henry L. Benning to members and guests of the Georgia legislature in Milledgeville, going into great detail on the amount of Southern wealth flowing north in the form of bounties, tariffs, subsidies, etc.

November 20, 1860

Georgia legislature approves bill for election of secession convention delegates on January 2, 1861, and convention itself to convene January 16, 1861.

November 21, 1860

Lincoln goes to Chicago from Springfield for five days to discuss cabinet appointments with his vice-president Hannibal Hamlin.

November 26, 1860

Mississippi Gov. Pettus advises a secession convention be called, and a bill was passed dealing with elections of delegates, setting dates, etc.

December 1, 1860

Florida legislature goes into special session that had been requested by secessionist Governor M. S. Perry to consider calling a secession convention.

December 3, 1860

The Thirty-sixth Congress of the United States, second session, begins in Washington, D.C.

December 4, 1860

Lame duck President James Buchanan gives State of the Union Message blaming fanatical abolitionism for destroying the country. He admits of the sovereignty of each state but that the Federal Government would defend the forts if attacked. He said slavery was on the way out, and he proposed a constitutional amendment protecting property rights in slaves. He condemned secession and said the election of one of our countrymen was no legitimate reason to leave the Union, but he admitted he had no power to coerce a state. The Committee of Thirty-three was created by the U. S. House of Representatives, composed of one representative from each of the 33 states, to analyze the crisis.

December 8, 1860

A South Carolina delegation of U. S. House members warn President Buchanan not to attempt the reinforcement of Fort Sumter, which would be an act of coercion and war. They implore him to negotiate with South Carolina commissioners so the state could get title to all federal property by paying for it.

December 10, 1860

The Botetourt Resolutions of Judge John J. Allen, President of the Supreme Court of Virginia, forty-nine detailed patriotic statements linking the South today with the times of the Founding Fathers, condemning the North for sectionalism and the promotion of hatred by pharisaical fanatics, and making it clear, among other things, that Virginia had always reserved the right of secession. It was adopted almost unanimously by the people of Botetourt County, Virginia.

In response to Louisiana Governor Thomas O. Moore's request, the Louisiana legislature met in Baton Rouge and two days later, on December 12, 1860, passed a bill setting January 7, 1861 as the day to elect delegates and January 23, 1861 as the date of a secession convention to be held in Baton Rouge.

South Carolina delegation presented President Buchanan with a written statement promising not to attack the forts but admonishing him not to try to reinforce them. The South Carolinians got the impression there would be no change in the military situation in Charleston Harbor and they promised to try and prevent any accidental confrontation.

Lincoln, despite having no voter mandate to not compromise with the South, wrote Sen. Lyman Trumbell, "Let there be no compromise on the question of extending slavery. If there be, all our labor is lost, and, ere long, must be done again. . . . The tug has to come & better now, than any time hereafter."

Lincoln and the Republicans did not want slavery in the West because they didn't want blacks in the West. As Lincoln said in the Lincoln-Douglas Debates, the West was to be reserved for white working men from all over the world. That was his promise to the North and the primary reason he was against the extension of slavery. Northern and Western States agreed and most already had statues that forbid even free blacks from living there. In Lincoln's Illinois, a free black person could only stay a few days then he was subject to arrest and imprisonment.

Most Northern abolitionists were racists who did not like slavery because they did not like blacks and did not want to associate with them. This is well-documented. A few abolitionists were sincere, such as William Lloyd Garrison. There was a huge economic and political component to Northern anti-slavery. As historian David Potter said, it was in no sense pro-black but was anti-black and designed to get rid of blacks. A better characterization is anti-South and not anti-slavery.

December 11, 1860

Lincoln to Rep. William Kellogg, "Entertain no proposition for a compromise in regard to the extension of slavery. The instant you do, they have us under again. . . ."

December 12, 1860

Committee of Thirty-three doing its job with a variety of proposals, bills and resolutions submitted.

December 13, 1860

Twenty-three representatives and seven senators from the South issue "a manifesto which urged secession and the organization of a Southern Confederacy." Lincoln continues his intense campaign against compromise with the South on slavery in the territories.

December 16, 1860

South Carolina legislature elects Francis Wilkinson Pickens governor. The next day he delivered his *Inaugural Message* emphasizing, among other things, that South Carolina will open her ports to the world and advocate free trade, that she has fine harbors and important commodities, that South Carolina acceded to the Constitution alone and will secede alone.

December 17, 1860

South Carolina secession convention (Convention of the People of South Carolina) opens at the Baptist Church in Columbia, but due to the presence of small-pox in Columbia, decides to reconvene the next day in Charleston. The Convention did vote on a resolution in favor of seceding and it passed 159 - 0. David F. Jamison opened the Convention and his speech included:

> I trust that the door is now forever
> closed to all further connection with our
> Northern confederates; for what guaran-
> tees can they offer us, more strictly
> guarded, or under higher sanctions, than
> the present written compact [the Consti-
> tution] between us? And did that sacred
> instrument protect us from the jealousy
> and aggressions of the North, com-
> menced forty years ago, which resulted
> in the Missouri Compromise? Did the
> Constitution protect us from the cupidity
> of the Northern people, who, for thirty-
> five years, have imposed the burden of
> supporting the General Government
> chiefly on the industry of the South?

December 18, 1860

South Carolina secession convention reconvenes in Institute Hall in Charleston. The United States Senate in Washington passed a resolution for a Committee of

Thirteen to investigate the country's problems. It would be similar to the House's Committee of Thirty-three.

Kentucky Senator John J. Crittenden presented his plan which became known as the Crittenden Compromise. It had widespread support North and South. Its main feature was the revival of the Missouri Compromise line which had worked well for 30 years. Slavery had been prohibited above the line (36° 30' north) and allowed below it. [156] Crittenden's Compromise was submitted to the new, official Committee of Thirteen two days later but Lincoln was against it for political reasons and would instruct Republicans to kill it.

December 20, 1860

South Carolina secedes by adopting 169 - 0 an "Ordinance To Dissolve the Union between the State of South Carolina and other States United with her under the Compact Entitled 'The Constitution of the United States of America.'"

Mississippi elects delegates to its secession convention.

---

[156] The Missouri Compromise became irrelevant when the Kansas-Nebraska Act passed and allowed slavery anywhere in the territories; and later, the Dred Scott decision of the Supreme Court said slavery could not be kept out of the territories.

Committee of Thirteen officially named in the United States Senate.

December 21, 1860

Lincoln writes to Democrat Francis P. Blair, Sr., "According to my present view if the forts shall be given up before the inauguration, the General [Scott] must retake them afterwards." He also wrote a similar letter to Rep. Elihu B. Washburne.

December 22, 1860

Election of delegates to the Florida Secession Convention.

South Carolina secession convention names three commissioners to negotiate the purchase of federal property in the state and put all the forts under South Carolina control. Lincoln wrote to Alexander Stephens saying he had no intention of interfering with slavery, only preventing its spread to the territories.

December 24, 1860

Declaration of the Immediate Causes Which Induce and Justify the Secession of South Carolina from the Federal Union adopted in Charleston, South Carolina by the South Carolina secession convention. It was written by Christopher Gustavus Memminger who served later as Confederate secretary of the treasury. It included many direct references to the right of seces-

sion going back to the Revolutionary War, such as the
following that starts out with a reference to the Articles of Confederation:

> Under this Confederation the war of
> the Revolution was carried on, and on
> the 3d September, 1783, the contest
> ended, and a definite Treaty was signed
> by Great Britain, in which she acknowl-
> edged the independence of the Colonies
> in the following terms:
> "Article 1 -- His Britannic Majesty
> acknowledges the said United States,
> viz: New Hampshire, Massachusetts
> Bay, Rhode Island and Providence Plan-
> tations, Connecticut, New York, New
> Jersey, Pennsylvania, Delaware, Mary-
> land, Virginia, North Carolina, South
> Carolina and Georgia, to be FREE, SOV-
> EREIGN AND INDEPENDENT
> STATES; that he treats with them as
> such; and for himself, his heirs and suc-
> cessors, relinquishes all claims to the
> government, propriety and territorial
> rights of the same and every part
> thereof.
> Thus were established the two great
> principles asserted by the Colonies,
> namely: the right of a State to govern
> itself; and the right of a people to abolish
> a Government when it becomes destruc-

tive of the ends for which it was insti-
tuted. And concurrent with the establishment of these principles, was the
fact, that each Colony became and was
recognized by the mother Country a
FREE, SOVEREIGN AND INDEPEND-
ENT STATE. (Memminger's emphasis.)

*The Address of the People of South Carolina, As-
sembled in Convention, to the People of the Slavehold-
ing States of the United States* adopted by the South
Carolina secession convention in Charleston, South
Carolina. It was written by *Charleston Mercury* editor
Robert Barnwell Rhett.

Delegates elected by Alabamians to the Alabama
Secession Convention.

New York Republican William H. Seward, soon to
be Lincoln's secretary of state, proposes a constitutional amendment to the effect that Congress can
never interfere with slavery in the states where it exists, and also that fugitive slaves be given jury trials,
and that the unconstitutional Personal Liberty Laws
on the books in many Northern states be revised.

December 26, 1860

Union Major Robert Anderson secretly moves from
Fort Moultrie on Sullivan's Island into the unfinished
Fort Sumter, making a tense national situation much
worse.

South Carolina secession convention proposed a convention meet in Montgomery, Alabama to create a constitution for the new Southern Confederacy.

December 27, 1860

Kentucky Governor Magoffin calls special secession of the legislature to meet January 17, 1861, to discuss federal relations.

Letter from Alabama Commissioner S. F. Hale, to Gov. Magoffin of Kentucky. Mr. Hale was a member of the Alabama House of Representatives and Alabama Secession Convention. His letter is one of the most thorough treatments of all the issues together in a persuasive package including Northern fanaticism, constitutional violations, use of the government for its own benefit with tariffs, bounties, subsidies, etc., John Brown and his Northern support, Emigrant Aid Societies, Lincoln's election by a sectional vote, etc.

December 31, 1860

Senate Committee of Thirteen reports that all proposals defeated in committee. As stated, Lincoln had instructed Republicans to kill it. The Crittenden Compromise was the only one that received serious attention.

January 1, 1861

Letter of Commissioner David Clopton of Alabama
to Delaware Gov. William Burton

January 2, 1861

Georgia election day for delegates to a secession
convention.

January 3, 1861

Florida secession convention convenes in Tallahassee.

Senate Republicans oppose Crittenden's proposal
that would allow the public to vote in a referendum on
his compromise , though it had some support.

Mid-Southern and border state congressmen meet
and form a committee to look at compromises.

January 5, 1861

South Carolina secession convention adjourns temporarily.

Missouri Senate calls for Federal Relations Committee to draft a bill for a secession convention.

A caucus of Southern senators from Florida, Arkansas, Texas, Louisiana, Mississippi, Alabama and

Georgia advise secession and a Southern Confederacy for their states.

January 7, 1861

Farewell Address of Sen. Robert Toombs of Georgia to the United States Senate.

Mississippi secession convention convenes in Jackson, Mississippi.

Alabama secession convention convenes in Montgomery.

Louisiana election of delegates to secession convention.

Tennessee Special Secession of the thirty-third legislature called by Governor Isham G. Harris meets in Nashville. Governor Harris delivers a long, passionate message outlining Northern aggressions against the South, from raising to martyrdom John Brown, to the North's harboring of one of his criminal fugitive sons. The legislature, among other things, agrees to allow a vote of the people "for or against" a secession convention, and at the same time to elect delegates to said convention.

Personal Explanation of the Hon. W. R. W. Cobb, of Alabama, delivered in the U.S. House of Representatives, pointing out, among other things, that the Republicans, elected by a minority of voters, have no mandate for anything.

Message on Federal Relations of Governor Letcher of Virginia to the Virginia legislature. Letcher points out Northern hatred of South and advocates a convention of Northern and Southern delegates to try and work out problems or separate peaceably. He rails against John Brown and says Brown should have been denounced by the North but was not. Points out history and New England's secessionist attempt with the Hartford Convention. Blames New England for all the nation's troubles. Includes glowing economic vision of free trade and rapidly growing Southern ports. Favors Southern independence.

Sen. John J. Crittenden speaks passionately in the U. S. Senate for his Compromise.

January 8, 1861

President Buchanan sends to Congress a message asking for pause, North and South, and saying the situation was beyond presidential control and the country needed to hear from the ballot box before a war started. He supports the Crittenden Compromise and the division of the territories by the old line of the Missouri Compromise.

January 9, 1861

The Mississippi secession convention passes a secession ordinance 84 - 15. The ensuing wild celebration is said to have inspired *The Bonnie Blue Flag* when Harry Macarthy spotted a blue silk flag with a single large white star in the middle, floating through the crowds.

The *Star of the West*, loaded with 250 troops and supplies, is fired on by South Carolina batteries as it tries to enter Charleston Harbor for the purpose of reinforcing Fort Sumter.

January 10, 1861

Florida secedes by a vote of 62 - 7 then, after taking care of other business, adjourns temporarily.

Union Lt. Adam J. Slemmer moved a small company of artillery a mile-and-a-half from Barrancas Barracks near the Navy Yard, where it had been stationed, into Fort Pickens at the mouth of Pensacola Bay, some six miles from Pensacola, Florida.

January 11, 1861

Speech of E. S. Dargan, in the Secession Convention of Alabama.

Alabama votes for secession 61 - 39.

Lincoln writes to Rep. James T. Hale of Pennsylvania stating "Now we are told in advance, the government shall be broken up, unless we surrender to those we have beaten, before we take the offices...".

New York Legislature passes anti-Southern resolution tendering aid to the president of the United
States in support of the Constitution and the Union
which starts "Whereas, treason, as defined by the Constitution of the United States, exists in one or more of
the States of this confederacy; and whereas, the insur-
gent State of South Carolina, . . .". It goes on to say
that the N.Y. Legislature "is profoundly impressed
with the value of the Union, and determined to preserve it unimpaired." A copy of this resolution was sent
to all the governors.

The reason New York was "profoundly impressed
with the value of the Union" is because the secession of
the Southern States proved to New York that its
wealth, power and employment were based on manufacturing for the South and shipping Southern cotton.
New York City without the South was headed for economic disaster.

New York City blamed the Republican Party for
the country's problems and had threatened to secede
from New York State and become an open city so it
could maintain its lucrative commercial relationship
with the South.

The entire North was suddenly "profoundly impressed" with the Union because they were headed for
economic annihilation without it.

January 12, 1861

In Pensacola, Florida, Navy Yard taken over by
Florida troops under Colonel W. H. Chase who

demanded that Fort Pickens surrender. Slemmer refused.

January 14, 1861

U.S. House Committee of Thirty-three unable to
reach agreement on a compromise. Ohio Rep. Thomas
Corwin, Chairman of the House Committee of Thirty-
three, proposed a constitutional amendment protecting
slavery forever, even beyond the reach of Congress, in
places where it already existed.

January 15, 1861

Mississippi secession ordinance signed.

Rep. John H. Reagan of Texas delivers fiery
speech in U.S. House of Representatives pointing out
Northern economic exploitation of the South and en-
visioning a powerful South with manufacturing, trade,
and agriculture. Reagan became Confederate postmaster general and served in Jefferson Davis's cabinet.

January 16, 1861

Georgia secession convention convenes in Milledgeville.

U. S. Senate kills Crittenden Compromise at the
behest of Abraham Lincoln, though it had widespread
support North and South, and historians admit it
would have likely prevented the war.

Arkansas legislature completes secession referendum bill.

January 17, 1861

Speech of C. Q. Lemmonds, Esq., of Union, North
Carolina on the Convention Bill [bill which called for
the convening of a secession convention] delivered in
the North Carolina House of Commons.

Kentucky legislature meets and its House tables a
convention bill, 54 - 36. Senate bill also died in committee. Resolutions encouraging Southern states to
stop seceding, as well as denouncing coercion by the
Federal Government were passed, then legislature adjourned until March 20th.

January 18, 1861

In Washington, "nine Southern senators" tried to
diffuse the situation in Pensacola, Florida and "urged
that no attack should be made on Fort Pickens." They
believed congressional Republicans wanted war to
start while Buchanan was still president, before Lincoln took office.

A copy of the New York resolutions supporting the
Union and pledging men and money to uphold it, while
accusing the South of treason, was received by Gov.
Joseph E. Brown of Georgia, who then presented the
resolution to the Georgia secession convention, which

was in session. Robert Toombs proposed a response, which was read and adopted:

> Resolved, unanimously, in response to
> the resolutions of New York, referred to
> in the Governor's message, that this con-
> vention highly approves the energetic
> and patriotic conduct of Governor Brown
> in taking possession of Fort Pulaski by
> Georgia troops, and requests him to hold
> possession until the relations of Georgia
> with the Federal Government be deter-
> mined by this convention; and that a
> copy of this resolution be transmitted to
> the Governor of New York.

Massachusetts legislature offers money and men to maintain the Union.[157]

January 19, 1861

Georgia, Empire State of the South, secedes by a vote of 208 - 89.

Virginia legislature adopts Governor Letcher's

---

[157] Contrast this with the War of 1812 in which treasonous Massachusetts withheld troops from the American war effort and aided and abetted the British. A secret delegation was sent by Gov. Caleb Strong to make a separate peace with the British because Massachusetts, again obsessed with its money over principle, was aggrieved by commercial losses due to the war. See footnote #152 on the Hartford Convention.

proposal for a national peace convention or conference. Also adopted around this time was a bill setting February 4th as date for election of delegates to a secession convention, and also to "decide whether the convention had to refer its actions to the voters for their approval." Adopted before this were "resolutions against coercion" and in support of going with the Cotton States if peace turned to war.

January 21, 1861

Farewell Address of Sen. Jefferson Davis of Mississippi to the United States Senate, along with withdrawal of four other Southern senators. Davis noted that the doctrine of secession has been asserted because the Northern States "have so acted as to convince us that they will not regard our constitutional rights."

New York legislature pledges support to the Union.

January 22, 1861

"Extracts from the message of Louisiana Governor Thomas O. Moore to the Louisiana State Legislature."

Legislatures of Wisconsin and other states pledge Union support inspired by previous action of New York legislature.

January 23, 1861

Georgia secession convention passes resolution calling for election of delegates to Confederate Provisional Congress in Montgomery, Alabama.

Louisiana secession convention convenes in Baton Rouge.

Massachusetts pledges support for the Union, following New York and other states.

January 24, 1861

Legislature of Pennsylvania pledges support for the Union.

January 26, 1861

Mississippi Secession Convention adopts *A Declaration of the Immediate Causes which Induce and Justify the Secession of the State of Mississippi from the Federal Union.* It includes the statement that the North "seeks not to elevate or to support the slave, but to destroy his present condition without providing a better." The convention adjourns temporarily.

Louisiana secedes by a vote of 113 - 17.

January 28, 1861

Georgia secession convention names commissioners to other slaveholding states not yet seceded.

A Monday on which the Convention of Texas was called by Texas leaders thanks to a grass roots movement that started back in November-December, 1860 when Governor Sam Houston refused, over and over, to call a convention. Article I of the Texas Bill of Rights was cited as giving them the power since it states "that all political power was inherent in the people and that they had at all times the right to alter, reform, or abolish their form of government as they deemed expedient."

January 29, 1861

Florida Senator Stephen R. Mallory "and others, with President Buchanan and his secretaries of War and the Navy" formed an agreement "to the effect that no reinforcement would be sent to Fort Pickens and no attack would be made upon it by the secessionists."

Georgia secession convention adopts Causes of Secession, written by Robert Toombs, then temporarily adjourns.

The North Carolina legislature votes to set February 28th as date to vote for or against a secession convention, and also for delegates to said convention.

January 30, 1861

Withdrawal Speech of the Hon. Williamson R. W. Cobb of Alabama from the United States House of Representatives

February, 1861

Washington dinner party of Sen. Stephen Douglas attended by Hon. John A. Campbell of the U.S. Supreme Court, French Minister Mercier, Sens. Crittenden and Seward, and Reps. Genl. Nielson and Miles Taylor, at which Campbell goes into some detail about slavery as a transient institution that was dying out. Seward was asked whether he knew that only 29 slaves had been carried into the New Mexico territory after 10 years of it being open to slavery. He answered, "Only twenty-four, sir."

February 1, 1861

Texas secession convention votes secession 166 - 8, pending ratification by the people.

Lincoln, concerned about the splintering of the Republican Party and likely election losses, continued to agitate on slavery in the territories, even though slavery was not expanding into the territories. As stated, many racist Northerners did not want slaves in the West because they didn't want blacks in the West. Historian David Potter pointed out that Northern anti-slavery was in no sense pro-black but was anti-black, designed to get rid of blacks, and that included keeping blacks out of the West.

The West was important because the North needed the West for its surplus population. Remember Horace Greeley's "Go west young man and grow up with the country!" Lincoln had said repeatedly that he wanted people to arrive in the West with Northern institutions in place, which meant no blacks allowed. Lincoln had made it clear in the Lincoln-Douglas Debates that the West was to be reserved for white people from all over the earth.

Many Northern working men were afraid of potential competition between free labor and slave labor in the West. They assumed that slave labor would undercut free labor and dominate work in the West.

But again, slavery was not expanding into the West. It was political posturing only. Republican James G. Blaine said that slavery in the West was "related to an imaginary Negro in an impossible place."

Nevertheless, Lincoln wrote Seward "I say now, however, as I have all the while said, that on the territorial question — that is, the question of extending slavery under the national auspices, — I am inflexible."

That inflexibility led us directly to war because historians know that the Crittenden Compromise would have passed and given the country time to work on ending slavery without the deaths of 800,000 people and maiming of a million more.

February 2, 1861

Texas secession convention issues *Declaration of Causes which Impel the State of Texas to Secede from the Federal Union.* Among the reasons noted are:

They [Northerners] have invaded Southern soil and murdered unoffending citizens, and through the press, their leading men and a fanatical pulpit have be-
stowed praise upon the actors and assas-
sins in these crimes, while the governors
of several of their States have refused to
deliver parties implicated and indicted
for participation in such offenses, upon
the legal demands of the States aggrieved. . . . They have, through the
mails and hired emissaries, sent sedi-
tious pamphlets and papers among us to
stir up servile insurrection and bring
blood and carnage to our firesides. . . .
They have sent hired emissaries among
us to burn our towns and distribute
arms and poison to our slaves for the
same purpose. . . . They have impover-
ished the slave-holding States by un-
equal and partial legislation, thereby
enriching themselves by draining our
substance.

*Speech of Florida Governor M. S. Perry to the
Florida House of Representatives, and Senate.* Includes many references to Northern gubernatorial and
legislative pledges of men and money to the Federal
Government for the purpose of coercing the South back
into Union.

February 4, 1861

Virginia elects mostly moderates and Unionists to secession convention, and decides any action by the convention would have to be ratified by the people.

Convention of representatives from South Carolina, Mississippi, Louisiana, Georgia, Florida and Alabama meet in Montgomery, Alabama and became first session of Provisional Confederate Congress.

Peace Convention called by Virginia convenes in Washington, D.C. with 131 members from 21 states, that included many prominent people such as former President John Tyler.

February 5, 1861

Farewell Address of Sen. Judah P. Benjamin of Louisiana to the United States Senate. Louisiana's other senator, John Slidell, also resigned. Benjamin later served the Confederacy as attorney general, chief of the War Department and secretary of state. A brilliant legal mind, Benjamin said in his address:

> The rights of Louisiana as a sovereign state are those of Virginia; no more, no less. Let those who deny her right [Louisiana's] to resume delegated powers, successfully refute the claim of Virginia to the same right, in spite of her [Virginia's] expressed reservation made and

notified to her sister states when she consented to enter the Union. And, sir, permit me to say that, of all the causes which justify the action of the Southern States, I know none of greater gravity and more alarming magnitude than that now developed of the denial of the right of secession. A pretension so monstrous as that which perverts a restricted agency [federal government], constituted by sovereign states for common purposes, into the unlimited despotism of the majority, and denies all legitimate escape from such despotism, when powers not delegated are usurped, converts the whole constitutional fabric into the secure abode of lawless tyranny, and degrades sovereign states into provincial dependencies.

February 7, 1861

Choctaw Indians proclaim their loyalty to the Southern States.

At the Montgomery Convention, Christopher Gustavus Memminger of Charleston, who had been appointed head of a committee to report to the convention the framework for a provisional government, issued his report, which was immediately taken up in secret session.

February 8, 1861

Confederates adopt a Provisional Constitution.

February 9, 1861

Confederate provisional president elected unanimously: former United States secretary of war and senator, Jefferson Davis of Mississippi, considered by most a moderate. He was not in attendance at the convention. Georgia's Alexander "Little Alec" Stephens is also elected unanimously, as vice-president.

Tennesseans vote against calling a secession convention 69,675 to 57,798.

February 10, 1861

Jefferson Davis is stunned to find out he has been elected president of the Confederate States of America. He had expected a military post. He immediately accepts and makes plans to leave for Montgomery.

February 11, 1861

Address of George Williamson, Commissioner from Louisiana to the Texas Secession Convention is written. It was actually delivered March 9, 1861.

Both Jefferson Davis and Abraham Lincoln leave their homes, Davis heads to Montgomery, and Lincoln to Washington, both taking circuitous routes. In Mont-

gomery, Alexander Stephens is inaugurated as vice-
president.

Texas secession convention votes to join the Confederacy and elected delegates to serve in the Confederate Congress.

February 12, 1861

Confederate Congress takes over decisions related
to all forts, from the various states.

February 13, 1861

Virginia secession convention assembles in Richmond.

February 18, 1861

Confederate president Jefferson Davis inaugurated in Montgomery, Alabama stating clearly that he
hoped for peace. It was only after reading Davis's inaugural that Lincoln began specifically saying that he
was for peace. Davis pointed out the words of the Declaration of Independence that were constantly spoken
everywhere in the South during the secession debate,
showing that the Confederacy was living proof that

> governments rest upon the consent of
> the governed, and that it is the right of
> the people to alter or abolish govern-
> ments whenever they become destruc-

tive of the ends for which they were established.

Davis also reiterated Southern economic strength and
plans for free trade.

Arkansians vote 27,412 to 15,826 in favor of calling a secession convention.

Missourians elect delegates to secession convention.

February 23, 1861

Texans vote decisively to ratify secession, 34,794
to 11,235.

February 25, 1861

*Letter from Georgia Commissioner A. R. Wright to
Governor Thomas H. Hicks of Maryland.* Ambrose
Ransom Wright served brilliantly as a Confederate
brigadier general under Lee. His persuasive letter includes much history, documents Northern hatred of
the South and agitation over slavery, why North can't
be trusted, the right of secession, economic strength of
an independent South pointing out that Baltimore
would be a great port rivaling New York, etc.

February 26, 1861

Florida secession convention reconvenes and ratifies Confederate Constitution 54 - 0.

February 27, 1861

Confederate President Jefferson Davis names A. B. Roman, John Forsyth and Martin J. Crawford as commissioners to Washington.

The Peace Convention reported to Congress six proposed constitutional amendments but none were accepted. The U.S. House of Representatives voted down one proposal after another. Lincoln finally kills the Crittenden Compromise.

February 28, 1861

North Carolinians reject a secession convention 47,323 to 46,672.

Missouri Secession Convention votes to move to St. Louis, where Unionist strength is larger.

U.S. Rep. Thomas Corwin's amendment that left black people in slavery forever and which stated that slavery could not be interfered with by the government, is passed overwhelmingly by the U.S. House of Representatives, with the blessing of the House Committee of Thirty-three, and is sent to Senate. Lincoln strongly supports this one.

March 1, 1861

Confederate government takes control of the military situation in Charleston, South Carolina.

March 2, 1861

Texas Ordinance of Secession takes effect.

United States Congress approves Morrill Tariff Act.

U.S. Congress also approves joint resolution to amend Constitution to protect slavery where it existed and that protection would be beyond amendment by Congress.

Senate rejects another attempt by John J. Crittenden, this one to adopt as a constitutional amendment, the result of the Peace Convention. This was Crittenden's last attempt at compromise.

March 3, 1861

Gen. Pierre Gustave Toutant Beauregard takes command of Confederate forces in Charleston, South Carolina.

March 4, 1861

Lincoln inaugurated in Washington, D.C. as the sixteenth president of the United States, the first purely sectional president in American history, having received not a single electoral vote in the South, and in fact was not even on the ballot in 10 Southern states. In his inaugural address, he gave strong assurances that slavery was protected in the Union, and that he supported the Corwin Amendment that left black peo-

ple in slavery forever, even beyond the reach of Congress, in places where slavery already existed.

Arkansas secession convention assembles in Little
Rock.

Missouri secession convention re-convenes in St.
Louis, advocates compromise, and takes anti-coercion
stance. It expressed Southern sympathy but does not
secede.

The first Confederate flag, reported by the Committee on the Confederate Flag in Montgomery, flies
over the state capitol of Alabama, which was also the
Confederate capitol at the time. It is known as the
Stars and Bars, three bars, red, white and red, with
seven white stars in a circle in a blue canton, one star
for each of the new Confederate states: South Carolina, Georgia, Florida, Alabama, Mississippi, Louisiana
and Texas.

March 5, 1861

Texas secession convention votes to unite with the
Confederate States of America.

March 8, 1861

Delaware legislature, after hearing from Confederate commissioners through the winter, and directing
its representatives to support the Crittenden Compromise, does not secede, and in fact Gov. Burton encour-

aged volunteers to serve the Union, and some 12,000
do.

The three Confederate commissioners, Roman,
Forsyth and Crawford, try to contact Seward through
Supreme Court Justice John A. Campbell.

March 9, 1861

Lincoln meets with his cabinet over Fort Sumter
and a long session ensues.

March 11, 1861

Confederate Congress adopts the Confederate
Constitution unanimously. Gen. Winfield Scott advises
Lincoln that Fort Sumter could not be reinforced with-
out a massive effort and twenty-five thousand troops.

March 12, 1861

Alabama secession convention had reconvened
March 5th, and on the 12th ratified the Confederate
Constitution 87 - 5, then adjourned sine die.

British newspapers and the public debate recognition of the Confederacy, and there was much support
for doing so.

March 13,1861

Lincoln advises Seward not to see the Confederate
commissioners, which would recognize their govern-

ment as legitimate. Lincoln meets with Gustavus Vasa
Fox on Fort Sumter resupply.

March 14, 1861

Lincoln's cabinet meets again on Fort Sumter.

March 15, 1861

Lincoln's cabinet meets and he asks them to sub-
mit in writing their positions on provisioning Fort
Sumter.

March 16, 1861

Georgia secession convention, which had reconvened on March 7th, ratifies Confederate Constitution
276 - 0.

Confederate Provisional Congress ends its first
session in Montgomery, having done an effective job
setting up the new nation. Three commissioners were
named to Britain: William Lowndes Yancy, Pierre A.
Rost, and A. Dudley Mann. Their job was to negotiate
official recognition. Arizona territory declares for the
Confederacy.

Lincoln receives the written recommendations
from his cabinet on Fort Sumter.

March 18, 1861

Texas Governor Sam Houston refuses to take oath to the Confederacy and is deposed.

Lincoln still "intensely perturbed over Fort Sumter."

March 20, 1861

Kentucky legislature convenes but does not vote on any secession topic other than to have another border state convention in May.

March 21,1861

Gustavus Vasa Fox visits Charleston and meets with Major Anderson.

March 23, 1861

Georgia secession convention adjourned for the last time.

Texas secession convention ratifies the Confederate Constitution then adjourns three days later, sine die.

March 25, 1861

Mississippi secession convention reassembled "to consider ratification of the Constitution of the Confederate States of America."

Lincoln confidant Col. Ward Hill Lamon, meets
with Gen. Beauregard and Gov. Pickens in Charleston.
Lamon's confidential mission was ostensibly to gauge
Unionist feeling in South Carolina, which was nil.
Charles W. Ramsdell believed Lamon's true mission
was to make sure that an attempt to reinforce Fort
Sumter would start the war. At this point, now that
the Morrill Tariff had kicked in and the economic catastrophe in the North was certain, war appeared to be
Lincoln's only way out. The Republican Party had severe problems that were getting worse and Lincoln's
cabinet had gone from being against reinforcing the
fort — because they had not wanted to take a chance
on starting the war — to being strongly for it. Many
aggressive Republican leaders could see no way out
but war and were anxious to get it started on their
own terms.

March 26, 1861

Louisiana secession convention adjourns after previously ratifying the Confederate Constitution 109 - 7.

Lincoln meets long with cabinet.

March 29, 1861

Mississippi secession convention ratifies Confederate Constitution.

Lincoln states that "I desire that an expedition, to
move by sea, be got ready to sail as early as the 6th of

April next" for the resupply and possible reinforcement of Fort Sumter.

March 30, 1861

Address of the Texas Secession Convention to the People of Texas.

March 31, 1861

Seward continues to mislead Confederate commissioners about the evacuation of Fort Sumter.

April 1, 1861

Lincoln signs orders for *U.S.S. Powhatan* to go to sea with sealed orders. There was confusion and the *Powhatan* ended up going to Fort Pickens instead of Fort Sumter.

Seward sends Lincoln a list of his opinions/positions and scolding Lincoln in the process. Seward states he would favor starting a foreign war to reunite the country. Lincoln writes back that the decision was his to make and not Seward's.

April 3, 1861

Lincoln's cabinet meets again over Fort Sumter. Allan B. Magruder sent to Richmond to talk to Virginia unionists, on behalf of Lincoln.

April 4, 1861

Virginia Secession Convention rejects secession 89 to 45, for the time being.

Lincoln meets secretly with Virginia unionist John B. Baldwin. It was reported he had hoped to exchange a state for a fort, meaning he hoped to keep Virginia in the Union in exchange for evacuating Fort Sumter.

Lincoln informs Fox the resupply/reinforcement mission would go. Lincoln drafts letter to Anderson letting him know and saying he hoped Anderson could make it until April 11 or 12 when the expedition "will endeavor also to reinforce you."

April 5, 1861

U.S. Navy Secretary Gideon Welles orders *U.S.S. Powhatan, Pawnee, Pocahontas,* and Revenue Cutter *Harriet Lane* to Charleston to resupply/reinforce Fort Sumter.

April 6, 1861

Lincoln sends Robert S. Chew, a State Department clerk, and Capt. Theodore Talbot, to Charleston to inform Gov. Pickens that Fort Sumter would be resupplied and if no resistance was given by the Confederates, then no troops would be thrown in. Otherwise, the fort would be reinforced as well as resupplied.

Lincoln learns that Fort Pickens had not been re-inforced. A messenger was sent the next day to Fort Pickens ordering the fort's immediate reinforcement.

Lincoln meets with at least seven and perhaps nine Republican governors including the governors of Indiana, Ohio, Maine, Pennsylvania, Illinois and Michigan, as well as with Virginia unionists.

April 7, 1861

Gen. Beauregard, suspecting that the Southerners were being misled by Seward's continued assertions that Fort Sumter would be evacuated, ends Anderson's cordial intercourse between the fort and city of Charleston, as the situation intensifies.

Lincoln meets with John Minor Botts, a Virginia unionist.

April 8, 1861

Virginia secession convention votes "to send a three-man commission to ask President Lincoln for a clear expression of his policy regarding the forts."

Lincoln representative Chew arrives in Charleston and reads Lincoln's message to Gov. Pickens and Gen. Beauregard.

Seward continues to mislead Confederate commis-sioners in Washington, so much so that they wired

Gov. Pickens that they believed Fort Sumter would be evacuated.

Revenue Cutter *Harriet Lane* departs from New York loaded with supplies amidst much publicity.

April 9, 1861

Gustavus V. Fox departs from New York aboard the steamer *Baltic,* headed for Fort Sumter.

April 10, 1861

South Carolina secession convention approves Jefferson Davis as president and Alexander H. Stephens as vice-president of the Confederate States of America, then adjourns, pending recall later by President Jamison.

Confederate Secretary of War Walker wired Beauregard in Charleston and told him if he was certain Fort Sumter was to be resupplied, then he was to demand its surrender and if it refused, "reduce it." Since all of Lincoln's representatives had lied to the Confederates for weeks about evacuating the fort, Southerners were unsure if it was finally a true statement that the fort was only to be resupplied.

The *U.S.S. Pawnee* departed Hampton Roads for Fort Sumter.

Lincoln meets with representative of the Chiriqui Improvement Company to discuss colonization of Negroes in what is today Panama, near Costa Rica.

Confederate floating battery is moved to a position near Sullivan's Island. Confederate troop activity around Charleston Harbor intensifies. All forts are manned.

April 11, 1861

Three Confederate representatives row over to Fort Sumter under a white flag of truce and demand its surrender. They are Col. James Chesnut, a former United States senator and husband of diarist Mary Boykin Chesnut; Capt. Stephen D. Lee, later an effective and beloved Confederate general; and Lt. Col. A. R. Chisolm, representing Gov. Pickens. Anderson refused to surrender but commented that he would be starved out in a few days if not battered to pieces. The Confederates, wanting to avoid war to the very last, wired Secretary of War Walker and told him of Anderson's comment. Walker telegraphed back, "Do not desire needlessly to bombard Fort Sumter. If Anderson will state the time at which, as indicated by him, he will evacuate, and agree that in the mean time he will not use his guns against us unless ours should be employed against Fort Sumter, you are authorized thus to avoid the effusion of blood. . . .". The three Confederate commissioners left Washington after realizing they had been lied to and misled by Seward.

April 12, 1861

Chesnut, Lee and Chisholm row back to Major Anderson arriving at Fort Sumter at 12:45 a.m. with Walker's message. At 3:15 a.m. they got Anderson's reply stating he would evacuate on the 15th but only if he did not receive supplies or additional instructions from his government. This response was unsatisfactory, with a hostile flotilla rapidly approaching Charleston. Chesnut, Lee and Chisholm wrote a reply to Anderson stating that they had the honor of informing him that Gen. Beauregard would commence firing in one hour, then they rowed over to Fort Johnson, arriving at 4:00 a.m. At 4:30 a.m., from Fort Johnson on James Island, a signal shot was fired by troops under Capt. George S. James alerting the other batteries to begin firing according to orders. Some of Fort Sumter's guns returned fire after daybreak but the small number of men under Anderson's command could do little more. The Confederate bombardment continued heavy all day. There were no deaths on either side. In Pensacola, Union troops were landed at Fort Pickens.

April 13, 1861

Fort Sumter surrenders at 2:30 p.m. after four thousand shells had been fired in thirty-four hours of bombardment. The federal fleet, now consisting of the *U.S.S. Baltic, U.S.S. Pawnee*, and *Harriet Lane*, stayed just out of danger and did not attempt to help Anderson.

April 14, 1861

Anderson formally surrenders and salutes his colors with drums beating and a fifty gun salute. An accidental explosion kills a man, the first to die in the war.

Lincoln's Cabinet approves of "his call for 75,000 militia" and a special July 4 session of Congress.

Virginia's three-man commission which had sought from Lincoln a statement of clear policy regarding the forts, returns and states that Lincoln was "firm in his resolve to hold the forts."

April 15, 1861

Lincoln issues public proclamation calling for seventy-five thousand volunteers to invade the South, and calling a special secession of Congress to meet July 4th.

April 17, 1861

Virginia secedes with its Ordinance to repeal ratification of the U. S. Constitution and resume all rights and powers granted under said Constitution. Vote was 88 - 55. Virginia's secession had absolutely nothing, whatsoever, to do with slavery. Virginia and the states that followed her out of the Union — North Carolina, Tennessee and Arkansas — seceded in response to Lincoln's call for 75,000 volunteers to invade the South

which they considered illegal, unconstitutional and immoral.

April 19, 1861

Maryland Gov. Hicks calls convention after Baltimore mob fights with Massachusetts troops.

Lincoln calls for blockade of first seven Confederates States. It was later extended to include Virginia
and North Carolina.

The blockade was Lincoln's purpose all along so
he could chill military and trade alliances between the
South and Europe as quickly as possible. The South
with European aid would be unbeatable just as French
aid in the American Revolution had turned the tide in
favor of the Colonists.

Every day that went by, the South had been getting stronger, and the North, on the verge of economic
collapse, weaker, so Lincoln had no reason whatsoever
to wait. He needed his war as quickly as he could get it
started. There had been a loud clamor for war among
Republicans and the business community in the North
for a while as hundreds of thousands of Northerners
became unemployed and businesses shut down amidst
the impending economic disaster. The North was on
the verge of panic, and governments know that an economic panic will progress geometrically into anarchy.
War is always preferable.

The astronomical Morrill Tariff, which had recently taken effect, was the second of a one-two punch
because now, in addition to losing its Southern manu-

facturing market, the North was about to lose its shipping industry in one fell swoop. The Morrill Tariff
made entry of goods into the North 37 to 50% higher
than entry into the South. This threatened to redirect
trade away from the high-tariff North and into the
South where protective tariffs were unconstitutional.
The world was beating a path to the South while goods
rotted on New York docks. Even Northern ship captains were leaving the North for Southern ports.

The Morrill Tariff was the result of extreme
Northern greed as well as ignorance of basic economics. They passed it in knee-jerk fashion thinking the
South would have to pay it, as in the past, but the
South was out of the Union and no longer had to pay
high Northern tariffs. This one fell on them alone, and
it contributed mightily to the feeling in the North that
war was their only way out. As Tennessee Representative Thomas A. R. Nelson, who had submitted the
Minority Report of the House Committee of Thirty-
three, said in his speech entitled "Speech of Hon. Thomas A. R. Nelson, of Tennessee, On the Disturbed condition of the Country"

> Commercial disaster and distress per-
> vade the land. Hundreds and thousands
> of honest laboring men have been
> thrown out of employment; gloom and
> darkness hang over the people; the
> **tocsin of war has been sounded; the**

clangor of arms has been heard.[158]
(Emphasis added.)

Charles W. Ramsdell proves in his famous treatise, *Lincoln and Fort Sumter*, that Lincoln knew that
attempting to reinforce the fort would start the war.
He had it first hand from his friend, Ward H. Lamon,
whom he had sent to Charleston a few days earlier to
make sure his reinforcement attempt *would* start the
war. Lamon had spoken face-to-face with Confederate
leaders and they told him point blank that a reinforcement attempt meant war.

The Fort Sumter crisis was the tensest hour in
American history. There is no way Lincoln's reinforcement mission would not start the war and Lincoln
knew it.

Northern newspapers knew it too. The Providence,
Rhode Island *Daily Post*, in an editorial April 13, 1861
entitled "WHY?", wrote:

> Mr. Lincoln saw an opportunity to inau-
> gurate civil war without appearing in
> the character of an aggressor.

Abraham Lincoln got the war started and announced his blockade before the smoke had cleared
from the bombardment of Fort Sumter.

Saving the country and working on ending slavery
were not even on Lincoln's radar. He was the first sec-

---

[158] Nelson, "Speech of Hon. Thomas A. R. Nelson, of Tennessee, On the Disturbed condition of the Country", 1-12.

tional president in American history and he was out to save his section and the rapidly splintering Republican Party that had so successfully used hatred and terrorism to get into power.

Even Lincoln's commander, Major Robert Anderson, inside Fort Sumter, emphatically blamed Lincoln for starting the war "which I see is to be thus commenced" by Abraham Lincoln.

Anderson's assessment from ground zero is irrefutable.

May 1, 1861

Associate Justice of the United States Supreme Court John A. Campbell, resigned. He later served as assistant secretary of war of the Confederacy.

May 6, 1861

Arkansas Secession Convention votes secession 65 - 5.

Tennessee legislature votes to secede, and sets June 8 as date for ratification of secession as well as acceptance of the Confederate Constitution.

Confederacy officially "recognizes state of war with United States."

Kentucky legislature meets in special session.

May 9, 1861

Tennessee legislature adopts address to the people explaining its action in seceding.

Maryland House Committee on Federal Relations adopts report, resigned to fact that situation was hope-less, but condemning the Union's war against the Con-federacy and calling for recognition of Southern inde-pendence. It passed the Maryland House the next day.

May 10, 1861

Arkansas Secession Convention adopts Confeder-ate Constitution 63 - 8.

May 13, 1861

North Carolinians elect delegates to a secession convention.

May 16, 1861

Kentucky House of Representatives votes 69 - 26 for neutrality, and also, by a vote of 89 - 4, not to fill Lincoln's quota for troops.

May 20, 1861

North Carolina secession convention meets in Ra-leigh and votes unanimously to secede, and to adopt the Confederate Constitution.

May 23, 1861

Virginians ratify secession by the vote of 125,950 to 20,373.

June 8, 1861

Tennesseans ratify secession 104,913 to 47,238.

Part III

Lincoln and Fort Sumter
by Charles W. Ramsdell

About Charles William Ramsdell

"In all that pertained to the history of the Southern Confederacy, his scholarship was decisive."[159]

In Memoriam
Charles William Ramsdell
University of Texas

From the Texas State Historical Association[160]

RAMSDELL, CHARLES WILLIAM (1877–1942). Charles William Ramsdell, historian, was born at Salado, Texas, on April 4, 1877. He entered the University of Texas in 1900, received a B.A. degree in 1903 and an M.A. in 1904, and finished his Ph.D. at Columbia University in 1910. From 1906 until his death he was a member of the history department at the Uni-

---

[159] *In Memoriam, Charles William Ramsdell*, Index of Memorial Resolutions and Biographical Sketches, The University of Texas at Austin, http://www.utexas.edu/faculty/council/pages/memorials.html, accessed October 1, 2014.

[160] J. Horace Bass, "RAMSDELL, CHARLES WILLIAM," Handbook of Texas Online (http://www.tshaonline.org/handbook/online/articles/fra25), accessed October 04, 2014. Uploaded on June 15, 2010. Published by the Texas State Historical Association.

versity of Texas, although he held visiting lectureships
in the state universities of Illinois, Colorado, West Virginia, Missouri, North Carolina, and Louisiana and in
Columbia, Northwestern, Western Reserve and Duke
universities. The Old South was his field of investigation, and he became such an authority on that epoch
that his colleagues commonly referred to him as the
"Dean" of Southern historians. Although classroom
teaching was his primary interest, Ramsdell wrote
widely. A bibliography of his publications includes
three books, two edited works, twenty-two articles and
monographs, seventeen contributions to American historical and biographical dictionaries, and numerous
book reviews. His books are *Reconstruction in Texas*, *A
School History of Texas* (in collaboration with Eugene
C. Barker and Charles S. Potts, and *Behind the Lines
in the Southern Confederacy* (published
posthumously). He was coeditor with Wendell Holmes
Stephenson in the planning stage of the multivolume *A
History of the South*, a joint endeavor of the Littlefield
Fund for Southern History at the University of Texas
and the Louisiana State University Press. The several
historical associations in which Ramsdell was active
recognized his eminence. He served as president of the
Mississippi Valley Historical Association in 1928–29.
The Southern Historical Association honored him with
its presidency in 1936. He was a member of the executive council of the American Historical Association
from 1931 to 1934. The Texas State Historical Association elected him treasurer annually from 1907 until

his death, and he was an associate editor of its Quarterly from 1910 to 1938. He died on July 3, 1942.

BIBLIOGRAPHY:
Wendell Holmes Stephenson, "Charles W. Ramsdell: Historian of the Confederacy," *Journal of Southern History* 26 (November 1960). Vertical Files, Dolph Briscoe Center for American History, University of Texas at Austin.

J. Horace Bass[161]

---

[161] See previous footnote.

Lincoln and Fort Sumter[162]
by Charles W. Ramsdell

We are to have civil war, if at all, be-
cause Abraham Lincoln loves a party
better than he loves his country. . . .
Mr. Lincoln saw an opportunity to in-
augurate civil war without appearing
in the character of an aggressor.

"WHY?"
Providence (R.I.) Daily Post
The day after the commencement of
the bombardment of Fort Sumter
April 13, 1861

When the Confederate batteries around Charleston
Harbor opened fire on Fort Sumter in the early morning hours of April 12, 1861, they signaled the beginning of the most calamitous tragedy in the history of
the American people. Because the Confederate authorities ordered the attack it is generally held that
they were directly responsible for the horrors of the

---

[162] Charles W. Ramsdell, "Lincoln and Fort Sumter," *The Journal of Southern History,* Vol. 3, Issue 3 (August, 1937), 259 -
288. Original copyright 1937, Southern Historical Association,
now in the public domain. This article with text and notes
comes verbatim from the original article.

ensuing four years. Certainly that was the feeling in the North, then and afterwards, and it became the verdict of austere historians.

Whether the war was inevitable, in any case, is a question that need not be raised here. It has been the subject of endless disputation and is one to which no conclusive answer can be given. But even though it be conceded that if the conflict had not arisen from the Fort Sumter crisis it would have sprung from some other incident growing out of the secession of the "cotton states," the actual firing of the "first shot" placed the Southerners under a great moral and material disadvantage. The general Northern conviction that the "rebels" had made an unprovoked attack upon the little Federal garrison added thousands of volunteers to the Union armies and strengthened the determination of the Northern people to carry the struggle through to the complete subjugation of the South.

The Confederate leaders who ordered the bombardment were not vicious, feeble-minded, irresponsible, or inexperienced men. As even a casual investigation will show, they had been fully aware of the danger of taking the initiative in hostilities and had hoped for peace. How then could they be so blind as to place themselves at this manifest disadvantage?

The story of the development of the Fort Sumter crisis has been told many times, but it is so full of complexities that there is little wonder that many of its most significant features have been obscured with a resultant loss of perspective. On the one hand, most accounts have begun with certain assumptions which have affected the interpretation of the whole mass of evidence; on the other, too little credit has been given to Abraham Lincoln's genius for political strategy, which is truly surprising in view of all the claims that have been made for the abilities of that very remarkable man. The purpose of this paper is to place the facts already known in their logical and chronological order and to re-evaluate them in that setting in the belief that when thus arranged they will throw new light upon this momentous affair.

The early stages of the Sumter problem can be dealt with in summary form. It is well known that six days after the secession of South Carolina Major Robert Anderson, who had been stationed at Fort Moultrie in command of all the United States forces in Charleston Harbor, abandoned Moultrie and moved his command into the new and still unfinished Fort Sumter where he thought his force would be better able to resist attack. The South Carolina authorities evidently had had no intention of attacking him for they thought they had an understanding with President Buchanan for maintaining the military status quo; but they immediately occupied Fort Moultrie and Castle Pinckney and made protest to Buchanan, demanding that Anderson be sent back to Moultrie. Buchanan refused to admit their ground of protest or to order Anderson back; then early in January he ordered relief to be sent secretly to the garrison on a merchant steamer. This vessel, *The Star of the West*, was forced back from the entrance of the harbor by the military authorities of the state, and the South Carolinians

were with some difficulty restrained by the leaders in
other Southern states from assaulting Fort Sumter.
Thereafter Buchanan refrained from the use of force,
partly because Anderson insisted that he was in no
danger, partly because he still hoped for some peaceful
adjustment, if not by Congress itself, then by the Peace
Conference which was soon to assemble in Washington, and partly because he was averse during the last
weeks of his term to beginning hostilities for which he
was unprepared.

By February 1 six other cotton states had passed
ordinances of secession and each of them, as a matter
of precaution and largely because of the happenings at
Charleston, seized the forts, arsenals, customs houses,
and navy yards within its own borders. There were two
exceptions, both in Florida. Fort Taylor, at Key West,
was left undisturbed; and Fort Pickens, at the entrance of Pensacola Bay and on the extreme western
tip of Santa Rosa Island, was occupied by a small Federal force much as Fort Sumter had been.

Since Fort Pickens plays a part in the development of the Sumter crisis, some explanation of the
situation at that point becomes necessary. In the beginning this fort was not occupied by troops, but a
company of artillery, under Lieutenant Adam J. Slemmer, was stationed at Barrancas Barracks, across the
neck of the bay about a mile and a half to the north of
Pickens, and close by the Navy Yard. The town of Pensacola was some six miles farther up the bay. On January 10 Lieutenant Slemmer, hearing that the governors of Florida and Alabama were about to send troops

to seize the forts and the Navy Yard and in accordance with instructions from General Winfield Scott, removed his small command to Fort Pickens. On the twelfth the Navy Yard capitulated to the combined state forces under Colonel W. H. Chase. Chase then demanded the surrender of Fort Pickens, which Slemmer refused. After some further correspondence between the two opposing officers, a group of nine Southern senators in Washington, on January 18, urged that no attack should be made on Fort Pickens because it was "not worth a drop of blood."[163] These senators believed that the Republicans in Congress were hoping to involve the Buchanan administration in hostilities in order that the war might open before Lincoln's inauguration. On January 29 an agreement was effected at Washington by Senator Stephen R. Mallory of Florida, and others, with President Buchanan and his secretaries of War and the Navy to the effect that no reinforcement would be sent to Fort Pickens and no attack would be made upon it by the secessionists.[164] The situation at Fort Pickens then became somewhat like that at Fort Sumter; but there were certain differences. Fort Pickens did not threaten the town of Pensacola as Fort Sumter did Charleston; it was easily accessible from the sea if reinforcements should be decided upon; and there was no such excitement over its

---

[163] *The War of the Rebellion: A Compilation of the Official Records of the Union and Confederate Armies* (Washington, 1880-1901), Ser. I, Vol. I, 445-46. Hereafter cited as *Official Records.*
[164] Ibid., 355-56.

continued occupation by the United States troops as there was about Sumter.

As soon as the new Confederate government was organized the Confederate Congress, on February 12, by resolution took charge of "questions existing between the several States of this Confederacy and the United States respecting the occupation of forts, arsenals, navy yards and other public establishments." This hurried action was taken in order to get the management of the Sumter question out of the hands of the impatient and rather headlong Governor Francis W. Pickens of South Carolina, who, it was feared, might precipitate war at any time.[165] In fact, the public mind, North and South, sensed accurately that the greatest danger to peace lay in Charleston Harbor.

This danger, of course, was in the irreconcilable views of the two governments concerning their respective claims to the fort. To the Washington officials Sumter was not merely the legal property of the Federal government; its possession was a symbol of the continuity and integrity of that government. To withdraw the garrison at the demand of the secessionists would be equivalent to acknowledging the legality of secession and the dissolution of the Union. There was also, especially with the military officials, a point of honor involved; they could not yield to threats of force. The attitude of the Southerners was based upon

---

[165] *Journal of the Congress of the Confederate States of America*, 7 vols. (Washington, 1904-1905), I, 47; Samuel W. Crawford, *The Genesis of the Civil War: The Story of Sumter* (New York, 1887), 261-62.

equally imperative considerations. In their view the Confederate States no longer had any connection with the government on the Potomac; they were as independent as that other seceded nation, Belgium. No independent government could maintain its own self-respect or the respect of foreign governments if it permitted another to hold an armed fortress within the harbor of one of its principal cities. When South Carolina had ceded the site for the fortification it had done so for its own protection. That protection was not converted into a threat, for the guns of Sumter dominated not only every point in the harbor but the city of Charleston itself. We may conceive an analogous situation by supposing that Great Britain at the close of the American Revolution had insisted upon retaining a fortress within the harbor of Boston or of New York. The Confederate government could not, without yielding the principle of independence, abate its claims to the fort.

During the last six weeks of Buchanan's term the situation at Charleston remained relatively quiet. Anderson and his engineers did what they could to strengthen the defenses of Sumter; while the state and Confederate officers established batteries around the harbor both to repel any future relief expedition and, in case of open hostilities, to reduce the fort. Although Governor Pickens had wished to press demands for surrender and to attack the fort if refused, he had first sought the advice of such men as Governor Joseph E. Brown of Georgia and Jefferson Davis of Mississippi. Both advised against any such action, partly because they still had some hope of peace and partly because they saw the danger of taking the initiative.[166] Although Anderson was under constant surveillance, he was allowed free use of the mails and was permitted to purchase for his men fresh meats and vegetables in the Charleston market. Other necessities, which under army regulations he must procure from the regular supply departments of the army, he was not allowed to receive because that would be permitting the Federal government to send relief to the garrison and involve an admission of its right to retain the fort. Anderson consistently informed the authorities at Washington during this time that he was safe and that he could hold out indefinitely. The Confederate government, having taken over from the state all negotiations concerning the fort, was moving cautiously with the evident hope of avoiding hostilities. On February 15 the Confederate Congress by resolution requested President Davis to appoint three commissioners to negotiate with the United States "all questions of disagreement between the two governments" and Davis appointed them on February 25.[167] They reached Washington on March 5, the day after Lincoln's inauguration.

Southern as well as Northern men waited anxiously to learn what policy would be indicated by the new President of the United States in his inaugural

---

[166] Crawford, *Genesis of the Civil War*, 263-68; Dunbar Rowland (ed.), *Jefferson Davis, Constitutionalist*, 10 vols. (Jackson, Miss., 1923), V, 36-37, 39-40.

[167] *Journal of the Congress of the Confederate States*, I, 46, 52, 55, 85-86.

address. It is not necessary to dwell long on what Abraham Lincoln said in that famous paper. He stated plainly that he regarded the Union as unbroken, the secession of the seven cotton states as a nullity. In this he merely took the position that Buchanan had taken. He also said that he would enforce the laws of the Union in all the states; but he immediately softened this declaration by saying that he would not use violence unless it should be forced upon the national authority. Then he added, "The power confided to me will be used to hold, occupy and possess the property and places belonging to the government, and to collect the duties and imposts; but beyond what may be necessary for these objects, there will be no invasion, no using of force against or among the people anywhere." And later on: "In your hands, my dissatisfied fellow countrymen, and not in mine, is the momentous issue of civil war. The government will not assail you. You can have no conflict without being yourselves the aggressors." How is it possible to reconcile the declaration that he would occupy "the property and places belonging to the government" with the promise that the government would not assail his dissatisfied fellow countrymen who either held or claimed the right to those places? While ostensibly addressing the Southerners, was he really directing these last soothing words to the anxious antiwar elements in the North? Although it is improbable that he had this early any definite plan in mind, his warning that the secessionists would be the aggressors, if civil war should come, may be significant in view of what he was to be engaged in exactly a month from that day.

But the inaugural should not be regarded as the declaration of a definite program; for while the new President was careful to lay down the general principle that the Union was legally unbroken, he refrained with equal care from committing himself to any course of action. If he hedged at every point where a state-ment of active policy was expected, it was because he could not know what he would be able to do. Caution was necessary; it was not merely political expediency, it was at that juncture political wisdom. Cautious reti-cence, until he knew his way was clear, was a very marked trait of Abraham Lincoln.[168] There is another characteristic quality in this address. Lincoln had de-veloped an extraordinary skill in so phrasing his public utterances as to arouse in each special group he sin-gled out for attention just the reaction he desired. To the extreme and aggressive Republicans the inaugural indicated a firm determination to enforce obedience upon the secessionists; to the Northern moderates and peace advocates, as well as to the anxious Unionists of

---

[168] This characteristic of Lincoln was attested to by numbers of his associates, sometimes with evident irritation. W. H. Hern-don once wrote, "He was the most secretive—reticent—shut-mouthed man that ever lived." Herndon to J. E. Remsburg of Oak Mills, Kansas, September 10, 1887 (privately printed by H. E. Baker, 1917). See also A. K. McClure, *Lincoln and Men of War-Times* (Philadelphia, 1892), 64-68, for statements of Leonard Swett, W. H. Lamon, A. K. McClure, and David Davis. Judge Davis said, "I knew the man well; he was the most reti-cent, secretive man I ever saw or expect to see."

the border slave states not yet seceded,[169] it promised a conciliatory attitude; in the seceded states it was interpreted as threatening coercion and had the effect of hastening preparations for defense.

In the latter part of the address Lincoln had counseled the people generally to avoid precipitate action and to take time to think calmly about the situation. He doubtless hoped to be able to take time himself; but he discovered within a few hours that there was one problem whose solution could not be long postponed. On the very day of his inauguration Buchanan's secretary of war, Joseph Holt, received a letter from Major Anderson in which for the first time the commander at Fort Sumter expressed doubt of his ability to maintain himself. More than this, Anderson estimated that, in the face of the Confederate batteries erected about the harbor, it would require a powerful fleet and a force of twenty thousand men to give permanent relief to the garrison. Since it was his last day in office, Buchanan had the letter referred to Lincoln; and when on March 5, Holt submitted it to the new President he accompanied it with a report sharply reviewing Anderson's pre-

---

[169] The "border states" Professor Ramsdell refers to in this treatise include Virginia, North Carolina, Tennessee and Arkansas since those future-Confederate states were still in the Union as the Fort Sumter drama played out. They did not secede until after the bombardment of Fort Sumter when Lincoln called for 75,000 volunteers to invade the South, and they did so, not in any way because of slavery, but because they did not believe the Federal Government had the constitutional, legal or moral right to coerce a sovereign state to do anything.

vious assurances of his safety.[170] Lincoln called General Scott into conference and the General concurred with Anderson. After a few days of further consideration Scott was of the same opinion and was sustained by General Joseph G. Totten, chief of the Army Engineers. These men considered the question primarily as a military problem, although Scott could not refrain from injecting political considerations into this written statement. In doing this the aged General was suspected of following the lead of Secretary William H. Seward who was already urging the evacuation of Sumter, in order to avoid precipitating hostilities at that point, and the reinforcement of Fort Pickens in order to assert the authority of the government. Lincoln accepted at least a part of Seward's plan, for on March 12, General Scott, by the President's direction, sent an order to Captain Israel Vogdes, whose artillery company was on board the U. S. Steamer *Brooklyn,* lying off Fort Pickens, directing him to land his company, reinforce Pickens, and hold it. Instead of sending the order overland, Scott sent it around by sea with the result that it did not reach its destination until April 1, and then the navy captain in command of the ship on which the artillery company was quartered refused to land the troops because the orders from the former Secretary of the Navy directing him to respect the truce with the Confederates had never been coun-

---

[170] Anderson's letter has net been located, but see *Official Records,* Ser. I, Vol. I, 197-202. For Holt's letter, Horatio King, *Turning on the Light* (Philadelphia, 1896), 126-128.

termanded. The fort was not reinforced at that time, a fact of which Lincoln remained ignorant until April 6. We shall return to the Fort Pickens situation later.

Meanwhile Lincoln was considering the Fort Sumter problem. He had learned that Anderson's supplies were running short and that the garrison could not hold out much longer without relief. Although both General Scott and General Totten had advised that the relief of the fort was impracticable with the forces available, Gustavus V. Fox, a former officer of the navy and a brother-in-law of Postmaster-General Montgomery Blair, believed that it would be possible to reach the fort by running small steamers past the Confederate batteries at the entrance to the harbor. Fox had first proposed this to Scott early in February; he now came forward again with the backing of Montgomery Blair and presented his plan and arguments to Lincoln on March 13. The President seems to have been impressed, for on March 15 he asked for the written opinions of his cabinet on the question whether, assuming that it was now possible to provision Sumter, it was wise to attempt it. All, save Montgomery Blair, advised against an expedition.[171] Apparently this overwhelming majority of his cabinet at first decided him against the plans, for there is considerable evidence,

---

[171] Secretary Chase favored a relief expedition, but only if it would not bring on an expensive war, a position that was so equivocal that he can hardly be said to stand with Montgomery Blair. John G. Nicolay and John Hay (eds.), *Abraham Lincoln: Complete Works,* 2 vols. (New York, 1894), II, 11-22, for replies of the cabinet.

although it is not conclusive, that he was about to order Anderson to evacuate. Certainly rumors of impending orders for evacuation were coming from various
high official circles in Washington, aside from those for
which Seward seems to have been responsible.[172]
There is the familiar story of how old Frank Blair,
brought to the White House by his son Montgomery,
found the President about to sign the evacuation order
and protested so vigorously that Lincoln did not sign
it.

Lincoln now found himself facing a most difficult
and dangerous situation and the more he considered it
the more troublesome it appeared. It seems reasonably
certain that he never wanted to give up Sumter. As
early as December 24, 1860, having heard a wild ru-
mor that the forts in South Carolina were to be surrendered by the order or consent of President Buchanan,
he had written from Springfield to Senator Lyman
Trumbull that he would, "if our friends at Washington
concur, announce publicly at once that they are to be
retaken after the inauguration."[173] After he had ar-

---

[172] The newspapers carried these reports almost every day
and the belief in their accuracy seems to have been general,
even among the war faction of the Republicans.

[173] Gilbert A. Tracy, *Uncollected Letters of Abraham Lincoln*
(Boston and New York, 1917), 173. Lincoln had written "con-
fidentially" to Major David Hunter on December 22, "If the forts
fall, my judgment is that they are to be retaken." A. B. Lapsley
(ed.), *The Writings of Abraham Lincoln*, 8 vols. (New York,
1905-1906), V, 199. It will be remembered that the original
draft of the inaugural had contained a declaration that he
would "reclaim the public property and places which have
fallen," but that this was changed at the suggestion of Orville

rived at Washington and had taken up the burden of office he saw that the problem was not so simple as it had looked from the frontier town of Springfield. His Secretary of State, a man of far greater political ex-perience than himself, was urging him to make his stand for the authority of the government at Fort Pick-ens and not Sumter, for Seward could not see how it would be possible to reinforce Sumter without putting the administration in the position of the aggressor. That would be a fatal mistake. Fort Pickens, on the other hand, could be relieved from the Gulf side with-out coming into direct conflict with the Confederates.

It would be extremely interesting to know what was passing through Lincoln's mind during those dif-ficult days when, bedeviled by importunate office seek-ers, he could find little time for considering what he should do about the re-establishment of Federal au-thority in the seceded states and especially about the imperiled fort at Charleston. As was his habit, he left few clues to his reflections and it is impossible to say with assurance what ideas he picked up, examined, and discarded. One plan which he seems to have enter-tained for a short while, just after the adverse cabinet vote on relieving Sumter, contemplated the collection of customs duties on revenue vessels, supported by ships of war, just outside the Confederate ports; and there were hints in the press that Anderson's force was to be withdrawn to a ship off Charleston. If it were se-

---

H. Browning to a more general and less threatening state-ment. John G. Nicolay and John Hay, *Abraham Lincoln, A History*, 10 vols. (New York, 1886-1892), III, 319, 333-34, n. 12.

riously considered, the plan was soon abandoned, possibly because of legal impediments or more probably
because it did not fully meet the needs of the
situation.[174] But although Lincoln kept his thoughts to
himself he must have studied public opinion closely,
and we may be able to follow his thinking if we examine for ourselves the attitudes of the several groups in
the North as they revealed themselves in those uncertain days of March.

It must not be forgotten that, notwithstanding
Lincoln's smashing victory in the free states in November, his party was still new and relatively undisci-
plined. His support had come from a heterogeneous

---

[174] Lincoln to Chase, Welles, and Bates, March 18, 1861, in
Nicolay and Hay (eds.), *Lincoln: Works*, II, 24-25. The Morrill
tariff, passed in February, had raised rates far above the former ones while the Confederate Congress had enacted a low
tariff. The difference in rates was causing anxiety to Northern
importers and shippers, and also to the administration, lest it
deflect imports to the South and stimulate smuggling across
the new border to the great injury of the Northern ports and the
loss of customs receipts. The tariff differential might even
swing some of the border states over to the Confederacy. The
New York *Times* was greatly disturbed at the prospect and
roundly condemned the Morrill tariff. The issues of the *Times*
for March 13, 15-20, and 22, intimated that the President was
considering the above-mentioned plan. The legal impediments
seem to have consisted in the absence of any law of Congress
permitting such a procedure and the nonexistence of local
Federal courts for the adjudication of cases arising out of the
enforcement of the revenue laws. This tariff question may
have had more influence upon the final determination of Lincoln's policy that the evidence now available shows. **[Author's
Note: Beyond the shadow of a doubt, Professor Ramsdell.]**

mass of voters and for a variety of reasons. The slavery issue, the drive for a protective tariff and internal improvements, the promise of free homesteads in the West, and disgust at the split among the Democrats had each played its part. Many voters had been persuaded that there was no real danger of a disruption of the Union in the event of his election. The secession of the border states had now thrown the former issues into the background and thrust to the front the question whether the discontented Southerners should be allowed to depart in peace or whether the government should, as Lincoln phrased it, "enforce the law" and in so doing bring on war with the newly formed Confederacy. As always, when a new and perilous situation arises, the crosscurrents of public opinion were confusing. As Lincoln, pressed on all sides, waited while he studied the drift, he could not fail to note that there was a strong peace party in the North which was urging the settlement of difficulties without resort to force. On the other hand the more aggressive party men among the Republicans, to whom he was under special obligations, were insisting that he exert the full authority of the government even to the extent of war. This group included some of the most active and powerful members of his party whom he could not afford to antagonize. One disturbing factor in the situation was the marked tendency of many voters who had supported him in November to turn against the Republicans, as was shown in a number of local elections in Ohio and New England. While the peace men attributed this reversal to fear of war, the more aggressive

Republicans insisted that it was caused by disgust at the rumors that Fort Sumter would be given up to the secessionists.[175] Reinforcing the Northern conservatives were the majorities in the eight border slave states who had thus far refused to secede but who were openly opposed to any "coercive" action against their brethren in the Lower South. The Virginia State Convention, which had convened on February 13 and was in complete control of the conditional Unionists, was still in session, evidently awaiting his decision. Therefore, if he should adopt a strongly aggressive policy he might find himself opposed by the large group of peace men in the North while he precipitated most if not all of the border slave states into secession and union with the Confederacy.[176] If, on the other hand, he failed to act decisively, he was very likely to alienate the radical Republicans who were already manifesting

---

[175] These elections were not actually held until April 1 in Ohio and Connecticut and April 3 in Rhode Island, but the pre-election evidences of defection had greatly alarmed the Republicans in the latter part of March. The fusion of the Democrats and other "Union-savers" carried all the larger cities of Ohio, defeated two radical Republican congressmen in Connecticut, re-elected Governor William Sprague in Rhode Island, and won a majority of the legislature in that state. Cincinnati *Commercial,* April 3, 1861; Columbus (Ohio) *Crisis,* April 4, 1861; New York *Times,* March 30, April 2, 4, 1861; J. H. Jordan to S. P. Chase, March 27, J. N. and J. B Antram to Chase, April 2, and W. D. Beckham to Chase, April 2, 1861, in Chase Papers, Library of Congress. I am indebted to Mrs. W. Mary Bryant of the University of Texas for copies of these letters.

[176] There are some indications, however, that at this time Lincoln overestimated the Unionist strength in the border slave states.

impatience. In either case he would divide his party at the very beginning of his administration and increase the risk of utter failure. There was, however, some cheering evidence among the business elements of a growing irritation against the secessionists because of the depression which had set in with the withdrawal of South Carolina; and if the Confederates should add further offense to their low tariff policy or adopt more aggressive tactics with respect to the forts, this feeling might grow strong enough to overcome the peace men.

He had promised to maintain the Union, but how was he to attempt it without wrecking his chances at the very outset? It was now too late to restore the Union by compromise because, having himself rejected all overtures in December, he could not now afford to offer what he had recently refused. Moreover, there was no indication that the Confederates would accept at this late date any compromise he might proffer. He must do something, for the gradual exhaustion of the supplies of the garrison in Fort Sumter would soon force his hand. He could not order Anderson to evacuate without arousing the wrath of the militant Unionists in the North. If he continued to let matters drift, Anderson himself would have to evacuate when his supplies were gone. While that would relieve the administration of any charge of coercion, it would expose the government to the accusation of disgraceful weakness and improve the chances of the Confederacy for foreign recognition.[177] If he left Anderson to his fate and made

---

[177] Lincoln's special message to Congress, July 4, 1861, indicates that he had weighed some of these considerations. "It

ostentatious display of reinforcing Fort Pickens, as
Seward was urging him to do, would he gain as much
as he lost? Was it not best, even necessary, to make his
stand at Sumter? But if he should try to relieve Anderson by force of arms, what was the chance of success?
Anderson, supported by the high authority of General
Scott, thought there was none. If, as Captain Fox believed, swift steamers could run the gauntlet of the
Confederate batteries and reach the fort with men and
supplies, would they then be able to hold it against attack? Failure in this military movement might seriously damage the already uncertain prestige of the administration. Would it not be looked upon as aggressive war by the border state men and perhaps by the
peace men in the North? Could he risk the handicap of
appearing to force civil war upon the country? In every
direction the way out of his dilemma seemed closed.

There was one remote possibility: the Confederates themselves might precipitate matters by attacking Sumter before Anderson should be compelled to
evacuate by lack of supplies. But the Confederates,
though watchful, were showing great caution. General

---

was believed, however, that to abandon that position [Sumter]
under the circumstances would be utterly ruinous; that the *necessity* under which it was to be done would not be fully understood; that by many it would be construed as a part of a *vol-
untary* policy; that at home it would discourage the friends of
the Union, embolden its adversaries, and go far to insure to
the latter a recognition abroad; that, in fact, it would be our
national destruction consummated. This could not be allowed."
J. D. Richardson (comp.), *Messages and Papers of the Presidents*, 10 vols. (Washington, 1896-1899), VI, 21.

P. G. T. Beauregard, in command at Charleston since March 6, was treating Major Anderson with elaborate courtesy. The government at Montgomery was in no hurry to force the issue, partly because it was quite well aware of the danger of assuming the aggressive and partly because it was waiting to see what its com‑ missioners would be able to effect at Washington, where Seward was holding out hopes to them of the eventual evacuation of Sumter. At some time, while turning these things over in his mind, this daring thought must have occurred to Lincoln: Could the Southerners be *induced* to attack Sumter, to assume the aggressive and thus put themselves in the wrong in the eyes of the North and of the world?[178] If they could, the latent irritation perceptible among the Northern moderates might flame out against the se‑ cessionists and in support of the government. The two

---

[178] It would be most surprising to find that such an idea never occurred to Lincoln, since not only were many Republicans suggesting it as a possibility, but various Republican newspa‑ pers were constantly reiterating the suggestion that if any clash came the secessionists would be responsible. The pre‑ dictions of the newspapers may have been "inspired," but if so, that fact makes it more certain that the idea was being dis‑ cussed in the inner circles of the administration. J. H. Jordan wrote Chase form Cincinnati, March 27, "In the name of God! why not hold the Fort? Will reinforcing & holding it cause the rebels to attack it, and thus bring on 'civil war'? What of it? That is just what the government ought to wish to bring about, and ought to do all it can . . . to bring about. Let them attack the Fort, if they will—it will then be *them* that commenced the war." The general idea of such an outcome was in the air; the contribution of Lincoln himself was the maneuver by which this desirable solution was brought about.

wings of his party would unite, some at least of the Democrats would come to his support, even the border-
state people might be held, if they could be convinced
that the war was being forced by the secessionists.
Unless he could unite them in defense of the authority
of the government, the peaceable and the "stiff-backed"
Republicans would split apart, the party would collapse, his administration would be a failure, and he
would go down in history as a weak man who had allowed the Union to crumble in his hands. As things
now stood, the only way by which the Union could be
restored, his party and his administration saved, was
by an unequivocal assertion of the authority of the government, that is, through war. But he must not openly
assume the aggressive; that must be done by the secessionists. The best opportunity was at Fort Sumter, but
the time left was short for Anderson was running short
of essential supplies.

Let us examine closely what Lincoln did after the
middle of March, taking care to place each movement
as nearly as possible in its exact sequence. We have
seen that Captain Fox made his argument to Lincoln
for a combined naval and military expedition on March
13 and that the cabinet, with the exception of Montgomery Blair and the equivocal Chase, had voted
against it on the fifteenth. Fox then offered to go in
person to Fort Sumter to investigate the situation and
Lincoln gave him permission. He arrived in Charleston
on March 21 and was allowed to see Anderson that
night. He and Anderson agreed that the garrison could
not hold out longer than noon of April 15. Although

Anderson seems to have remained unconvinced of its feasibility, Fox returned to Washington full of enthusiasm for his plan.

On the very day that Fox arrived in Charleston, Lincoln had dispatched to that city a close friend and loyal supporter, Ward H. Lamon, a native of Virginia and his former law partner in Illinois. This sending of Lamon on the heels of Fox is an interesting incident. The precise nature of his instructions has never been fully revealed. Lamon himself, in his *Recollections*, merely says he was sent "on a confidential mission" and intimates that he was to report on the extent of Unionist feeling in South Carolina. He arrived in Charleston on the night of Saturday, March 23; visited James L. Petigru, the famous Unionist, on Sunday and learned from him that there was no Unionist strength in the state, that "peaceable secession or war was inevitable"; and on Monday morning obtained an interview with Governor Pickens. In reply to questions the Governor stated very positively that any attempt on the part of President Lincoln to reinforce Sumter would bring on war, that only his "unalterable resolve *not* to attempt any reinforcement" could prevent war. Lamon, whether through innocence or guile, left the impression with the Governor, and also with Anderson whom he was permitted to visit, that the garrison would soon be withdrawn and that his trip was merely to prepare the way for that event. He left Charleston on the night of the twenty-fifth, arrived in Washington on the twenty-seventh, and reported to Lincoln what

he had learned.[179] What had he been sent to Charleston to do? There must have been some purpose and it
could hardly have been to prepare the way for Anderson's evacuation.[180] Does it strain the evidence to suggest that it was chiefly to find out at first hand how
strong was the Southern feeling about relief for Fort
Sumter and that this purpose was camouflaged by the
vague intimations of evacuation? But it is quite probable that Lamon himself did not understand the real
purpose, for it is altogether unlikely that the cautious
Lincoln would have divulged so important a secret to
his bibulous and impulsive young friend. But if there
was such an ulterior purpose, Lincoln now had the information directly from Charleston that any sort of relief would result in an attack upon the fort.

According to Gideon Welles, whose account of
these events was written several years later, Lincoln
sometime in the latter half of March had informed the
members of his cabinet that he would send relief to

---

[179] Ward H. Lamon, *Recollections of Abraham Lincoln* (Washington, 1911), 68-79.

[180] On April 1 Lincoln sent word, through Seward, to Justice
John A. Campbell that Lamon had no authority to make such a
promise. Not only that but, according to the same source, he
stated that "Lamon did not go to Charleston under any commission or authority from Mr. Lincoln." Henry G. Connor, *John
Archibald Campbell* (Boston and New York, 1920), 127. The
words "commission or authority" may have been a mere technical evasion of responsibility, for Lamon himself recounts the
conversation between Lincoln, Seward, and himself when Lincoln asked him to go. It is possible, of course, that Justice
Campbell misunderstood the exact language or meaning of
Seward.

Sumter. During a cabinet meeting on March 29 (two days after Lamon's return), when the matter was again discussed, Lincoln, at the suggestion of Attorney General Edward Bates, again requested each member to give his opinion in writing on the question of relieving Sumter. Whether Lincoln's known determination, political pressure, or some other influence had effected it, there was a marked change from the advice given just two weeks earlier. Now only Seward and Caleb Smith were for evacuating Sumter, but they both wished to reinforce Fort Pickens. Bates proposed to strengthen Pickens and Key West and said that the time had come either to evacuate Sumter or relieve it. The rest were unequivocally for a relief expedition. Later that day Lincoln directed the secretaries of War and the Navy to co-operate in preparing an expedition to move by sea as early as April 6. The destination was not indicated in the order, but it was Charleston.[181]

On the same day Seward, intent upon the reinforcement of Fort Pickens, brought Captain M. C. Meigs of the Engineers to Lincoln to discuss an expedition to that place. On March 31 Meigs and Colonel Erasmus D. Keyes, of General Scott's staff, were directed to draw up a plan for the relief of Fort Pickens. They took it to Lincoln who had them take it to Scott to be put into final form and executed. On the next day, April 1, Seward, Meigs, and Lieutenant D. D. Porter of the

---

[181] Howard K. Beale (ed.), *The Diary of Edward Bates, 1859-1866*, in American Historical Association, *Annual Report, 1930* (Washington, 1933), IV, 180; Nicolay and Lay (eds.), *Lincoln: Works*, II, 25-28.

navy went to the Executive Mansion and after consul-
tation with Lincoln finished the plans for the Pickens
expedition. It was to be conducted with such absolute
secrecy, lest information leak out to the Confederates,
that even the secretaries of War and the Navy were to
know nothing of it. The orders were signed by the
President himself. It was only because the same ship,
the *Powhatan*, was selected for both expeditions that
the Secretary of the Navy learned of the expedition to
the Gulf of Mexico.[182] Energetic preparations began in
New York and Brooklyn to collect vessels, men, arms,
and provisions for the two expeditions.

In the first days of April came the disquieting returns from the elections in Ohio, Connecticut, and
Rhode Island. April 4 proved to be an important day.
Early that morning Lincoln seems to have had a mys-
terious conference with a group of Republican governors, said to be seven or nine in number. Among them
were Andrew G. Curtin of Pennsylvania, William Dennison of Ohio, Richard Yates of Illinois, Oliver P. Mor-
ton of Indiana, Israel Washburn of Maine, and Austin
Blair of Michigan.[183] How did all these governors hap-

---

[182] John T. Morse (ed.), *The Diary of Gideon Welles*, 3 vols.
(Boston and New York, 1911), I, 23-25. Hereafter cited as
Welles, *Diary*. David D. Porter, in *Incidents and Anecdotes of
the Civil War* (New York, 1885), 13-14, tells a lively and rather
amusing story of the conference with Lincoln on April 1.
[183] New York *World*, April 5, 1861; New York *Herald*, April 5, 7,
1861; Philadelphia *Enquirer*, April 6, 1861; James Ford Rhodes, *History of the United States Since the Compromise of
1850*, 8 vols. (New York, 1910 edition) III, 346, n. 3. John B.
Baldwin, who had an interview with Lincoln later that morning,

pen to be in Washington at the same time? The newspapers, in so far as they noticed the presence of these
gentlemen, assumed that they were looking after pa-
tronage; but rumors were soon current that they had
gone to demand of the President that he send relief to
the garrison at Fort Sumter. This is not improbable
since all these men belonged to the aggressive group of
Republicans who had been alarmed at the rumors of
evacuation and they could hardly have known what
Lincoln had already planned. Several questions arise
here. If Lincoln was still hesitating, did they bring
pressure upon him and force him to a decision? Or did
Lincoln allow them to think they were helping him to
decide? Or, if the President had not actually sum-
moned them to a conference, did he seize the opportunity to make sure of their powerful support in case the
Confederates should show fight? Were mutual pledges
of action and support exchanged that morning?

Later that same morning occurred the much-dis-
cussed Lincoln-Baldwin interview. On April 2, apparently at the suggestion of Seward, Lincoln had sent
Allan B. Magruder, a Virginia Unionist living in Washington, to Richmond to ask G. W. Summers, the leader
of the Unionists in the State Convention, to come to

---

testified on February 10, 1866, "At the time I was here I saw,
and was introduced to, in the President's room, a number of
governors of states. It was at the time the nine governors had
the talk here with the President." *Report of the Joint Committee on Reconstruction* (39 Cong., 1 Sess., House Report No.
30), 105. As several of these governors were in Washington
for three or four days, it is possible that the conferences extended over several days, from about April 3 to 6.

see him at once or to send some other representative
from that group. Magruder reached Richmond the next
day. As Summers could not leave, John B. Baldwin,
another leader of the group, was selected; and Baldwin
and Magruder were in Washington early on the morning of April 4. They went to Seward who conducted
Baldwin to Lincoln at eleven o'clock. Lincoln took
Baldwin alone into a bedroom, locked the door and exclaimed "You have come too late!" In the conversation
which followed, according to Baldwin's statement, the
President asked why the Unionists in the Virginia
Convention did not adjourn sine die, as the continu-
ance of the session was a standing menace to him.
Baldwin replied that if they should so adjourn without
having accomplished anything for the security of the
state, another convention would certainly be called
and it would be more strongly secessionist. He then
urged the President to assure peace to the country and
strengthen the border-state Unionists by evacuating
both Sumter and Pickens and calling upon the whole
people to settle their differences in a national convention. Lincoln replied that his supporters would not permit him to withdraw the garrisons. Baldwin then
warned him that if a fight started at Fort Sumter, no
matter who started it, war would follow and Virginia
would go out of the Union in forty-eight hours. Lincoln
became greatly excited and exclaimed, "Why was I not
told this a week ago? You have come too late!" This is

Baldwin's account;[184] but it is substantiated by several other Virginia Unionists, at least to the extent that it was what Baldwin told them when he returned to Richmond the next day.

But John Minor Botts, a violent Virginia Unionist who by invitation talked with Lincoln on the night of April 7, insisted that Lincoln then told him that he had offered to Baldwin to withdraw Anderson's force from Sumter if the Virginia Convention would adjourn sine die, that he would gladly swap a fort for a state; but that Baldwin refused the offer. When Botts offered to take the proposition to Richmond at once Lincoln replied, "Oh, it is too late; the fleet has sailed and I have no means of communicating with it."[185]

Baldwin always denied that Lincoln had made any such proposal as Botts reported. Did Baldwin lie? He seems to have had a much better reputation for accuracy than Botts and his account of his journey to Washington is accurate as far as it can be checked, whereas Botts' story is full of minor inaccuracies.[186] Besides, Baldwin was a sincere Unionist and voted against secession to the last. Why should he have re-

---

[184] Baldwin's testimony, *Report of Joint Committee on Reconstruction*, 102-107; J. B. Baldwin, *Interview between President Lincoln and John B. Baldwin, April 4, 1861* (Staunton, VA., 1866).

[185] Botts' testimony, *Report of Joint Committee on Reconstruction*, 114-19; John Minor Botts, *The Great Rebellion* (New York, 1866), 194-202.

[186] The most recent and also the most judicial summary of all the evidence is by Henry T. Shanks, *The Secession Movement in Virginia, 1847-1861* (Richmond, 1934), 192-95.

fused Lincoln's offer and failed to report it to his fellow
Unionists in Richmond? Did Botts lie about what Lincoln told him? His extreme prejudices and frequently
unwarranted statements on other matters would easily
bring this conclusion into the range of possibility, were
it not for the fact that Lincoln seems to have told much
the same story to others. If Lincoln did, then the question whether the President offered to evacuate Sumter
at this stage of his plan becomes an issue of veracity
between Lincoln and Baldwin, which obviously places
the Virginian at a great disadvantage. But let us consider other factors in the situation. Lincoln had just
been holding conferences with the militant Republican
governors and evidently had come to some agreement
with them, else why should he greet his visitor with
the exclamation, repeated later in the conversation,
"You have come too late"? Certainly he could not have
referred to the final orders to Fox, for those orders
were given later that day. And why did he refuse on
the night of April 7, if the Botts story is correct, to permit Botts to take his proposition to Richmond, alleging
that the fleet had sailed, when in fact none of the vessels left New York until the next night? Is there not
some basis for suspecting that Lincoln had not actually
made the offer to Baldwin to evacuate Sumter because
he was already bound by some sort of agreement with
the Republican governors to send the expedition forward; and that later, desiring above all things to leave
the impression that he had done everything in his
power to avoid a collision, he dropped hints about an
offer which had been flatly refused?

During the afternoon of April 4 Lincoln saw Captain Fox, who was to have charge of the Sumter expedition, and told him of his final determination to send relief to Anderson and that notification of the relief expedition would be sent to the Governor of South Carolina before Fox could possibly arrive off Charleston Harbor.[187] Fox hurried back to New York to push his preparations. At some time that same day Lincoln drafted a letter to Major Anderson, which was copied and signed by the Secretary of War, informing him that relief would be sent him.[188]

On the afternoon of April 6 Secretary Welles received a letter from Captain Henry A. Adams of the navy, stationed off Fort Pickens, explaining that he had not landed the artillery company at the fort in accordance with General Scott's order of March 12 because of controlling orders from the former Secretary of the Navy to respect the truce of February 29, but stating that he was not ready to obey if ordered to land the men. Welles consulted the President and then hurried off Lieutenant John L. Worden with verbal orders to Captain Adams to land the men at once.[189] This incident gave occasion for a strange statement of Lincoln which deserves notice. In his special message to Congress of July 4, he stated that the expedition for the

[187] Crawford, *Genesis of the Civil War*, 404; William E. Smith, *The Francis Preston Blair Family in Politics*, 2 vols. (New York, 1933), II, 12-13.
[188] Nicolay and Hay, *Abraham Lincoln*, IV, 27-28.
[189] Welles, *Diary*, I, 29-32. Worden reached Captain Adams' ship on April 12 and the men were landed that night, the very day on which the firing began at Sumter.

relief of Sumter was first prepared "to be ultimately used or not according to circumstances," and intimated that, if Pickens had been relieved in March, Sumter would have been evacuated, and that it had not been decided to use the expedition until word came that Fort Pickens had not been reinforced in accordance with the order of March 12.[190] The strange thing about this statement is that word was not received from Adams until April 6, while positive orders had been given two days before to Captain Fox to go ahead with his expedition and at the same time Anderson had been notified to expect it. Had Lincoln become confused about the order of these events? It does not seem probable. Or was he, for effect upon public opinion, trying to strengthen the belief that his hand had been forced, that his pacific intentions had been defeated by circumstances?

On April 1 Lincoln had passed the promise through Seward and Justice John A. Campbell to the Confederate Commissioners in Washington that he would notify Governor Pickens if any relief expedition should be sent to Fort Sumter.[191] When they learned of it, several members of his cabinet objected to such notification, but Lincoln insisted; he had his own reasons for so doing. The formal notice which he drafted with his own hand, dated April 6, is interesting not only for

---

[190] Richardson (comp.), *Messages and Papers*, VI, 21-22.
[191] Connor, *John Archibald Campbell*, 127-28. Lincoln chose to send the notification to the Governor, not the Confederate officers, because he could recognize the former and not the latter.

its careful phrasing but for the evident importance which he attached to it. It was embodied in a letter of instruction to R. S. Chew, an official of the state department who was to be accompanied by Captain Theodore Talbot, directing him to proceed to Charleston where, if he found that Fort Sumter had not been evacuated or attacked and that the flag was still over it, he was to seek an interview with Governor Pickens, read to him the statement and give him a copy of it. If he found the fort evacuated or attacked he was to seek no interview but was to return forthwith. The message to Governor Pickens was in these words:

"I am directed by the President of the United States to notify you to expect an attempt will be made to supply Fort Sumter with provisions only; and that, if such an attempt be not resisted, no effort to throw in men, arms, or ammunition will be made without further notice, or in case of an attack upon the fort."[192]

Was the purpose of this message merely to fulfill a promise? Is there no special significance in the fact that Lincoln entrusted the form of it to no one else, but carefully drafted it himself? It is unnecessary to call attention again to the fact that Lincoln was a rare master of the written word, that he had the skill of an artist in so phrasing a sentence that it conveyed pre-

[192] Nicolay and Hay, *Abraham Lincoln*, IV, 34.

cisely the meaning he wished it to convey. He could do
more than that: he could make the same sentence say
one thing to one person and something entirely different to another and in each case carry the meaning he
intended. It is obvious that the message to be read to
Governor Pickens was intended less for that official
than for General Beauregard and the Confederate government at Montgomery. But it was intended also for
the people of the North and of the border states. To the
suspicious and apprehensive Confederates it did not
merely give information that provisions would be sent
to Anderson's garrison — which should be enough to
bring about an attempt to take the fort — but it carried a threat that force would be used if the provisions
were not allowed to be brought in. It was a direct challenge! How were the Southerners expected to react to
this challenge? To Northern readers the same words
meant only that the government was taking food to
hungry men to whom it was under special obligation.
Northern men would see no threat; they would understand only that their government did not propose to
use force if it could be avoided. Is it possible that a
man of Lincoln's known perspicacity could be blind to
the different interpretations which would be placed
upon his subtle words in the North and in the South?

The message was not only skillfully phrased, it
was most carefully timed. It was read to Governor
Pickens in the presence of General Beauregard on the
evening of April 8. News of the preparation of some
large expedition had been in the newspapers for a
week; but as the destination had not been officially di-

vulged, newspaper reporters and correspondents had guessed at many places, chiefly the coast of Texas and revolutionary Santo Domingo. It was not until April 8 that the guessing veered toward Charleston, and not until the next day was any positive information given in the press of the notice to Governor Pickens.[193] The Confederate officials had regarded these preparations at New York with suspicion while conflicting reports came to them from Washington concerning Lincoln's designs about Sumter. The first of Captain Fox's vessels were leaving New York Harbor at the very hour that Chew read the notification to Governor Pickens. The Confederates were given ample time, therefore, to act before the fleet could arrive off Charleston. They did not know that a portion of the vessels which had left New York were really destined not for Charleston but for Fort Pickens at Pensacola. The utmost secrecy was maintained about the Pensacola expedition, thus permitting the Confederates to believe that the whole force was to be concentrated at Charleston.

The tables were now completely turned on the Southerners. Lincoln was well out of his dilemma while they, who had heretofore had the tactical advantage of being able to wait until Anderson must evacuate, were suddenly faced with a choice of two evils. They must either take the fort before relief could arrive, thus taking the apparent offensive which they had hoped to avoid, or they must stand by quietly and

---

[193] New York *Times*, April 8, 1861; Baltimore *Sun*, April 8, 1861. The Richmond *Examiner* asserted as early as April 6 that the expedition was for the purpose of relieving Sumter.

see the fort provisioned. But to allow the provisioning meant not only an indefinite postponement to their possession of the fort which had become as much a symbol to them as it was to Lincoln; to permit it in the face of the threat of force, after all their preparations, would be to make a ridiculous and disgraceful retreat.[194] Nor could they be sure that, if they yielded now in the matter of "Provisions only," they would not soon be served with the "further notice" as a prelude to throwing in "Men, arms, and ammunition." This, then, was the dilemma which they faced as the result of Lincoln's astute strategy.

Events now hurried to the inevitable climax. As soon as President Lincoln's communication was received General Beauregard telegraphed the news to the Confederate secretary of war, L. P. Walker. Walker at once ordered that the Sumter garrison be isolated by stopping its mails and the purchase of provisions in Charleston. On this same day the Confederate commissioners at Washington had received a copy of a memorandum filed in the state department by Seward, dated March 15, in which the Secretary declined to hold any official intercourse with them. They tele-

---

[194] Evidently Lincoln did not expect them to retreat, for on April 8 he wrote Governor Curtin of Pennsylvania, one of the recent conferees, "I think the necessity of being *ready* increases. Look to it." From "Lincoln Photostats," Library of Congress; also in Paul M. Angle, *New Letters and Papers of Lincoln* (Boston and New York, 1930), 266. Governor Dennison of Ohio, who was still in Washington, was quoted as promising, on the same date, support to "a vigorous policy." Mt. Vernon (Ohio) *Democratic Banner*, April 16, 1861.

graphed the news to their government and at once, feeling that they had been deceived and knowing that their mission had failed, prepared to leave Washington. Jefferson Davis was thus, on April 8, apprised of two movements by the Federal government which, taken together or singly, looked ominous. On the following day Beauregard seized the mails as they came from Fort Sumter and discovered a letter from Anderson to the war department which disclosed that he had been informed of the coming of Fox's expedition and indicated that the fleet would attempt to force its way into the harbor. This information also was at once communicated to the Montgomery government. On the tenth came the news that the fleet had sailed from New York. Walker then directed Beauregard, if he thought there was no doubt of the authorized character of the notification from Washington (meaning Lincoln's), to demand the evacuation of Fort Sumter and, if it should be refused, "to reduce" the fort. The Davis administration had waited two full days after receiving word of Lincoln's notification before deciding what to do. It is said that Robert Toombs, secretary of state, objected vigorously to attacking the fort. "It is unnecessary; it puts us in the wrong; it is fatal!"[195] If Toombs

---

[195] That Toombs protested against the attack seems to be based wholly upon the statement in Pleasant A. Stovall, *The Life of Robert Toombs* (New York, 1892), 226. Stovall cites no source and U. B. Phillips in his *Life of Robert Toombs* (New York, 1913), 234-35, gives no other citation than Stovall. Richard Lathers attributed the same words to Toombs several days before this crisis arose in a letter which he wrote to the New York *Journal of Commerce* from Montgomery. See Alvan F.

protested, he was overruled because Davis and the rest believed that Lincoln had already taken the aggressive and they regarded their problem now as a military one. To them it was the simple question whether they should permit the hostile fleet to arrive before they attacked the fort or whether they should take Sumter before they had to fight both fort and fleet.

At two o'clock on the eleventh Beauregard made the demand upon Anderson, who rejected it but added verbally to the officer sent to him that if not battered to pieces, he would be starved out in a few days. When Beauregard reported this remark to Walker, that official informed him that the government did "Not desire needlessly to bombard Fort Sumter" and that if Major Anderson would state when he would evacuate, Beauregard should "avoid the effusion of blood." Evidently the Montgomery officials thought there was still a chance to get the fort peaceably before the fleet could arrive. Had not Lincoln so carefully timed his message with the movement of Fox there might have been no attack. But late in the afternoon of the same day Beauregard received information from a scout boat that the *Harriet Lane*, one of Fox's ships, had been sighted a few miles out of the harbor. It was expected

---

Sanborn, *Reminiscences of Richard Lathers* (New York, 1907), 164-65. Nevertheless, that Toombs was greatly concerned over the dangers in the situation is attested by the Confederate secretary of war, L. P. Walker, who quotes Toombs as saying at the cabinet meeting on April 10, "The firing upon that fort will inaugurate a civil war greater than any the world has yet seen; and I do not feel competent to advise you." Crawford, *The Genesis of the Civil War*, 421.

that all the fleet would be at hand by next day. Nevertheless, Beauregard about midnight sent a second
message to Anderson, in accordance with Walker's instructions, saying that if he would state the time at
which he would evacuate and would agree not to use
"your guns against us unless ours should be employed
against Fort Sumter, we will abstain from opening fire
upon you." To this Anderson replied that he would
evacuate by noon on the fifteenth and would in the
meantime not open fire upon Beauregard's forces
unless compelled to do so by some hostile act "against
the fort or the flag it bears, should I not receive prior
to that time controlling instructions from my government or additional supplies." This answer was conditional and unsatisfactory for it was clear that, with
Fox's fleet arriving, Anderson would not evacuate.
Thereupon the two aids who had carried Beauregard's
message, in accordance with their instructions from
that office, formally notified Anderson — it was now
3:20 in the morning of the twelfth — that fire would be
opened upon him in one hour's time.

What followed we all know. The bombardment
which began at 4:30 on the morning of April 12 ended
in the surrender of Anderson and his garrison during
the afternoon of the following day. The three vessels[196]

---

[196] These were the *Baltic*, the *Harriet Lane*, and the *Pawnee*.
The *Pocahontas* did not arrive until the 13th. It is an interesting
question whether the Northern reaction would have been different if the Confederates had ignored Fort Sumter and concentrated their efforts upon trying to keep the fleet from enter-
ing the harbor. The fact that their chief naval officer, Captain
Henry J. Hartstene, reported on April 10 that the Federals

of the fleet which lay outside were unable to get into
the harbor because of the high seas and the failure of
the rest of the fleet — the tugboats and the *Powhatan*
— to arrive. Although there were no casualties during
the bombardment, the mere news that the attack on
the fort had begun swept the entire North into a roar-
ing flame of anger. The "rebels" had fired the first
shot; they had chosen to begin war. If there had been
any doubt earlier whether the mass of the Northern
people would support the administration in suppressing the secessionists, there was none now. Lincoln's
strategy had been completely successful. He seized at
once the psychological moment for calling out the militia and committing the North to support of the war.
This action cost him four of the border slaves states,
but he had probably already discounted that loss.

    Perhaps the facts thus far enumerated, standing
alone, could hardly be conclusive evidence that Lincoln, having decided that there was no other way than
war for the salvation of his administration, his party,
and the Union, maneuvered the Confederates into firing the first shot in order that they, rather than he,
should take the blame of beginning bloodshed. Though
subject to that interpretation, they are also subject to
the one which he built up so carefully. It there other
evidence? No one, surely, would expect to find in any
written word of his a confession of the stratagem; for

---

would be able to reach the fort in boats at night and that he
had no vessels strong enough to prevent the entrance of the
fleet may have determined the Confederates to take the fort
first. *Official Records*, Ser. I, Vol. I, 299.

to acknowledge it openly would have been to destroy the very effect he had been at so much pains to pro-duce. There are, it is true, two statements by him to Captain Fox which are at least suggestive. Fox relates that in their conference of April 4 the President told him that he had decided to let the expedition go and that a messenger would be sent to the authorities at Charleston before Fox could possibly get there; and when the Captain reminded the President of the short time in which he must organize the expedition and reach the destined point, Lincoln replied, "You will best fulfill your duty to your country by making the attempt." Then, again, in the letter which Lincoln wrote the chagrined Captain on May 1 to console him for the failure of the fleet to enter Charleston Harbor, he said: "You and I both anticipated that the cause of the country would be advanced by making the attempt to provision Fort Sumter, even if it should fail; and it is no small consolation now to feel that our anticipa-tion is justified by the result."[197] Was this statement merely intended to soothe a disappointed commander, or did it contain a hint that the real objective of the expedition was not at all the relief of Sumter?

Lincoln's two secretaries, John G. Nicolay and John Hay, in their long but not impartial account of the Sumter affair come so close to divulging the es-sence of the stratagem that one cannot but suspect

---

[197] Crawford, *Genesis of the Civil War*, 404; Robert Means Thompson and Richard Wainwright (eds.), *Confidential Correspondence of Gustavus Vasa Fox*, 2 vols. (New York, 1918), I, 43-44; Nicolay and Hay (eds.), *Lincoln: Works*, II, 41.

that they knew of it. In one place they say, with reference to Lincoln's solution of this problem of Sumter,
"Abstractly it was enough that the Government was in
the right. But to make the issue sure, he determined
that in addition the rebellion should be put in the
wrong." And again, "President Lincoln in deciding the
Sumter question had adopted a simple but effective
policy. To use his own words, he determined to 'send
bread to Anderson'; if the rebels fired on that, they
would not be able to convince the world that he had
begun the civil war." And still later, "When he finally
gave the order that the fleet should sail he was master
of the situation . . . master if the rebels hesitated or
repented, because they would thereby forfeit their
prestige with the South; master if they persisted, for
he would then command a united North."[198]

Perhaps not much weight should be given to the
fact that before the expedition reached Charleston his
political opponents in the North expressed suspicion of
a design to force civil war upon the country in order to
save the Republican party from the disaster threatened in the recent elections and that after the fighting
began they roundly accused him of having deliberately
provoked it by his demonstration against Charleston.
And perhaps there is no significance in the further fact
that the more aggressive members of his own party
had demanded action to save the party and that the
administration newspapers began to assert as soon as

---

[198] Nicolay and Hay, *Abraham Lincoln*, IV, 33, 44, 62.

the fleet sailed that, if war came, the rebels would be the aggressors.[199]

---

[199] Predictions, on the one hand, that the "rebels" would soon start a war and charges, on the other, that, to save the Republican party, Lincoln was demonstrating against Charleston in order to force the Southerners to attack Sumter are to be . found in administration and antiadministration papers, respectively, during the week before the fort was fired upon. See, for instance, the Columbus (Ohio) *Crisis*, April 4, 1861; New York *Times*, April 8, 10, 1861; Baltimore *Sun*, April 10, 1861. When the news came of the bombardment at Charleston, the Providence *Daily Post*, April 13, 1861, began an editorial entitled "WHY?" with: "We are to have civil war, if at all, because Abraham Lincoln loves a party better than he loves his country." And after commenting on what seemed to be a sudden change of policy with respect to Sumter, "Why? We think the reader will perceive why. Mr. Lincoln saw an opportunity to inaugurate civil war without appearing in the character of an aggressor. There are men in Fort Sumter, he said, who are nearly out of provisions. They ought to be fed. We will attempt to feed them. Certainly nobody can blame us for that. . . . The secessionists, who are both mad and foolish, will resist us. They will commence civil war. Then I will appeal to the North to aid me in putting down rebellion, and the North must respond. How can it do otherwise? And sure enough, how can we do otherwise?" A photostatic copy of this editorial was furnished me through the kindness of Professor E. M. Coulter of the University of Georgia.

One story that seems to have had some currency was related by Alexander Long, a Democratic congressman from Ohio, in an antiadministration speech before the House on April 8, 1864, to the effect that when Lincoln first heard the news that the Confederates had opened fire on Fort Sumter, he exclaimed, "I knew they would do it!" *Congressional Globe*, 38 Cong., I Sess., 1499 *et seq*. Long's speech aroused much excitement among the Republicans who attempted to expel him from the House on the ground that he was a sympathizer with the rebellion.

There is evidence much more to the point than any
of these things. Stephen A. Douglas, senator from Illinois, died on June 3, 1861. On June 12 the Republican governor of that state, Richard Yates, appointed to
the vacancy Orville H. Browning, a prominent lawyer,
a former Whig, then an ardent Republican, and for
more than twenty years a personal friend of Abraham
Lincoln. Browning was one of the group who from the
first had favored vigorous measures and had opposed
compromise. He was to become the spokesman of the
administration in the Senate. On July 2, 1861, Browning arrived in Washington to take his seat in the Senate for the special session which had been called to
meet on July 4. On the evening of the third he called at
the White House to see his old acquaintance. Now
Browning for many years had kept a diary, a fact that
very probably was unknown to Lincoln since diarists
usually conceal this pleasant and useful vice. In the
entry for July 3 Browning relates the conversation he
had with the President that evening, for after reading
the new Senator his special message to Congress, Lincoln laid aside the document and talked. The rest of
the entry best be given in Browning's own words:

> He told me that the very first thing
> placed in his hands after his inaugura-
> tion was a letter from Majr Anderson
> announcing the impossibility of defend-
> ing or relieving Sumter. That he called
> the cabinet together and consulted Genl
> Scott — that Scott concurred with

Anderson, and the cabinet, with the exception of P M Genl Blair were for
evacuating the Fort, and all the troubles
and anxieties of his life had not equaled
those which intervened between this
time and the fall of Sumter. He himself
conceived the idea, and proposed sending supplies, without an attempt to reinforce giving notice of the fact to Gov
Pickens of S.C. The plan succeeded.
They attacked Sumter — it fell, and thus
did more service than it otherwise
could.[200]

This statement, condensed from the words of Lincoln himself by a close friend who wrote them down
when he returned that night to his room at "Mrs.
Carter's on Capitol Hill," needs no elaboration. It completes the evidence.

It is not difficult to understand how the usually
secretive Lincoln, so long surrounded by strangers and
criticized by many whom he had expected to be help-
ful, talking that night for the first time in many
months to an old, loyal, and discreet friend, though a
friend who had often been somewhat patronizing, for
once forgot to be reticent. It must have been an emotional relief to him, with his pride over his consum-
mate strategy bottled up within him for so long, to be

---

[200] Theodore Calvin Pease and James G. Randall (eds.), *The
Diary of Orville H. Browning*, 2 vols. (Springfield, Ill., 1927), I,
475-76.

able to impress his friend Browning with his success in meeting a perplexing and dangerous situation. He did not suspect that Browning would set it down in a diary.

There is little more to be said. Some of us will be content to find new reason for admiration of Abraham Lincoln in reflecting on this bit of masterful strategy at the very beginning of his long struggle for the preservation of the Union. Some, perhaps, will be reminded of the famous incident of the Ems telegram of which the cynical Bismarck boasted in his memoirs. And some will wonder whether the sense of responsibility for the actual beginning of a frightful war, far more terrible than he could possibly have foreseen in that early April of 1861, may have deepened the melancholy and the charity toward his Southern foemen which that strange man in the White House was to reveal so often before that final tragic April of 1865.

Author's Final Assessment

Any historian who does not think the annihilation of the Northern economy is the true cause of the War Between the States is like a detective who needs to solve a crime but is too stupid to consider *motive* in his investigation.

The annihilation of the Northern economy and the rise of the South are what drove all actions of all participants, North and South, in the spring of 1861 when the war started. Ending slavery was nowhere on the Northern radar. Northerners were seeing their world crumble before their very eyes with bankruptcy and anarchy at the end of the tunnel.

Southerners were seeing 1776 and the re-founding of the American republic but with constitutionally protected free trade, low tariffs, and even more emphasis on States' Rights. In the South, power belonged to the people in their respective states — not to a centralized government representing, as the Founding Fathers warned over and over, the tyranny of the majority.

I am interested in historical truth, and in this age of political correctness, we do not have it. Northerners, as this book proves beyond the shadow of a doubt, did not go to war to end slavery, and Southerners did not go to war to preserve it. With all that the South had to gain by being a free, independent nation on this earth,

249

only a dull person would think that protecting slavery was all the South wanted.[201]

The Confederate States of America was about powerful sovereign states in which free people governed themselves. It was united by a weak federal government that was subservient to the states and the people in those states, and was not their master.

That is the main issue of the war. The North believed in a powerful central government, and the South did not.

Basil Lanneau Gildersleeve (1831–1924) of Charleston, South Carolina was a Confederate soldier during the War Between the States. He is, today, "still regarded as the greatest American classical scholar of all times."[202] His 1915 book, *The Creed of the Old South*, is so beautifully written, so heartfelt and sincere, that you know immediately — whether you are from the North or the South — that it is the truth and this is what happened. It is actually a reprint of an es-

---

[201] Besides, the U.S. Constitution strongly protected slavery. Slavery was not in danger in the Union, and 94% of Southerners didn't own slaves anyway. Also, the Confederate Constitution allowed free states to join. Slavery was not required. Southerners wanted free states to join for economic reasons and anticipated that many would. This worried Lincoln to death.

[202] Clyde N. Wilson, Abstract, *The Creed of the Old South* by Basil L. Gildersleeve, Society of Independent Southern Historians, http://southernhistorians.org/the-societys-southern-life-recommended-reading/11-southern-literature/11-09-southern-literature-southern-view-of-southern-culture/11-09-04/, accessed 10/11/2014.

say that was published in 1892, only 27 years after the war. He writes:

> A friend of mine, describing the crowd
> that besieged the Gare de Lyon in Paris,
> when the circle of fire was drawing
> round the city, and foreigners were has-
> tening to escape, told me that the press
> was so great that he could touch in every
> direction those who had been crushed to
> death as they stood, and had not had
> room to fall. Not wholly unlike this was
> the pressure brought to bear on the Con-
> federacy. It was only necessary to put
> out your hand and you touched a corpse;
> and that not an alien corpse, but the
> corpse of a brother or a friend.[203]

So much of Southern history today is not truth and is not what really happened. Esteemed historian Eugene D. Genovese had it right:

> Rarely these days, even on southern
> campuses, is it possible to acknowledge
> the achievements of the white people of
> the South. The history of the Old South
> is now often taught at leading univer-
> sities, when it is taught at all, as a pro-
> longed guilt-trip, not to say a prologue to

---

[203] Gildersleeve, *The Creed of the Old South*, 26-27.

the history of Nazi Germany. . . . **To
speak positively about any part of this
southern tradition is to invite charges of
being a racist and an apologist for slavery and segregation. We are witnessing
a cultural and political atrocity** — an
increasingly successful campaign by the
media and an academic elite to strip
young white southerners, and arguably
black southerners as well, of their heritage, and, therefore, their identity. They
are being taught to forget their forebears
or to remember them with shame.[204]
(Emphasis added.)

Nobody who wants a career in history in this day
and age can say anything good about the South. They
can't risk being called a racist. We no longer learn
from much of the historical discussion because so much
is banned or censored, leaving a false record. The "pro-
gressives" who bring up the McCarthy era with hate-
America glee are a thousand times worse with their
political correctness. They represent an Orwellian
anti-intellectual, anti-knowledge movement and it's
cowardly because they want to control the debate
through intimidation, not by producing the best scholarship and ideas.

Much of this liberal political correctness goes back
to today's politics. The PC crowd believes in a giant all-

---

[204] Genovese, *The Southern Tradition*, Preface, xi-xii.

powerful federal government, and that was unquestionably the main issue of the War Between the States. The North wanted a powerful federal government that it would control with its majority for its own wealth and aggrandizement.

The South wanted powerful sovereign states — States' Rights — and a weak federal government, which is what the Founding Fathers intended.

It is no coincidence that the blue states of the big government Democrat Party of today are mostly the old Union states of the North and West, while most of the red states, who take a Reaganesque view of the Federal Government — "Government is not the solution to our problem, government is the problem"[205] — are in the South.

So, this politically correct anti-South view of history benefits the liberal Democrat Party that worships federal power and is enthusiastically embraced by liberals who make up 80 to 90% of academia. It's partly the dirty politics of today and not a truthful examination of history.

Who controls the past controls the future: who controls the present controls the past.[206]

---

[205] President Ronald Reagan, *First Inaugural*, January 20, 1981.

[206] George Orwell, *1984* (New York: New American Library, 1950), 32. This was one of the slogans of Big Brother's English Socialist Party of Oceania, INGSOC.

Big Brother is absolutely correct. That's why the moral-superiority argument, that the good North went to war to end slavery, must be maintained at all costs, though they actually went to war to establish the supremacy of the Federal Government (they were called "Federals" during the war) and destroy the republic of the Founding Fathers. Truth, and the deaths of 800,000 people and wounding of over a million, are a cheap price to pay. The ends justify the means, or so the PC argument goes, and the South must be vilified that much more.

The charge of racism will not only intimidate and keep many from doing meaningful research on the South, but it also casts aspersions on much great writing of the past so that nothing is left except what the PC crowd wants you to believe — and that is always something favorable to the growth of liberal politics and federal power.

As Winston Smith laments in *1984*:

> Every record has been destroyed or falsified, every book has been rewritten, every picture has been repainted, every statue and street and building has been repainted, every statue and street and building has been renamed, every date has been altered. And that process is continuing day by day and minute by minute. History has stopped. Nothing

exists except an endless present in
which the Party is always right.[207]

That's why David H. Donald said there has been
no Southern view among professional historians for
over a half-century. There *is* a powerful Southern view
but it has been subverted in an attempt to erase and
rewrite history as Big Brother demands.

Charleston's William Gilmore Simms, according to
Edgar Allan Poe, was the greatest American writer of
the 19th century yet he is not studied in depth, and in
most places, not at all, because he was a slaveowner.
Simms wrote 82 book-length works including history
and poetry. He was an expert on the American Revolution and wrote a fantastic series of big, thick Revolutionary War novels, mostly set in and around
Charleston, and they cause the Revolution to jump off
the pages. You are suddenly there in Charleston in
1776.

What is lost in Charleston alone by not studying
William Gilmore Simms in depth, is a crime. There is a
bust of Simms at the Battery, high up on a pedestal,
but that's where the study of Simms ends.

The primary reason for the viciousness against the
South is to cover up the enormity of the North's crime
of destroying the republic of the Founding Fathers and
killing 800,000 men and wounding over a million. Historians admit that the Northern victory destroyed the

---

[207] Ibid, 128.

republic of sovereign states of the Founders and centralized power in the Federal Government.

That was not what the Founding Fathers had in
mind in all their wisdom. A nation of sovereign states
with a weak national government is where they saw
true freedom and self-determination. That's what
States' Rights are about and that is why the South
fought. Centralization would give us the tyranny of the
majority as the Founding Fathers warned.

So, rather than giving the South any credit, Big
Brother's PC hordes must rewrite history. The Southern cause must be changed from independence to vile
slavery, and the North's guilt in bringing most of the
slaves here and building the infrastructure of the Old
North on profits from the slave trade should be forgotten.

It is extremely enlightening to read the excellent
book, *Complicity, How the North Promoted, Prolonged,
and Profited from Slavery.* This is an important book,
not only because it is well-researched and fearless, but
because it is written by Northerners, and recently. It
was written by Anne Farrow, Joel Lang, and Jenifer
Frank of *The Hartford Courant* and published in 2005.

This book had come about when *The Hartford
Courant* published a story with headline "Aetna 'Reg-
rets' Insuring Slaves."

This shocked them, to think that a Northern company and Northerners could have had anything to do
with slavery. Slavery was the sin of the South, wasn't
it?

To their credit, they began investigating and found that *The Hartford Courant* itself had run ads support-ing the sale and capture of slaves. They found out that "Connecticut's role in slavery was not only huge, it was a key to the success of the entire institution," then the floodgates opened and as a result, this is what they wrote in the Preface:

> What was true of Connecticut turned out to be overwhelmingly true of the entire North. Most of what you'll read here was gleaned from older, often out-of-print texts, and from period newspapers, largely in Connecticut, New York, and Massachusetts.
>
> We are Journalists, not scholars, and want to share what surprised, and even shocked, the three of us. We have all grown up, attended schools, and worked in Northern states, from Maine to Maryland. We thought we knew our home. We thought we knew our country. We were wrong.[208]

Let me suggest some other topics that would enlighten the country historically. How about a book on the laws in most of the Northern and Western States that forbid black people from living there. Add Northern racism in general.

---

[208] See Preface of Farrow, Lang, Frank, *Complicity,* xvii - xix.

How about a book on the racist nature of Northern anti-slavery, which was mostly economic and political, featuring Northern greed and racism at its worst. Even Ralph Waldo Emerson wrote in his diary: "The abolitionist wishes to abolish slavery, but because he wishes to abolish the black man."[209]

How about a book on the racist nature of Lincoln's "extension of slavery into the West" argument, which was racist to the core. Neither slaves nor free blacks were allowed because the West was to be reserved for white people from all over the world, and Northern in-stitutions. That's why Lincoln and the Republicans did not want slavery in the West, because they did not want blacks in the West. Lincoln wanted to send them back to Africa, which is another huge issue.

How about more books on Lincoln's strong belief that black people should be sent back to Africa or into a place suitable for them. If Lincoln had had his way, there would be no blacks in America. African-Ameri-can scholar, Lerone Bennett, Jr.'s *Forced Into Glory, Abraham Lincoln's White Dream,* is a good start.

How about more books on Republican Party ha-tred and greed, which President James Buchanan said was the main cause of the war.

How about more books examining the North's eco-nomic dependence on the South, on manufacturing for the South and shipping Southern cotton. Add to that

---

[209] Ralph Waldo Emerson, diary entry, in Clyde N. Wilson, "Our History and Their Myth: Comparing the Confederacy and the Union," *Confederate Veteran*, Vol. 72, No. 2, March/April, 2014, 19.

the Northern abuse of the economic system with tariffs, monopolies, bounties, and subsidies from the Federal Treasury that benefited the North at the expense
of the South. Examine the unfair taxation issue in detail. Taxes were supposed to be uniform but Southerners ended up paying most of them while most of the
tax money was spent in the North.

How long do you think Northerners would put up
with paying 3/4ths of the country's taxes while 3/4ths
of the tax money was spent in the South?

The economic system was hugely unfair to the
South, but I understand how Northern businessmen
would be aggressive within the system in pursuit of
profits. I don't fault them for that. I fault historians
today for perpetuating the fraud that Northerners
were more concerned about ending slavery than profits
or free land in the West.

There is no other way to look at the Morrill Tariff
than pure Northern greed. It passed the Northern
Congress in a knee-jerk fashion because Northerners,
without even thinking, figured it would fall on the
South. Southerners would have to pay it. It would be
like more free Southern money for the North.

But the South was out of the Union and no longer
had to pay astronomical Northern tariffs. This one fell
on the North alone and it made entry of goods into the
North 37 to 50% higher than entry into the South. It
instantly rerouted U.S. trade away from the high-tariff
North and into the low-tariff South where protective
tariffs were unconstitutional. This threatened to destroy the Northern shipping industry in one fell swoop.

Northern ship captains began moving South where
they were guaranteed cargoes because of the South's
free trade philosophy and low tariff. This added
greatly to panic in the North and the North's call for
war.

When the Morrill Tariff and destruction of the
North's shipping industry is added to the loss of its
manufacturing market because of secession, it meant
the Northern economy would not recover. The Republican Party of the North pledged against the South was
in serious political trouble. War was Lincoln's only way
out.

In many ways, historical interpretations are like
politics. People in different places see things differ-
ently. Evidence and logic should rule but most of the
time they don't. You pull for your home team no matter what.

That's fine, but good scholarship — truth — demands a vigorous discussion and analysis with all
sides presented accurately. If we don't have that, then
we don't have history. We have propaganda and filthy
politics. That's why they call this modern fraud, "political" correctness, and it is the opposite of truth.

When you get down to it, the only thing that matters is the right of secession. If the South had the right
to secede from the Union, then Southerners are the
heroes of American history and Northerners the vil-
lains who started a bloody fratricidal war for commercial gain.

That is how it was largely viewed in Europe during the war, as Charles Dickens proves, and after.

British Lord Acton (John Dalberg Acton) wrote this to Gen. Robert E. Lee a year-and-a-half after Appomattox:

> . . . I saw in State Rights the only availing check upon the absolutism of the sovereign will, and secession filled me with hope, not as the destruction but as the redemption of Democracy. The institutions of your Republic have not exercised on the old world the salutary and liberating influence which ought to have belonged to them, by reason of those defects and abuses of principle which the Confederate Constitution was expressly and wisely calculated to remedy. I believed that the example of that great Reform would have blessed all the races of mankind by establishing true freedom purged of the native dangers and disorders of Republics. Therefore I deemed that you were fighting the battles of our liberty, our progress, and our civilization; and I mourn for the stake which was lost at Richmond more deeply than I rejoice over that which was saved at Waterloo.[210]

---

[210] John Dalberg-Acton to Gen. Robert E. Lee, November 4, 1866, The Acton-Lee Correspondence, http://archive.lewrockwell.com/orig3/acton-lee.html, accessed November 10, 2014.

Of course the South had the right to secede from the Union. Anybody who believes in the Declaration of Independence has to believe in the right of secession. The Declaration of Independence is the greatest Ordinance of Secession ever written.

The fact that the Constitution did not prohibit secession, and three states — Virginia, New York and Rhode Island — reserved the right of secession before acceding to the U.S. Constitution, proves the right of secession. Virginia, New York and Rhode Island's reserved right of secession was acknowledged and approved by the other states, which means that they had it too because all the states are equal. Horace Greeley certainly believed in the right of secession. The other overwhelming evidence is icing on the cake.

The secession debate in the South in the months before they left the Union, the calling of conventions, the votes, the formation of a new nation on this earth, was, as I said, the greatest expression of democracy and self-government in the history of the world. The Colonists of 1776 were a great expression too but the South in 1860-61 was so much larger and covered a continent-size landmass and represented the exact same argument as 1776, so I would give the South one up.

Or perhaps a tie.

But a tie with the Founding Fathers puts the South in pretty damn good company.

This book proves, beyond the shadow of a doubt, that the North did not go to war to end slavery or free the slaves.

The annihilation of the Northern economy and the rise of the South are what drove all actions of all participants, North and South, in the spring of 1861 when the war started.

Abraham Lincoln started the war the North demanded, as the *Providence Daily Post* asserted, "because Abraham Lincoln loves a party better than he loves his country," and 800,000 men had to die, and over a million had to be maimed.

Southerners are patriotic Americans and our ancestors accepted the verdict of the battlefield, though it was not a just verdict. We fought well and were proud of ourselves for standing with George Washington, Thomas Jefferson, Patrick Henry and all the others who believed in States' Rights.

There was an ad that ran often in the back of the original *Confederate Veteran* magazine of 1893 to 1932 and it said, "One Country, . . . One Flag."

We, in the South, are enormously proud of that country and flag, but the truth of our glorious Southern history is going to be told.

Additional Resources for the Study of Southern History and Literature

America was founded in the South, in Virginia. The Founding Fathers from the South include Thomas Jefferson, Author of the Declaration of Independence, James Madison, Father of the Constitution and Author of the Bill of Rights, and George Washington, Father of His Country. Nobody can even begin to understand American history without a thorough understanding of Southern history.

Southerners so thoroughly dominated the Federal Government right up to war time, it was a major source of jealousy and hatred in the North. A Southerner was president "forty-nine out of seventy-two years, or better than two-thirds of the time." Despite its smaller population, "twenty-four of the thirty-six speakers of the House and twenty-five of the thirty-six presidents pro tem of the Senate" were Southerners as well as "twenty of thirty-five Supreme Court Justices." The South had had a majority on the Supreme Court the entire time of the country's existence.[211]

Despite impediments put up by politically correct cowards who won't say anything good about the South because they are afraid of being called a racist, there is

---

[211] Jeffrey Rogers Hummel, *Emancipating Slaves, Enslaving Free Men, A History of the American Civil War* (Chicago: Open Court, 1996), 131.

much good exciting history out there that is easily accessible. Much of it was written in the past and served
as college texts or well-respected general histories before Orwellian political correctness began erasing
truthful history.

There are also several outstanding organizations
of scholars who study, speak, write and publish on
Southern historical and literary topics. I want to mention two: The Abbeville Institute,[212] and The Society of
Independent Southern Historians.[213] Both organizations include many who have had long careers as professors and who have written many books, essays, articles and reviews.

Dr. Don Livingston, Professor Emeritus of Philosophy at Emory University in Atlanta, founded the Abbeville Institute in 2003. He is a David Hume scholar
and author.

The Principles of the Abbeville Institute are on
their website and include:

> The mission of the Abbeville Institute is
> to preserve and present what is true and
> valuable in the Southern tradition. The
> fellowship has grown to over 170 schol-
> ars and associates. Among other activi-
> ties, the Institute has conducted annual
> summer schools for college and graduate

---

[212] The Abbeville Institute website is
www.abbevilleinstitute.org.
[213] The Society of Independent Southern Historians website is
www.SouthernHistorians.org.

students, conferences for academics, and educational programs for the public.[214]

Some of the Institute's most accomplished faculty include Thomas Woods, Thomas DiLorenzo, and Clyde Wilson.

Thomas E. "Tom" Woods, Jr. is a New York Times best-selling author of *The Politically Incorrect Guide to American History* and ten other books.

DiLorenzo, a professor of economics at Loyola University in Maryland, has written several books including two on Abraham Lincoln: *The Real Lincoln: A New Look at Abraham Lincoln, His Agenda, and an Unnecessary War*; and *Lincoln Unmasked: What You're Not Supposed to Know About Dishonest Abe.*

Clyde N. Wilson is Emeritus Distinguished Professor of History at the University of South Carolina and edited most of *The Papers of John C. Calhoun.* Dr. Wilson has written and edited many books in his long career including *Carolina Cavalier: The Life and Mind of James Johnston Pettigrew*; *From Union to Empire: Essays in the Jeffersonian Tradition*; and *Defending Dixie: Essays in Southern History and Culture.*

Dr. Wilson is also the founder of the Society of Independent Southern Historians along with historian Howard Ray White. The Society has created a massive bibliographical framework for Southern historical and

---

[214] Principles, The Abbeville Institute, http://www.abbevilleinstitute.org/principles/, accessed October 13, 2014.

literary works so that they can identify and categorize every good work of Southern history and literature out there. The website already lists hundreds, perhaps thousands, of books, movies, videos, articles, essays, and by the time it is filled out, it will contain hundreds of thousands, and that is the goal: to create a massive, easily accessible and searchable bibliography of the best works ever produced on the South along with brief information on each one.

Here's how I found *The Creed of the Old South*, which I have wanted to read forever. On the website of The Society of Independent Southern Historians, I clicked on Item 11:

11 The Society's Recommended Reading for
Southern Literature up to 1940

I got the following list:

11.00 Encyclopedia and Works That Cover
a Long Span of Time

11.01 Literature Set in the Colonial Era,
Perhaps Longer (4)

11.02 Literature Set in the Revolutionary
Era (3)

11.03 Literature Set Prior to the War Between the States (3)

11.04 Literature Set During the War Between the States (4)

11.05 Literature Set During Political Reconstruction (4)

11.06 Literature Set From 1877 to 1913 (4)

11.07 Literature Set From 1914 to 1940 (4)

11.08 Poetry (8)

11.09 Southern View of Southern Culture (3)

11.10 Southern View of Northern Culture
(3)

11.11 Southern Books for Youth and Children

11.12 Essays Discussing Important Writers
and Their Works

I then clicked on 11.09, out of curiosity:

11.09 SOUTHERN LITERATURE, Southern
View of Southern Culture

I got the following list:

11.09.01 : Brooks, Cleanth, *The Language of
the American South*, published in 1985.
[Click on Number to Read Review.]

11.09.02 : Wilson, Clyde N., editor, *Chronicles of the South*, Volume 1: *Garden of the
Beaux Arts,* Volume 2: *In Justice to so Fine*

a *Country*, published in 2011. [Click on
Number to Read Review]

11.09.03 : Haley, Alex, *Roots, The Saga of
an American Family*, [To Understand why
Roots is among the Society's Listings, please
Read the Review. To Read, Just Click on
the Number]

11.09.04 : Gildersleeve, Basil Lanneau, *The
Creed of the Old South, 1865-1915*, pub-
lished in 1915. [Click on Number to Read
Review]

11.09.05 : Garrett, George P., Two Books of
Essays: *The Sorrows of Fat City: A Selection
of Literary Essays and Reviews* (written
1957-1990), and *Going to See the Elephant:
Pieces of a Writing Life*, published in 1992
and 2002, respectively. [Click on Number to
Read Review]

11.09.06 : Tindall, George B., *Pursuit of
Southern History: Presidential Addresses of
the Southern Historical Association, 1935-
1963*, published in 1964. [Click on number
to read review]

11.09.07 : Allen, Ward S., *What Makes
Southern Manners Peculiar*, a pamphlet re-
published in 2012. [Click on number to read
review]

11.09.08 : Landess, Thomas H., *Life, Literature, and Lincoln: A Tom Landess Reader*,
edited by Clyde N. Wilson and Mary Beth

Landess, published in 2014. [Click on number to read review]

11.09.09 : Babcock, Havilah, *My Health is
Better in November*, published in 1947
[Click on number to read review]

11.09.10 : Elliott, William, *Carolina Sports
by Land and Water*, published in 1846 [Click
on number to read review]

I then clicked on:

11.09.04 Gildersleeve, Basil Lanneau, *The
Creed of the Old South, 1865-1915*, published in 1915. Notes Concerning the Author

And got this:

Basil Lanneau Gildersleeve (1831–1924), is
today still regarded as the greatest American classical scholar of all times. He was
born in Charleston, South Carolina, graduated from Princeton in 1849, and after several years of study in Germany received a
doctorate from Geotingen University in
1853. He was a professor at the University
of Virginia, 1856–1876, and then at Johns
Hopkins. Gildersleeve's contributions to the
study of Greek and Latin gave him international status. He founded what is still a
leading journal in the field, the AMERICAN
JOURNAL OF PHILOLOGY. He produced
textbooks, translations, definitive texts of
various classical works, and many articles.

He was also the author of many popular essays for general readers.

Abstract

In *The Creed of the Old South* Gildersleeve
recalls his youth as a Confederate soldier
(wounded in action) and explains to later
generations the spirit and thinking that mo-
tivated Southerners in their War of Independence. The book also contains a compan-
ion essay, "A Southerner in the Peloponne-
sian War."

Availability of this Book

You will have no problem getting this book
as a used or new print book or as a Kindle e-
book. The Kindle book is presently free.

CNW

The Abbeville Institute, in addition to their ongo-
ing classes, lectures and activities, is doing something
similar. This is their main list of topics:

GENERAL WORKS

SECTIONAL CONFLICT AND THE WAR FOR
SOUTHERN INDEPENDENCE

STATES RIGHTS AND THE ORIGINAL CON-
STITUTION

RECONSTRUCTION

THE COLONIAL SOUTH AND THE EARLY
FEDERAL PERIOD

PLANTATIONS AND PLAIN FOLK

BIOGRAPHIES

SOUTHERN LITERATURE

POLITICAL AND SOCIAL COMMENTARY

SOUTHERN CULTURE

THE NEW SOUTH

I clicked on GENERAL WORKS and got this:

1. Francis Butler Simkins,
A History of the South

An essential one-volume history of
the Southern people.

2. James Ronald Kennedy and Walter Donald Kennedy, *The South Was Right!*

The most popular history of the
South in the modern era. Hard hit-
ting, fast paced, and politically incorrect, every Southerner should
have a copy.

3. John Shelton Reed, *The Enduring South:
Subcultural Persistence in Mass Society*

A scholarly explanation of the cultural distinctiveness of the American South.

4. M.E. Bradford, *Remembering Who We
Are: Observations of a Southern Conserva-
tive*

A series of essays by the great
Southern scholar on the founding
and origins of Southern conservatism.

5. Clyde N. Wilson, ed., *A Defender of
Southern Conservatism: M.E. Bradford and
His Achievements*

Ten essays in honor of Bradford
and his contribution to Southern
intellectual history.

6. Richard M. Weaver, *The Southern Essays
of Richard M. Weaver*

A rich collection of material from
one of the most important Southern scholars of the twentieth century.

7. Richard M. Weaver, *The Southern Tradition at Bay: A History of Postbellum
Thought*

> Equally as important as the pre-
> vious work, this was Weaver's first
> full defense of the South as the in-
> tellectual center of American con-
> servative thought.

8. Basil L. Gildersleeve, *The Creed of the
Old South 1865-1915:* Civil War Classic Library

> The author was the greatest
> American classical scholar and a
> Confederate soldier who explained
> things to fair-minded Northerners
> after Reconstruction.

I clicked on the next section, SECTIONAL CON-
FLICT AND THE WAR FOR SOUTHERN INDEPEND-
ENCE, and got these outstanding titles. I have seen
Clyde Wilson also highly recommend *North Against
South* by Ludwell Johnson.

1. Ludwell Johnson, *North Against South:
The American Iliad, 1848-1877*

> The best one volume study of the
> late antebellum period, the War,
> and Reconstruction from a South-
> ern perspective. It could be used as
> a textbook on mid-nineteenth cen-
> tury American history.

2. Marshall DeRosa, *The Confederate Constitution of 1861: An Inquiry into American
Constitutionalism*

> The only study of its kind on the
> Confederate Constitution of 1861.

3. E. Merton Coulter, *Confederate States of
America (History of the South)*

> The definitive one volume study of
> the Confederacy by one of the best
> Southern historians of the twen-
> tieth century.

4. Robert Selph Henry, *The Story of the
Confederacy*

> A riveting one volume narrative of
> the War and the Southern struggle
> for independence.

5. Shelby Foote, *Civil War Volumes 1-3* Box
Set

> A multi-volume masterpiece. Foote
> implored historians to learn to
> write, and according to first-hand
> accounts, loved to sing "I'm a Good
> Ol' Rebel."

6. Walter Brian Cisco, *War Crimes Against Southern Civilians*

The only sweeping history of the crimes committed against South-ern civilians during the War.

7. Charles Adams, *When in the Course of Human Events: Arguing the Case for South-ern Secession*

A stunning post-revisionist (or un-Reconstructed) history of the War. Tariffs and economics take center stage.

8. Gary Gallagher, *The Confederate War*

Gallagher skillfully shows that the men and women who defended the South did so gallantly and that Southern nationalism was not cre-ated by a simple defense of slavery.

9. James McPherson, *For Cause and Com-rades: Why Men Fought in the Civil War*

McPherson uncharacteristically explains why Southern (and North-ern) soldiers fought in the War, and it wasn't slavery for most.

10. Thomas DiLorenzo, *The Real Lincoln: A New Look at Abraham Lincoln, His Agenda, and an Unnecessary War*

AND

11. Thomas DiLorenzo, *Lincoln Unmasked:
What You're Not Supposed to Know About
Dishonest Abe*

> Definitive revelations about the
> real as opposed to the mythical
> Lincoln.

12. Edgar Lee Masters, *Lincoln the Man*

> A major American poet who was
> born, raised, and lived in Lincoln's
> home country in Illinois gives a
> unique view of the American icon's
> life and legacy.

13. Avery O. Craven, *The Coming of the
Civil War*

> A classic balanced account of the
> causes of the great War Between
> the States.

14. Michael Holt, *The Political Crisis of the
1850s*

> Holt places the issues of the 1850s
> within the context of power poli-
> tics. Controlling the Congress took
> center stage, particularly for the
> North.

15. Marshall DeRosa, ed., *The Politics of Dissolution: The Quest for A National Identity and the American Civil War*

> Southerners of 1861 explain their reasons for independence from the North.

16. Susan-Mary Grant, *North Over South: Northern Nationalism and American Identity in the Antebellum Era*

> A new look of the source of the aggressions that led to the War Between the States.

17. Herman Belz, ed., *The Webster-Hayne Debate on the Nature of the Union: Selected Documents*

> Actual documents from the period give a different view of Webster's alleged triumphal claim of federal supremacy.

18. D. Jonathan White, ed., *Northern Opposition to Mr. Lincoln's War*

> Nine essays on Lincoln's Northern opponents during the War Between the States.

19. Raimondo Luraghi, *A History of the Confederate Navy*

A leading European historian of
the American war of 1861—1865
chronicles the heroic exploits and
the scientific and technical achieve‑
ments of Southern navy men.

20. Richard Bensel, *Yankee Leviathan: The
Origins of Central State Authority in Amer‑
ica, 1859‑1877*

Bensel shows how the North used
the War to solidify the Hamilto‑
nian economic system and force it
on a reluctant America.

21. Douglas Southall Freeman, *Lee's Lieu‑
tenants: A Study in Command,* 3 Volumes

An unmatched study on leadership
and command by the master
Southern historian.

22. Bart Rhett Talbert, *Maryland: The
South's First Casualty*

The only history of Maryland that
correctly explains the State's real
sympathies before the War.

23. Sara Agnes Rice Pryor, *Reminiscences of
Peace and War*

24. Raphael Semmes, *Memoirs of Service Afloat, During the War Between the States*

25. Richard Taylor, *Destruction and Reconstruction*

Confederate Memoirs by literate
and thoughtful participants in the
War for Southern Independence,
more representative and authentic
than the novelized Mary Chestnut
"diary" so often used by historians.

26. Howard Ray White, *Bloodstains, An Epic History of the Politics that Produced and Sustained the American Civil War and the Political Reconstruction that Followed*, Set of 4 Volumes

This very original 4-volume study
of the War For Southern Independence, its causes and aftermath,
contains much generally unfamil-
iar information and insight.

27. Edmund Wilson, *Patriotic Gore: Studies in the Literature of the American Civil War*

A classic and controversial study of
writings by both sides in the War
of Southern Independence, by a
major American critic.

Visit the websites of the Abbeville Institute and
The Society of Independent Southern Historians. Join

both of these excellent organizations and support them. Go through their entire lists and become familiar with the resources available.

One of the best things to do when studying the South is go straight to primary sources: the newspapers, letters, diaries, documents, photographs, drawings, government records, the official records of the war and other things written and produced by the people of the past.

One problem with today's often erroneous scholarship is the application of today's standards to the past. You can not understand the past and the people of the past by applying today's standards, or lack thereof. You have to look at the past the way the people of the past looked at it. That's how you truly understand the past.

One outstanding primary source of American and Southern history, the war, and the years after the war, is the original *Confederate Veteran* magazine founded by S. A. Cunningham. It was published from 1893 to 1932 by which time the old Confederate veterans were dying out and there wasn't enough circulation to continue the magazine. Broadfoot Publishing Company of Wilmington, North Carolina[215] is the main publisher of the complete collection of original *Confederate Veteran* magazines in their original size and in a hardback, handsomely bound, 43 volume set. Broodfoot's offers numerous other complete sets, all with indices, as well

---

[215] Broadfoot Publishing Company's website is www.BroadfootPublishing.com, accessed October 19, 2014.

as scores of individual titles, many of which are rare or out of print.

The original *Confederate Veteran* magazine had a large circulation and drew contributions from Confederate veterans all over the country. There is fundraising for Confederate monuments all over the South, notices of deaths, notices of upcoming United Confederate Veteran reunions and events, and advertising, which is a history lesson in itself — but the great thing about this magazine is that every imaginable topic related to the War Between the States is discussed by average soldiers who were in the middle of the hottest battles of the war, or on ships, even in the CSS Hunley, the first submarine in history to sink an enemy ship in combat. There are articles by officers, political leaders, and women as well. There are drawings, photographs, plenty of flags, lots of beautiful poetry. One can see clearly the spirit and personalities of Confederate soldiers and Southerners in general including women and children as they honored their dead and rebuilt the South from America's bloodiest war. You will find no better first-hand accounts of battles of the War Between the States by people who were in them.

If you want to understand Southern history and the war, read *Confederate Veteran* and it will be as if you are sitting in a circle talking face to face with Southerners from that period, most of whom were in the war, many of whom were wounded, all of whom lost friends and family. It was heartwarming for me and made me even more proud to be a Southerner and descendent of numerous Confederate soldiers.

Definitely visit Broadfoot Publishing Company's website at www.BroadfootPublishing.com and view all the lengthy sets of major primary sources that are available to you. Tom Broadfoot has made a *mighty* contribution to American history and especially Southern history. And all the sets are beautiful. They are perfectly made, heavy hardback sets that are exciting to the eyes and touch.[216]

Here are some of Broadfoot's Reference Sets. They are the sole supplier of most of these.

---

[216] Here's what Broadfoot's has to say on the "About Us" page of their website:

> Broadfoot's has been in the Civil War book business for over 40 years. We are a sole-source publishing company that specializes in multivolume reference sets suitable for libraries and genealogical research facilities, but we also publish individual books on various aspects and theaters of the war. Indexing is also our specialty, and our books provide thorough, cross-referenced indices, which typically include unusual or hard-to-find subjective detail.
>
> Our main office is located in Wilmington, N.C. We also have a retail outlet in Wendell, N.C. (15 miles east of Raleigh). This is a 7,000-square-foot facility with a large stock of Civil War material, new and old, and discounted books and sets; there you will also find the best selection of new North Carolina books available anywhere.
>
> Browse through our listings and please visit our web site often. Whether your interest is genealogy or Civil War, new books, or old books, you will find Broadfoot's publications are of the highest standards.

The South Carolina Regimental-Roster Set

WAR OF THE REBELLION. OFFICIAL RE-
CORDS OF THE UNION AND CONFEDERATE
ARMIES — 128 Vols. Individual Volumes
Available. Army Official Records.

OFFICIAL RECORDS OF THE UNION AND
CONFEDERATE NAVIES IN THE WAR OF
THE REBELLION — 31 Vols. Government
Document. Navy Official Records.

COLONIAL & STATE RECORDS OF NORTH
CAROLINA — 30 Vols. in 28 books. NC Colonial Records.

CONFEDERATE CENTENNIAL STUDIES —
28 Vols. Individual Volumes Available.

CONFEDERATE MILITARY HISTORY. EX-
TENDED EDITION — 19 Vols. Individual
Volumes. Confederate Military History.

CONFEDERATE STATE ROSTER — 27 Vols.
Individual States Available. Goverment
Document.

CONFEDERATE VETERAN — 43 Vols. Confederate Veteran.

HISTORIES OF THE SEVERAL REGIMENTS &
BATTALIONS FROM NORTH CAROLINA IN
THE GREAT WAR 1861-'65 — 5 Vols. Individual Volumes Available. Histories of the Several Regiments-NC.

MEDICAL AND SURGICAL HISTORY OF THE
CIVIL WAR — 15 Vols. Now Indexed!!! Gov-
ernment Document. Medical and Surgical
History of the Civil War.

NORTH CAROLINA TROOPS

1861-1865: A Roster — Volumes 1-18.
These volumes are the best rosters of Civil
War soldiers published by any state at any
time.

REPORT OF THE JOINT COMMITTEE ON
THE CONDUCT OF WAR — 9 Vols. Goverment Document. Conduct of the War.

ROSTER OF CONFEDERATE SOLDIERS 1861-
1865 — 16 Vols. Goverment Document. Roster of Confederate Soldiers 1861-1865.

ROSTER OF CONFEDERATE AND UNION
SOLDIERS 1861-1865 — Combo. Best Buy

BIOGRAPHICAL ROSTERS OF FLORIDA'S
CONFEDERATE & UNION SOLDIERS 1861-65
— 6 Vols.

SHOOTING AND FISHING, 1885-1906 — 45
vols. in 42 books, includes 3 vol. index.

THE SOUTH CAROLINA REGIMENTAL-ROS-
TER SET — 10 Vols. of projected 50 volume
set.

SOUTHERN BIVOUAC — 6 Vols. Southern
Bivouac.

SOUTHERN HISTORICAL SOCIETY
PAPERS — 55 Vols. Southern Historical Society Papers.

SUPPLEMENT TO THE OFFICIAL RECORDS
OF THE UNION AND CONFEDERATE ARMIES
— 100 Vols. Reviews. Goverment Document.
The Supplement to the Official Records.

I studied the secession debate in the South that
began in earnest around a year before South Carolina
seceded. South Carolina seceded on December 20, 1860
and immediately sent commissioners to other Southern States to encourage them to secede. Several states
called conventions and six seceded and sent more commissioners out.

Study the secession debate in the South and the
secession conventions. MUCH American history is included because Southerners based all their secession
arguments on the country's founding and the beliefs of
the Founding Fathers, especially the Declaration of
Independence: that governments derive their just powers from the consent of the governed. The secession
debate gives one a crystal clear view of why Southerners seceded, and the reason they seceded was independence and self-government.

The bibliography of this book includes many important speeches and documents from the secession
debate and they are all first-rate primary sources for
understanding the position of the South and the important issues in play.

Here are a few more books that are excellent. They
are by no means a comprehensive list.

As previously mentioned, the 2005 book, *Complicity, How the North Promoted, Prolonged, and Profited
from Slavery*, by *Hartford Courant* journalists Anne
Farrow, Joel Lang and Jenifer Frank. This is an outstanding book and it is even more outstanding because
it is recent and written by Northerners. This is from
the inside front cover:

> Slavery in the South has been docu-
> mented in volumes ranging form exhaus-
> tive histories to bestselling novels. But
> the North's profit from—indeed, depend-
> ence on—slavery has mostly been a
> shameful and well-kept secret . . . until
> now. In this startling and superbly re-
> searched new book, three veteran New
> England journalists demythologize the
> region of American known for tolerance
> and liberation, revealing a place where
> thousands of people were held in bond-
> age and slavery was both an economic
> dynamo and a necessary way of life.[217]

As stated many times, read anything by the great
Southern writer, William Gilmore Simms. Edgar Allan
Poe said Simms was the greatest American novelist of
the 19th century. There is a monument to him in

---

[217] Farrow, Lang, and Frank, *Complicity,* inside front cover.

White Point Gardens at the Battery in Charleston: a
bust of Simms in a Byronic pose high up on a pedestal.
Simms is buried at Magnolia Cemetery in Charleston.
He wrote 82 book length works including much poetry.
Twenty of his books are extremely important in Ameri-
can history and literature according to his biographer,
John Caldwell Guilds, who wrote *Simms, A Literary
Life*. Dr. Guilds also edited a superb collection of es-
says entitled *Long Years of Neglect, The Work and
Reputation of William Gilmore Simms*. Dr. James
Everett Kibler, Jr., edited *Selected Poems of William
Gilmore Simms*. A lot of other scholars have written on
Simms as well. There is also a William Gilmore Simms
Society.[218]

Simms wrote a series of Revolutionary War novels
mostly set in the Lowcountry around Charleston because he was an expert on the American Revolution.
They are brilliant and give a clear picture of life in
Charleston during the Revolutionary War. This is how
to really understand history, as if you are watching it
before your very eyes.

Simms was in Columbia, South Carolina when
Sherman burned it, and he wrote about it. He also
wrote several frontier novels when the frontier was
Alabama.

Simm's house and library of thousands of books,
his manuscripts, much correspondence with his Northern publishers — a virtual history of the American

---

[218] The William Gilmore Simms Society website is:
http://www.westga.edu/~simms/.

publishing industry of the 19th century — was lost
when the barbaric Union Army burned his house and
library to the ground.

Emma Holmes Diary is a magnificent account of
life in Charleston and South Carolina just before and
during the war by a fiery patriotic young Charleston
woman who witnessed the bombardment of Fort Sumter, sewed battle flags with her own hands along with
the ladies of Charleston, and wrote almost every day
from February 1861 until 1866. It is best to get the
original typed manuscript from the South Caroliniana
Library at the University of South Carolina in Columbia rather than the LSU publication that is cut 25%
and edited heavily.

Definitely buy and read African-American scholar,
Lerone Bennett, Jr.'s book, *Forced Into Glory, Abraham Lincoln's White Dream.* It is 656 pages of energy
and outrage over Abraham Lincoln's false status as the
great emancipator.

Black Bondage in the North by Edgar J. McManus
(New York: Syracuse University Press, 1973) is excel-
lent as is the good Foner, Philip S. Foner, and his book
*Business & Slavery, The New York Merchants & the
Irrepressible Conflict* (Chapel Hill: The University of
North Carolina Press, 1941).

The Coming of the Glory by John Shipley Tilley is
superb on slavery, secession and Reconstruction. Tilley
also wrote *Lincoln Takes Command* and proves, as
Ramsdell does, that Lincoln deliberately started the
war by manipulating events in Charleston Harbor. We
now know why, because the North's economy would

have been annihilated without a war and the North
would likely have ended up in anarchy. *The Coming of
the Glory* was published in 1995 by Bill Coats, Ltd.,
1406 Grandview, Nashville, TN 37215-3030, who also
published *Lincoln Takes Command* in 1991.

Black Confederates compiled and edited by
Charles Kelly Barrow, J. H. Segars, and R. B. Rosen-
burg, published by Pelican Publishing Company,
Gretna, Louisiana, 2004, is outstanding.

*Mixed Up with All the Rebel Horde: Why Black
Southerners Fought for the South in the War Between
the States* is an excellent two-DVD set featuring Professor Edward C. Smith of American University who is
one of the foremost scholars in the country on black
participation in all American wars, and why. He explains well that black people considered America home
and were willing to fight because they were a part of
Southern communities despite slavery. This DVD is
produced by me and published by Charleston Athenaeum Press and Bonnie Blue Publishing. It is available on www.BonnieBluePublishing.com.

*The Secession Movement in the Middle Atlantic
States* by William C. Wright is eye-opening and extremely valuable. It was published by Fairleigh Dickinson University Press in 1973 and lists Rutherford as
the place of publication.

*Northern Editorials on Secession, Volumes 1 and
2*, edited by Howard Cecil Perkins, is an outstanding
two-volume hardback set published originally in 1942
by the American Historical Association. It was reprinted in 1964 by Peter Smith, Gloucester, Massachu-

setts. It is over 1,100 pages of newspaper editorials, organized and indexed. This is a great set to have in your library.

There are numerous excellent historical organizations that one can join and should. Join a Sons of Confederate Veterans camp, a chapter of the United Daughters of the Confederacy and/or the Order of Confederate Rose. Join a reenactment unit. All of these organizations promote a serious and enjoyable study of Southern history and literature and camaraderie with those who love the South. Most publish newsletters and hold conventions and there are many scholars and knowledgeable people participating. All can be found on the Internet and Facebook these days.

Good luck!

Bibliography

Professor Ramsdell's sources from "Lincoln and Fort Sumter" are not included in this bibliography.

Primary Sources

Address of the People of South Carolina, Assembled in Convention, to the People of the Slaveholding States of the United States. Adopted 24 December 1860 by the South Carolina Secession Convention, Charleston, S.C. In John Amasa May and Joan Reynolds Faunt, *South Carolina Secedes.* Columbia: University of South Carolina Press, 1960.

Address to the People of Texas. 30 March 1861. In *The War of the Rebellion: A Compilation of the Official Records of the Union and Confederate Armies.* Washington: Government Printing Office, 1900. Reprint, Historical Times, Inc., 1985, Series IV, Volume 1.

Acton, Lord. Sir John Dalberg-Acton. Letter to Gen. Robert E. Lee, November 4, 1866. The Acton-Lee Correspondence. http://archive.lewrockwell.com/orig3/acton-lee.html. Accessed November 10, 2014.

Allen, John J. *The Botetourt Resolutions of Judge John J. Allen.* Botetourt County, Virginia 10 December 1860. In *Southern Historical Society Papers.* Reprint, Broadfoot Publishing Company, Morningside Bookshop, 1990, Volume 1, January-June, 1876.

Benjamin, Judah P. *Farewell Address to the U. S. Senate.* Delivered 5 February 1861. In Edwin Anderson Alderman and Joel Chandler Harris, eds., *Library of Southern Literature.* Atlanta: The Martin and Hoyt Company, 1907.

Benning, Henry L. "Henry L. Benning's Secessionist Speech, Monday Evening, November 19." In William W. Freehling and Craig M. Simpson, *Secession Debated, Georgia's Showdown in 1860.* New York: Oxford University Press, 1992.

Bledsoe, Albert Taylor. *Is Davis a Traitor; or Was Secession a Constitutional Right Previous to the War of 1861?.* Baltimore: Innes & Company, 1866. Reprint, North Charleston: Fletcher and Fletcher Publishing, 1995.

Boston Transcript, The, Editorial. 18 March 1861. In Charles Adams, *When in the Course of Human Events, Arguing the Case for Southern Secession.* Lanham: Rowman & Littlefield Publishers, Inc., 2000, 65.

Brown, Joseph E. "Special Message of Governor Joseph
E. Brown on Federal Relations, delivered to the
Georgia Senate and House of Representatives in
Milledgeville, Georgia, on November 7, 1860." In
Allen D. Chandler, *The Confederate Records of the
State of Georgia.* Volume I. Atlanta: Charles P.
Byrd, State Printer, 1909.

Buchanan, James. "Republican Fanatacism as a Cause
of the Civil War." In Edwin C. Rozwenc, ed., *The
Causes of the American Civil War.* Boston: D. C.
Heath and Company, 1961.

Calhoun, John C. "A Discourse on the Constitution." In
Richard Cralle, ed., *The Works of John C. Calhoun.*
New York: D. Appleton and Company, 1851-1856,
Volume 1.

————. "Letter to John McLean, August 4, 1828." In
Meriwether et al., eds., *The Papers of John C. Calhoun,* Vol. X, 407.

Campbell, John A. "Memoranda Relative to the Seces-
sion Movement in 1860-61." In "The Papers of Hon.
John A. Campbell—1861-1865." *Southern Historical
Society Papers.* New Series—Number IV, Volume
XLII, September, 1917. Richmond: James Power
Smith, Secretary. Reprint, Broadfoot Publishing
Company and Morningside Bookshop, 1991.

Chicago Times, The. "Value of the Union." December
10, 1860. In Howard Cecil Perkins, ed., *Northern
Editorials on Secession.* Gloucester: Peter Smith,
1964, Volume II.

Clopton, David. "Letter of Commissioner David Clopton of Alabama to Delaware Governor William Burton." In *The War of the Rebellion: A Compilation of
the Official Records of the Union and Confederate
Armies.* Washington: Government Printing Office,
1900. Reprint, Historical Times, Inc., 1985, Series
IV, Volume 1.

Cobb, Thomas R. R. "Thomas R. R. Cobb's Secessionist
Speech, Monday Evening, November 12." In Wil-
liam W. Freehling and Craig M. Simpson, *Secession
Debated, Georgia's Showdown in 1860.* New York:
Oxford University Press, 1992.

Cobb, Williamson R. W. *Personal Explanation of the
Hon. W. R. W. Cobb, of Alabama.* Delivered in the
United States House of Representatives, January 7,
1861. Washington: W. H. Moore, 1861.

————. *Withdrawal of the Hon. Williamson R. W. Cobb
of Alabama.* 30 January 1861. United States House
of Representatives. Washington: W. H. Moore, 1861.

Confederate Veteran. Founder, S. A. Cunningham.
1893 to 1932. Reprint: Broadfoot Publishing Company, Wilmington, North Carolina, 1987, 1988,
43 vols.

Cornhill Magazine. "The Dissolution of the Union." 4,
July-October 1861, 153. Quoted in Charles Adams,
*When in the Course of Human Events, Arguing the
Case for Southern Secession.* Lanham: Rowman &
Littlefield Publishers, Inc., 2000, 72.

Corwin Amendment. Introduced in U.S. House of Representative by Thomas Corwin. Introduced in U.S. Senate by William H. Seward. Passed United States Congress March 2, 1861. http://en.wikipedia.org/wiki/Corwin_Amendment. Accessed March 26, 2014.

Davis, Jefferson. "Farewell Address to the United States Senate." 21 January 1861. In Lynda Lasswell Crist, ed., *The Papers of Jefferson Davis.* Baton Rouge: Louisiana State University Press, 1992, Volume 7.

————. "Inaugural Address." Provisional President of the Confederate States of America. 18 February 1861. Montgomery, Alabama. In Lynda Lasswell Crist, ed., *The Papers of Jefferson Davis.* Baton Rouge: Louisiana State University Press, 1992, Volume 7.

————. *The Rise and Fall of the Confederate Government.* New York: D. Appleton and Company, 1912.

Davis, Jefferson, Papers of, The. Lynda Lasswell Crist. ed. Baton Rouge: Louisiana State University Press, 1992, Volume 7.

Declaration of Causes which Impel the State of Texas to Secede from the Federal Union. Adopted 2 February 1861 by the Texas Secession Convention, Austin, Texas. In E. W. Winkler, ed., *Journal of the Secession Convention of Texas*, Austin: 1912.

*Declaration of the Immediate Causes Which Induce
and Justify the Secession of South Carolina from
the Federal Union.* Adopted 24 December 1860 by
the South Carolina Secession Convention, Charleston, S.C. In John Amasa May and Joan Reynolds
Faunt, *South Carolina Secedes.* Columbia: University of South Carolina Press, 1960.

*Declaration of the Immediate Causes Which Induce
and Justify the Secession of the State of Mississippi
from the Federal Union.* Adopted 26 January 1861
by the Mississippi Secession Convention. In *Journal
of the State Convention.* Jackson: E. Barksdale,
State Printer, 1861.

Declaration of Independence. In Henry Steele Commager, ed., *Documents of American History.* Sixth ed.
New York: Appleton-Century-Crofts, Inc., 1958.

*Democratic Speaker's Hand-Book: Containing every
thing necessary for the defense of the national democracy in the coming presidential campaign, and
for the assault of the radical enemies of the country
and its constitution.* Compiled by Matthew Carey,
Jr. Cincinnati: Miami Printing and Publishing Company, 1868.

Dickens, Charles. "American Disunion." In Charles Adams, *When in the Course of Human Events, Arguing the Case for Southern Secession.* Lanham: Rowman & Littlefield Publishers, Inc., 2000, 90-91.

———. "Letter to W. W. De Cerjat." 16 March 1862. In Graham Storey, ed., *The Letters of Charles Dickens*. Oxford: Clarendon Press, 1998, Volume Ten, 1862-1864.

———. "The Morrill Tariff." *All the Year Round*, 28 December 1861, 328-330. In Charles Adams, *When in the Course of Human Events, Arguing the Case for Southern Secession*. Lanham: Rowman & Littlefield Publishers, Inc., 2000, 90-91.

Emerson, Ralph Waldo. Diary entry. In Clyde N. Wilson, "Our History and Their Myth: Comparing the Confederacy and the Union." *Confederate Veteran*, Vol. 72, No. 2, March/April, 2014, 19.

Gildersleeve, Basil L. *The Creed of the Old South*. Baltimore: The Johns Hopkins Press, 1915. Reprint: BiblioLife, Penrose Library, University of Denver (no date given).

Greeley, Horace. *The American Conflict*. Hartford: O. D. Case and Company, 1865, Volume 1.

Hale, S. F. "Letter of Commissioner S. F. Hale of Alabama to Kentucky Governor B. Magoffin, 27 December 1860." In *The War of the Rebellion: A Compilation of the Official Records of the Union and Confederate Armies*. Washington: Government Printing Office, 1900. Reprint, Historical Times, Inc., 1985, Series IV, Volume 1.

Helper, Hinton Rowan. *The Impending Crisis of the South: How to Meet It*. Reprint, New York: Collier Books, 1963.

*History and Debates of the Convention of The People
of Alabama, The.* William R. Smith, Delegate, ed.
Montgomery: White, Pfister & Co., 1861. Reprint,
Spartanburg: The Reprint Company, Publishers,
1975.

Holmes, Emma. *Private Journal, Commenced February 13th, 1861, Charleston, So. Ca.* Unedited, typed
manuscript from the original diary in its entirety.
South Caroliniana Library, University of South
Carolina, Columbia, SC.

Jamison, David F. "Opening speech by then temporary
president of the South Carolina Secession Convention, General David F. Jamison." 17 December
1860, the First Baptist Church, Columbia, South
Carolina. In John Amasa May and Joan Reynolds
Faunt, *South Carolina Secedes.* Columbia: University of South Carolina Press, 1960.

Jefferson, Thomas. "A Summary View of the Rights of
British America." 1774. In James L. Huston, *Securing the Fruits of Labor, The American Concept of
Wealth Distribution, 1765-1900.* Baton Rouge: Louisiana State University Press, 1998, 17.

Joint Resolutions of the General Assembly of Alabama.
Adopted 24 February 1860. In William R. Smith,
Delegate, *The History and Debates of the Conven-
tion of The People of Alabama.* Montgomery: White,
Pfister & Co., 1861. Reprint, Spartanburg, SC: The
Reprint Company, Publishers, 1975.

Kettell, Thomas Prentice. *Southern Wealth and North-
ern Profits, as Exhibited in Statistical Facts and
Official Figures: Showing the Necessity of Union to
the Future Prosperity and Welfare of the Republic.*
New York: Geo. W. & John A. Wood, 1860. Reprint,
University, AL: University of Alabama Press, 1965.

Letcher, John. "Governor John Letcher's Message on
Federal Relations to the legislature of Virginia in
extraordinary secession on 7 January 1861." In
*Journal of the House of Delegates of the State of
Virginia, for the Extra Session, 1861.* Richmond:
William F. Ritchie, Public Printer, 1861, Doc. I.

Lincoln, Abraham. "A House Divided." 16 June 1858.
Republican State Convention, Springfield, Illinois.
In Roy P. Basler, ed., *The Collected Works of Abra-
ham Lincoln,* History Book Club edition. New
Brunswick: Rutgers University Press, 1953, Vol. II.

———. "Campaign Circular from Whig Committee."
March 4, 1843. In Roy P. Basler, ed., *The Collected
Works of Abraham Lincoln.* History Book Club edition. New Brunswick: Rutgers University Press,
1953, Volume I.

———. 1847 Congressional Debate in the United
States House of Representatives in Goldwin Smith,
*The United States: An Outline of Political History,
1492-1871.* New York and London: 1893, 248.

———. *Emancipation Proclamation.* January 1, 1863.
http://www.archives.gov/exhibits/
featured_documents/emancipation_proclamation/.
Accessed May 4, 2014.

————. *First Inaugural Address.*
http://en.wikisource.org/wiki/
Abraham_Lincoln%27s_First_Inaugural_Address.
Accessed March 27, 2014.

————. "Letter to Francis P. Blair." December 21,
1860. In E. B. Long with Barbara Long. *The Civil
War Day by Day, An Almanac 1861-1865.* New
York: Da Capo Press, 1971. Reprint, New York: Da
Capo Press, 1985.

————. "Letter to Horace Greeley." August 22, 1862. In
Roy P. Basler, ed., *The Collected Works of Abraham
Lincoln.* New Brunswick, NJ: Rutgers University
Press, 1953, V:388.

————. "Letter to Lyman Trumbull." December 10,
1860. In Earl Schenck Miers, ed., *Lincoln Day by
Day, A Chronology, 1809 - 1865.* Washington: Lincoln Sesquicentennial Commission, 1960, Volume
II, 1849-1860.

————. "Lincoln-Douglas Debate, The Seventh." 15 October 1858.

————. *Preliminary Emancipation Proclamation.*
September 22, 1862. http://www.archives.gov/
exhibits/american_originals_iv/setions/
transcript_preliminary_emancipation.html.
Accessed May 4, 2014.

Lincoln, Abraham, *The Collected Works of.* Roy P. Basler, ed. History Book Club edition. New Brunswick:
Rutgers University Press, 1953.

Liverpool Daily Post. 11 March 1862. In Charles Adams, *When in the Course of Human Events, Arguing the Case for Southern Secession.* Lanham: Rowman & Littlefield Publishers, Inc., 2000.

Locke, John. *The Second Treatise of Government.* In Peter Laslett, *John Locke, Two Treatises of Government, A Critical Edition with an Introduction and Apparatus Criticus.* Second edition. Cambridge: University Press, 1970.

London Times, The. 7 November 1861. In Jeffrey Rogers Hummel, *Emancipating Slaves, Enslaving Free Men, A History of the American Civil War.* Chicago: Open Court, 1996.

Madison, James. *The Madison Papers.* Philadelphia: 1840. In H. Newcomb Morse, "The Foundations and Meaning of Secession." *Stetson Law Review*, Stetson University College of Law, Volume. XV, No. 2, 1986.

Manchester (N.H.) Union Democrat. "Let Them Go!" 19 February 1861. In Howard Cecil Perkins, *Northern Editorials on Secession.* Gloucester: Peter Smith, 1964, Volume II, 592.

Marshall, John, Chief Justice. *Gibbons v. Ogden*, 22 U.S. (9 Wheat.) 1 (1824), 200. In H. Newcomb Morse, "The Foundations and Meaning of Secession." *Stetson Law Review*, Stetson University College of Law, Volume. XV, No. 2, 1986.

Marx, Karl. "The North American Civil War." In Karl
   Marx and Frederick Engels, *The Civil War in the
   United States.* Reprint: New York: International
   Publishers, 1971.

Marx, Karl and Frederick Engels. *The Civil War in the
   United States.* Reprint: New York: International
   Publishers, 1971.

Moore, Thomas O. "Extracts from the message of the
   governor of Louisiana to the State Legislature,
   January 22, 1861." In *The War of the Rebellion: A
   Compilation of the Official Records of the Union and
   Confederate Armies.* Washington: Government
   Printing Office, 1880, Series I, Volume 1.

Nelson, Thomas A. R. "Minority Report of the Committee of Thirty-three." United States House of Representatives. Washington: H. Polkinhorn, 1861.

————. "Speech of Hon. Thomas A. R. Nelson, of Tennessee, On the Disturbed Condition of the Country."
   Washington: H. Polkinhorn, 1861.

New York Commercial Advertiser. March 2 - 21, 1861.
   In Philip S. Foner, *Business & Slavery, The New
   York Merchants & the Irrepressible Conflict.*
   Chapel Hill: The University of North Carolina
   Press, 1941, 278.

New York Courier and Enquirer. March 2 - 21, 1861.
   In Philip S. Foner, *Business & Slavery, The New
   York Merchants & the Irrepressible Conflict.*
   Chapel Hill: The University of North Carolina
   Press, 1941, 278.

New York Daily News. March 2 - 21, 1861. In Philip S. Foner, *Business & Slavery, The New York Merchants & the Irrepressible Conflict.* Chapel Hill: The University of North Carolina Press, 1941, 278.

New-York Daily Tribune, The. "The Right of Secession." 17 December 1860. In Howard Cecil Perkins, ed., *Northern Editorials on Secession.* Gloucester: Peter Smith, 1964, 199-201.

New York Evening Post, March 2 - 21, 1861. In Philip S. Foner, *Business & Slavery, The New York Merchants & the Irrepressible Conflict.* Chapel Hill: The University of North Carolina Press, 1941, 278.

New York Evening Post. "What Shall Be Done for a Revenue?" 12 March 1861. In Howard Cecil Perkins, ed., *Northern Editorials on Secession.* Gloucester: Peter Smith, 1964, Volume II, 599.

New York Herald. March 2 - 21, 1861. In Philip S. Foner, *Business & Slavery, The New York Merchants & the Irrepressible Conflict.* Chapel Hill: The University of North Carolina Press, 1941, 278.

New York Journal of Commerce. March 2 - 21, 1861. In Philip S. Foner, *Business & Slavery, The New York Merchants & the Irrepressible Conflict.* Chapel Hill: The University of North Carolina Press, 1941, 278.

New-York Times, The. "Concurrent resolutions tendering aid to the President of the United States in support of the Constitution and the Union passed by the New York State Assembly, January 11, 1861." *The New-York Times.* January 12, 1861.

New-York Times, The. Editorial. 22-23 March, 1861 In
Charles Adams, *When in the Course of Human
Events, Arguing the Case for Southern Secession.*
Lanham: Rowman & Littlefield Publishers, Inc.,
2000, 65.

Oglesby, Richard. "Speech of Oglesby" in *Chicago
Press and Tribune,* August 1, 1860. In James L.
Huston, "Property Rights in Slavery and the Com-
ing of the Civil War," *Journal of Southern History,*
Vol. LXV, No. 2, May, 1999.

*Ordinance to repeal the ratification of the Constitution
of the United States of America by the State of Virginia, and to resume all the rights and powers
granted under said Constitution.* Adopted by the
Virginia Secession Convention, 17 April 1861. In
*The War of the Rebellion: A Compilation of the Of-
ficial Records of the Union and Confederate Armies.*
Washington: Government Printing Office, 1900. Reprint, Historical Times, Inc., 1985, Series IV, Volume 1.

Perry, M. S. "Address by Florida Governor M. S. Perry
to the Florida Senate and House of Representatives
in Tallahassee on 2 February 1861." In *The War of
the Rebellion: A Compilation of the Official Records
of the Union and Confederate Armies.* Washington:
Government Printing Office, 1900. Reprint, Historical Times, Inc., 1985, Series IV, Volume 1.

Pickens, Francis Wilkinson. "Inaugural Message of
South Carolina Governor Francis Wilkinson Pickens." Published 18 December 1860 in *The (Charleston, S.C.) Courier.*

Quarterly Review, The. "The Confederate Struggle."
112 (1862): 537. In Charles Adams, *When in the
Course of Human Events, Arguing the Case for
Southern Secession.* Lanham: Rowman & Littlefield
Publishers, Inc., 2000, 81-82.

Reagan, John H. "Letter from Hon. John H. Reagan,
member of the United States House of Representatives from Texas, 19 October 1860." In *The Texas
(Marshall) Republican.* 3 November 1860.

―――. "Speech of Representative John H. Reagan of
Texas, January 15, 1861." In *Congressional Globe,*
36 Congress, 2 Session, I, 391.

Report on the Causes of the Secession of Georgia.
Adopted by the Georgia Secession Convention,
Tuesday, 29 January 1861. In the *Journal of the
Georgia Convention.* In *The War of the Rebellion: A
Compilation of the Official Records of the Union and
Confederate Armies.* Washington: Government
Printing Office, 1900. Reprint, Historical Times,
Inc., 1985, Series IV, Volume 1.

Republican Party Platform, The 1860. In Marshall L.
DeRosa, ed., *The Politics of Dissolution, The Quest
for a National Identity & the American Civil War.*
New Brunswick: Transaction Publishers, 1998.

Resolutions on Secession from Floyd County, Georgia.
Adopted November, 1860. In Allen D. Chandler, *The
Confederate Records of the State of Georgia.* At-
lanta: Charles P. Byrd, State Printer, 1909, Vol. 1.

Secession, Northern Editorials on. Howard Cecil Perkins, ed. Two Vols. The American Historical Association, 1942. Reprint with permission of Appleton-Century-Crofts, Inc. Gloucester, Mass.: Peter Smith, 1964.

Second Confiscation Act. July 17, 1862. http://www.freedmen.umd.edu/conact2.htm. Accessed May 6, 2014.

Saturday Review. "The American Tariff Bill." 9 March 1861, 234-235. In Charles Adams, *When in the Course of Human Events, Arguing the Case for Southern Secession.* Lanham: Rowman & Littlefield Publishers, Inc., 2000, 90-91.

Seward, William H. "On the Irrepressible Conflict." Rochester, New York speech, October 25, 1858. Quoted in James Buchanan, "Republican Fanatacism as a Cause of the Civil War." In Edwin C. Rozwenc, ed., *The Causes of the American Civil War.* Boston: D. C. Heath and Company, 1961.

Shaffner, Taliaferro P. *The War in America: being an Historical and Political Account of the Southern and Northern States: showing the Origin and Cause of the Present Secession War.* London: Hamilton, Adams, 1862.

Simms, William Gilmore. "Antagonisms of the Social Moral. North and South., The." Unpublished 1857 lecture housed in the Charles Carroll Simms Collection of the South Caroliniana Library, University of South Carolina, Columbia.

————. "Our Social Moral," also labeled "The Social Moral. Lecture 2." Unpublished 1857 lecture housed in the Charles Carroll Simms Collection of the South Caroliniana Library, University of South Carolina, Columbia.

————. "South Carolina in the Revolution. The Social Moral. Lecture 1." Unpublished 1857 lecture housed in the Charles Carroll Simms Collection of the South Caroliniana Library, University of South Carolina, Columbia.

Smith, Robert H. *An Address to the Citizens of Alabama on the Constitution and Laws of the Confederate States of America.* Mobile: 1861, 20. In Marshall L. DeRosa, *The Confederate Constitution of 1861, An Inquiry into American Constitutionalism.* Columbia: University of Missouri Press, 1991.

Tocqueville, Alexis de. *Democracy in America.* New York: Everyman's Library, Alfred A. Knopf, Inc., 1945, 1972, 1994.

Toombs, Robert. "On Secession." The last address of Georgia Sen. Robert Toombs in the United States Senate, 7 January 1861. In John Vance Cheney, ed., *Memorable American Speeches,* Volume IV, Secession, War, Reconstruction. Chicago: The Lakeside Press, 1910.

————. "Secessionist Speech, Tuesday Evening, November 13." Delivered to the Georgia legislature in
Milledgeville, November 13, 1860. In William W.
Freehling, and Craig M. Simpson, *Secession Debated, Georgia's Showdown in 1860*. New York: Oxford University Press, 1992.

War Aims Resolution. Also known as the Crittenden-
Johnson Resolution or just the Crittenden Resolu-
tion. United States Congress, July, 1861.
http://en.wikipedia.org/wiki/
Crittenden-Johnson_Resolution.
Accessed March 29, 2014.

*War of the Rebellion, The: A Compilation of the Offi-
cial Records of the Union and Confederate Armies*.
Washington: Government Printing Office, 1900. Reprint, Historical Times, Inc., 1985, Series IV, Volume 1.

Williamson, George. *Address of George Williamson,
Commissioner from Louisiana, to the Texas Secession Convention*. 9 March 1861. In E. W. Winkler,
ed., *Journal of the Secession Convention of Texas*.
Austin, 1912.

Wood, Fernando. "Mayor Fernando Wood's Recommen-
dation for the Secession of New York City." January
6, 1861. In Henry Steele Commager, ed., *Documents
of American History*, Seventh Edition. New York:
Appleton-Century-Crofts, 1963.

Wright, A. R. "Letter of Commissioner A. R. Wright of Georgia to Governor Thomas H. Hicks of Maryland, 25 February 1861." In *The War of the Rebellion: A Compilation of the Official Records of the Union and Confederate Armies.* Washington: Government Printing Office, 1900. Reprint, Historical Times, Inc., 1985, Series IV, Volume 1.

Yancy, William Lowndes. "The Constitution and the Union." Speech in Montgomery, Alabama, 10 November 1860. In Edwin Anderson Alderman and Joel Chandler Harris, eds., *Library of Southern Literature.* Atlanta: The Martin and Hoyt Company, 1907, Vol. 13.

————. "Equal Rights in a Common Government." Speech in Washington, D.C., September 21, 1860. In Edwin Anderson Alderman and Joel Chandler Harris, eds., *Library of Southern Literature.* Atlanta: The Martin and Hoyt Company, 1907, Volume 13.

Secondary Sources

Ackroyd, Peter. *Dickens.* London: Sinclair-Stevenson, 1990.

Adams, Charles. *When in the Course of Human Events, Arguing the Case for Southern Secession.* Lanham: Rowman & Littlefield Publishers, Inc., 2000.

Barrow, Charles Kelly, ed., and J. H. Segars, ed., and R. B. Rosenburg, ed. *Black Confederates.* Gretna, LA: Pelican Publishing Company, 2001.

Beard, Charles A. and Mary R. Beard. *The Rise of American Civilization.* New York: The MacMillan Company, 1936.

Bennett, Lerone, Jr. *Forced Into Glory: Abraham Lincoln's White Dream.* Chicago: Johnson Publishing Company, 2000.

Benson, Lee. "Explanations of American Civil War Causation." In Lee Benson *Toward the Scientific Study of History.* Philadelphia: J. B. Lippincott, 1972.

Boles, John B. and Evelyn Thomas Nolen, eds. *Interpreting Southern History, Historiographical Essays in Honor of Sanford W. Higginbotham.* Baton Rouge: Louisiana State University Press, 1987.

Bradford, M. E. *Original Intentions, On the Making and Ratification of the United States Constitution.* Athens: The University of Georgia Press, 1993.

Casualties of War, United States Military. http://en.wikipedia.org/wiki/ United_States_military_casualties_of_war. Accessed August 1, 2014.

Cheney, John Vance. ed., *Memorable American Speeches*, Volume IV, Secession, War, Reconstruction. Chicago: The Lakeside Press, 1910.

Cisco, Walter Brian. *War Crimes Against Southern Civilians*. Gretna, LA: Pelican Publishing Company, 2007.

Cohn, David L. *The Life and Times of King Cotton*. New York: Oxford University Press, 1956.

Coker, Rachel. "Historian revises estimate of Civil War dead." September 21, 2011. Binghampton University Research News — *Insights and Innovations from Binghampton University*. http://discovere.binghamton.edu/news/civilwar-3826.html. Accessed July 7, 2014.

Commager, Henry Steele. *Commager on Tocqueville*. Columbia, MO: University of Missouri Press, 1993.

————. ed., *Documents of American History*, Seventh Edition. New York: Appleton-Century-Crofts, 1963.

Coward, Barry. *The Stuart Age, England, 1603-1714*. Second Edition. London: Longman Group, Ltd., 1994.

Current, Richard N. *The Lincoln Nobody Knows*. New York: McGraw-Hill Book Company, Inc., 1958.

Curtis, George M., III and James J. Thompson, Jr., eds. *The Southern Essays of Richard M. Weaver*. Indianapolis: LibertyPress, 1987.

DeRosa, Marshall L. *The Confederate Constitution of 1861, An Inquiry into American Constitutionalism*. Columbia: University of Missouri Press, 1991.

————, ed. *The Politics of Dissolution, The Quest for a National Identity & the American Civil War.* New Brunswick: Transaction Publishers, 1998.

————. Book Review: *The Rule of Law v. The Misrule of Ideology: The Confederacy and Constitutional Interpretation.* Reprinted from Texas Law Review, Vol. 77, No. 3, February, 1999.

DiLorenzo, Thomas J. *Lincoln Unmasked: What You're Not Supposed to Know About Dishonest Abe.* New York: Crown Forum, 2006.

————. *The Real Lincoln: A New Look at Abraham Lincoln, His Agenda, and an Unnecessary War.* Roseville, CA: Prima Publishing, 2002.

Dobson, John M. *Two Centuries of Tariffs: The Background and Emergence of the U.S. International Trade Commission.* Washington: United States International Trade Commission, 1976.

Egnal, Marc. *Clash of Extremes, The Economic Origins of the Civil War.* New York: Hill and Wang, 2009.

Farrow, Anne, Joel Lang, and Jenifer Frank. *Complicity, How the North Promoted, Prolonged, and Profited from Slavery.* New York: Ballantine Books, 2005.

Faulkner, Ronnie W. "The Impending Crisis of the South." 2006 NCpedia sketch on Hinton Rowan Helper's book, *The Impending Crisis of the South: How to Meet It* (New York: Burdick Brothers, 1857). NCpedia. Encyclopedia of North Carolina. The University of North Carolina Press. http://ncpedia.org/print/2723. Accessed July 31, 2014.

Faust, Patricia L., ed. *Historical Times Illustrated Encyclopedia of the Civil War*. New York: Harper & Row, Publishers, 1986.

Fehrenbacher, Don E. ed., *Abraham Lincoln, Speeches and Writings, 1832-1858*. New York: Library Classics of the United States, Inc., 1989.

Fogel, Robert William and Stanley L. Engerman. *Time on the Cross, The Economics of American Negro Slavery*. Little, Brown and Company, Inc., 1974. Reprint, New York: W. W. Norton & Company, 1989, 1995.

Foner, Philip S. *Business & Slavery, The New York Merchants & the Irrepressible Conflict*. Chapel Hill: The University of North Carolina Press, 1941.

Freehling, William W. and Craig M. Simpson. *Secession Debated, Georgia's Showdown in 1860*. New York: Oxford University Press, 1992.

Garrison, Webb. *Lincoln's Little War*. Nashville: Rutledge Hill Press, 1997.

Genovese, Eugene D. *The Southern Front, History and Politics in the Cultural War.* Columbia, MO: University of Missouri Press, 1995.

———. *The Southern Tradition, The Achievement and Limitations of an American Conservatism.* Cambridge, MA and London: Harvard University Press, 1994.

Guilds, John Caldwell. *Simms, A Literary Life.* Fayetteville: The University of Arkansas Press, 1992.

———. ed. *Long Years of Neglect, The Work and Reputation of William Gilmore Simms.* Fayetteville, AR: The University of Arkansas Press, 1988.

Hartford Convention. http://en.wikipedia.org/wiki/ Hartford_Convention. Accessed August 26, 2014.

Hinkle, Don. *Embattled Banner, A Reasonable Defense of the Confederate Battle Flag.* Paducah, KY: Turner Publishing Company, 1997.

Hofstader, Richard. *America at 1750, A Social Portrait.* New York: Vintage Books, 1973.

Hummel, Jeffrey Rogers. *Emancipating Slaves, Enslaving Free Men, A History of the American Civil War.* Chicago: Open Court, 1996.

Huston, James L. *The Panic of 1857 and the Coming of the Civil War.* Baton Rouge: Louisiana State University Press, 1987.

———. "Property Rights in Slavery and the Coming of the Civil War." *Journal of Southern History*, Volume LXV, Number 2, May, 1999.

———. *Securing the Fruits of Labor, The American Concept of Wealth Distribution, 1765-1900.* Baton Rouge: Louisiana State University Press, 1998.

Johnson, Ludwell H. *North Against South, The American Illiad 1848-1877.* Columbia, SC: The Foundation for American Education, 1993, 1995.

Jordan, Ervin L., Jr. *Black Confederates and Afro-Yankees in Civil War Virginia.* Charlottesville: University Press of Virginia, 1995.

Kershaw, Jack. "Flags as Symbols." *Chronicles, A Magazine of American Culture*, 1994.

Knoles, George Harmon. ed. *The Crisis of the Union, 1860-1861.* Baton Rouge: Louisiana State University Press, 1965.

Koger, Larry. *Black Slaveowners, Free Black Slave Masters in South Carolina, 1790-1860.* Columbia: University of South Carolina Press, 1985.

Long, E. B. with Barbara Long. *The Civil War Day by Day, An Almanac 1861-1865.* New York: Da Capo Press, 1971. Reprint, New York: Da Capo Press, 1985.

Lloyd, Christopher. *The Navy and the Slave Trade.*
London, 1949. In Brian Jenkins, *Britain & the War
for the Union.* London: McGill's-Queen's University
Press, 1974, Volume 1.

Masters, Edgar Lee. *Lincoln, the Man.* New York:
Dodd, Mead & Co., 1931. Reprint, Columbia, SC:
The Foundation for American Education, 1997.

May, John Amasa and Joan Reynolds Faunt.
South Carolina Secedes. Columbia: University of
South Carolina Press, 1960.

McCawley, Patrick J. *Artificial Limbs for Confederate
Soldiers.* Columbia: South Carolina Department of
Archives & History, 1992.

McDonald, Forrest. *States' Rights and the Union, Im-
perium in Imperio, 1776-1876.* Lawrence, KS:
University Press of Kansas, 2000.

McManus, Edgar J. *Black Bondage in the North.*
New York: Syracuse University Press, 1973.

McPherson, James M. *Battle Cry of Freedom.*
New York and Oxford: Oxford University Press,
1988.

————. "Lincoln the Devil." Book review of Lerone
Bennett Jr.'s *Forced into Glory, Abraham Lincoln's
White Dream. New York Times* on the Web, August
27, 2000. http://www.nytimes.com/
books/00/08/27/reviews/000827.27mcphert.html.
Accessed 7/4/2014.

McPherson, James M. and William J. Cooper, Jr., eds. *Writing the Civil War, The Quest to Understand.* Columbia: University of South Carolina Press, 1998.

Miller, John. *The Glorious Revolution.* Second edition. London: Longman, 1997.

Mixed Up with All the Rebel Horde, Why Black Southerners Fought for the South in the War Between the States. August 12, 1993, Professor Edward C. Smith Address to SCV National Convention, Lexington, Kentucky. DVD. Two Vols. Produced by Bonnie Blue Publishing. http://www.BonnieBluePublishing.com.

Morse, H. Newcomb. "The Foundations and Meaning of Secession." *Stetson Law Review*, Stetson University College of Law, Volume. XV, No. 2, 1986.

NAACP Anti-Confederate-Battle-Flag Resolutions. 1987 and 1991. In Don Hinkle, *Embattled Banner, A Reasonable Defense of the Confederate Battle Flag.* Paducah, KY: Turner Publishing Company, 1997, 23-25, and 157-186, respectively.

Orwell, George. *1984.* New York: New American Library, 1950.

Owsley, Frank L. "The Irrepressible Conflict." In *I'll Take My Stand, The South and the Agrarian Tradition*, by Twelve Southerners. Harper & Brothers, 1930. Reprint: Baton Rouge: Louisiana State University Press, Louisiana Paperback Edition, 1977, sixth printing, 1990.

Paskoff, Paul F. and Daniel J. Wilson, eds. *The Cause of the South, Selections from De Bow's Review, 1846-1867.* Baton Rouge: Louisiana State University Press, 1982.

Potter, David M. *The Impending Crisis, 1848-1861.* Completed and edited by Don E. Fehrenbacher. New York: Harper & Row, Publishers, 1976.

————. *Lincoln and His Party in the Secession Crisis.* New Haven: Yale University Press, 1942, 1979.

Ramsdell, Charles W. "Lincoln and Fort Sumter." *Journal of Southern History*, Volume 3, Issue 3, August, 1937.

————. "The Natural Limits of Slavery Expansion." In Edwin C. Rozwenc, ed., *The Causes of the American Civil War.* Boston: D. C. Heath and Company, 1961.

Ramsdell, Charles William. Bio by J. Horace Bass. Handbook of Texas Online. http://www.tshaonline.org/handbook/online/articles/ fra25. Uploaded June 15, 2010. Texas State Historical Association. Accessed October 04, 2014.

Ramsdell, Charles William, In Memoriam. Index of Memorial Resolutions and Biographical Sketches. The University of Texas at Austin, http://www.utexas.edu/faculty/council/pages/ memorials.html. Accessed October 1, 2014.

Randall, James G. and David H. Donald,
The Civil War and Reconstruction. Lexington, Mass:
D.C. Heath, 1969.

Roland, Charles P. *An American Iliad, The Story of
the Civil War.* Lexington, KY: University Press of
Kentucky, 1991.

Rollins, Richard. "Black Southerners in Gray," edition
ed. for *Black Southerners in Gray, Essays on Afro-
Americans in Confederate Armies, Journal of Confederate History,* Vol. XI, Dr. John McGlone, series
ed.

―――. *"The Damed Red Flags of the Rebellion," The
Confederate Battle Flag at Gettysburg.* Redondo
Beach, CA: Rank and File Publications, 1997.

Scott, Otto. *The Secret Six, John Brown and the Abolitionist Movement.* Murphys, CA: Uncommon
Books, 1979.

Shillingsburg, Miriam J. "Simms's Failed Lecture Tour
of 1856: The Mind of the North." In John C. Guilds,
ed., *Long Years of Neglect, The Work and Reputation of William Gilmore Simms.* Fayetteville: The
University of Arkansas Press, 1988.

Sifakis, Stewart. *Who Was Who in the Civil War.*
New York: Facts on File Publications, 1988.

Simkins, Francis Butler & Charles Pierce Roland. *A
History of the South,* Forth Edition. New York:
Alfred A. Knopf, 1972.

Smith, Goldwin. *The United States: An Outline of
Political History, 1492-1871.* New York and London:
1893.

Stampp, Kenneth M. ed. *The Causes of the Civil War,*
3rd revised edition. New York: Simon & Schuster,
1959, 1991.

―――. *The Imperiled Union, Essays on the Background of the Civil War.* New York: Oxford University Press, 1980.

Tarbell, Ida M. *The Tariff in Our Times.* New York:
The Macmillan Company, 1911.

Taylor, Joe Gray. "The White South from Secession to
Redemption." In John B. Boles and Evelyn Thomas
Nolen, *Interpreting Southern History, Historiograp-
hical Essays in Honor of Sanford W. Higginbotham.*
Baton Rouge: Louisiana State University Press,
1987.

Thornton, Mark and Robert B. Ekelund, Jr. *Tariffs,
Blockades, and Inflation, The Economics of the Civil
War.* The American Crisis Series. Books on the Civil
War Era, No. 15. Wilmington, DE: Scholarly Re-
sources, Inc., 2004.

Tilley, John Shipley. *The Coming of the Glory.*
Nashville: Bill Coats, Ltd., 1995.

―――. *Lincoln Takes Command.*
Nashville: Bill Coats, Ltd., 1991.

Vanauken, Sheldon. *The Glittering Illusion, English Sympathy for the Southern Confederacy.* Washington: Regnery Gateway, 1989.

Van Deusen, John G. *Economic Bases of Disunion in South Carolina.* New York: Columbia University Press, 1928, 1970.

Walther, Eric H. *The Fire-Eaters.* Baton Rouge: Louisiana State University Press, 1992.

Walvin, James. *Slavery and the Slave Trade, A Short Illustrated History.* Jackson: University Press of Mississippi, 1983.

Williams, Eric. *Capitalism & Slavery.* Chapel Hill: University of North Carolina Press, 1944, 1994.

Wilson, Clyde N. Abstract. *The Creed of the Old South* by Basil L. Gildersleeve. Society of Independent Southern Historians. http://southernhistorians.org/ the-societys-southern-life-recommended-reading/ 11-southern-literature/11-09-southern-literature- southern-view-of-southern-culture/11-09-04/. Accessed 10/11/2014.

Wilson, Clyde N. "Our History and Their Myth: Comparing the Confederacy and the Union." *Confederate Veteran*, Vol. 72, No. 2, March/April, 2014.

Wooster, Ralph A. *The Secession Conventions of the South.* Princeton: Princeton University Press, 1962.

Wright, Gavin. *The Political Economy of the Cotton South, Households, Markets, and Wealth in the Nineteenth Century.* New York: W. W. Norton & Company, 1978.

Wright, William C. *The Secession Movement in the Middle Atlantic States.* Rutherford: Fairleigh Dickinson University Press, 1973.

Yanak, Ted and Pam Cornelison. *The Great American History Fact-Finder.* Boston: Houghton Mifflin Company, 1993.

Yearns, W. Buck, ed. *The Confederate Governors.* Athens: University of Georgia Press, 1985.

Colophon

Most of the text in this book is 11 point Century with 1.3 leading and .3 paragraph indentation. The chapter titles and other titles are bold Century and most are 14 point.

The words and Roman numerals that designate each of the three sections — Part I, Part II and Part III — in both the Contents and on each section's first page, are CasablancaAntique.

The footnotes are 10 point Arial with 1.1 leading.

The front cover title and author's name are Lea‌mington‌-Light, as are the interior half titles and title page.

The back cover text is Century.

Index

A full index will soon be part of this book. For those who purchased before the index was complete, there will be a downloadable printable PDF file containing the complete index, on our websites.

I apologize for the inconvenience.

Gene Kizer, Jr.

Fiction by Gene Kizer, Jr.

An Amazon Kindle eBook

Charleston '86

Short Stories

THE CITADEL

SOUTH CAROLINA CORPS OF CADETS

Six Tales
of Courage,
Love, the War
Between the
States, Satire,
Ghosts &
Horror from
the Holy City

Gene Kizer, Jr.

Volume
One

Finis

Made in the USA
Lexington, KY
21 March 2015